D1563371

Praise for *My Life in Jewish Renewal*

"In this wonderful and important memoir, we see why Reb Zalman is viewed by so many as one of the key Jewish figures and influencers of the last century. In intimate detail, the book affords us glimpses into the friendships, relationships, and shared experiences he has had with some of the most compelling (and at times lesser known) spiritual teachers and leaders of this era, as well as his own experiences and personal history—and how those many and varied interconnections have shaped his worldview and inner life. I recommend this book very highly to anyone interested in the evolution of a soul and the formation of a modern mystic." —**Rabbi Niles Goldstein,** director of external relations at the Council for a Parliament of the World's Religions; author of *Gonzo Judaism: A Bold Path for Renewing an Ancient Faith*

"Reb Zalman is a deeply beloved, unique figure, founder of the Jewish Renewal movement, who has single-handedly inspired several generations of Jews to rediscover their own rich heritage. In this compelling memoir, Reb Zalman (assisted by Edward Hoffman) recounts his remarkable life story, revealing the personal evolution that made it possible for him to serve as an authentic Hasidic rebbe in the modern era. This fascinating book is like a long, delicious visit with Reb Zalman as he recounts, with exceptional honesty and affection, the events that have shaped his life." —**Howard Schwartz,** author of *Tree of Souls: The Mythology of Judaism*

"Judaism is a living religion of endless reinvention. From Abraham to Moses, and Moses to Micah, and Micah to Hillel, and Hillel to Luria, and Luria to the Baal Shem Tov, and the Baal Shem Tov to Reb Zalman ours is a civilization rooted in creativity, innovation, imagination, and experimentation. Reb Zalman's story is a testament to Jewish creativity rooted in the richest soil of the past and fearlessly branching out into the as yet unknown dimensions of the future. If there is hope for a Jewish future, Reb Zalman carries it; if there is a rabbi for the twenty-first century, Reb Zalman is it." —**Rabbi Rami Shapiro,** author of *The Sacred Art of Lovingkindness*

"Reb Zalman, the Master Teacher of Jewish Renewal has given us access to the wisdom of the past appreciation of the technological present and insights for a luminous future now he is giving us the inside view of his amazing life presented as an engaging personal narrative those who have enjoyed his teachings will find this a 'must read' book." —**Rabbi Leah Novick,** author of *On the Wings of Shekhinah: Rediscovering Judaism's Divine Feminine*

"To be in the presence of Rabbi Zalman Schachter-Shlom is to be in the presence of a fountain that is forever bubbling up with new nsights and fresh discoveries. The next best thing to being with him is to have this book which describes the fascinating journey that Reb Zalman has travelled in his life—so far. The Lubavitcher Rebbe and the Dali Lama, the diamond cutters of Antwerp and the Trappist monks of Kentucky, Shlomo Carlbach and Timothy O'Leary are among some of the travelling companions whom he introduces us to, as he tells us of the adventures he has lived through in his travels from world to world in search of Truth. This is a book that anyone who wants to understand the twists and turns of the spiritual life of our time simply has to read." —**Rabbi Jack Riemer**, editor of *The World of the High Holy Days* and *So That Your Values Live On*

"In this radiant book, Reb Zalman Schachter accompanied by Edward Hoffman, take us on the majestic tour of Reb Zalman's exhilarating life. This tour comprises a treasure-trove of wise and diversified souls, beginning with Reb Zalman himself, from his discoveries as a youth in Hitler's Vienna to his education as a rabbi to his meetings with some of the most remarkable minds of the past 100 years. And weaved throughout we are gifted with the clarification and articulation of Reb Zalman's crowning theological achievement—Jewish Renewal—and the hope for a more inclusive, awe-based, and appreciative world." —**Kirk Schneider**, author of *Existential-Humanistic Therapy*

"Few writers have so accurately described Jewish boyhood in Vienna, the doubts and fears, the fascination with a world that overnight turned from friendly Gemütlichkeit to hostility and hatred. And none that I know of has had such accurate recall of names, places, people and happenings as Reb Zalman. What this revered rabbi became has much to do with what he was as a boy. After decades of sharing with us thoughts, views, insights and teachings, I am grateful that he has decided to share the journey of his life." —**Theodore Bikel**, actor, musician, Yiddishist

"What a marvelous collection of memories, told with warmth and affection! We who know and love Reb Zalman have all heard parts of his story, but seeing it all together is quite magnificent. May he live to write still more unexpected chapters!" —**Art Green**, Hebrew College

My Life in Jewish Renewal

My Life in Jewish Renewal

A Memoir

Rabbi Zalman M. Schachter-Shalomi

with Edward Hoffman

ROWMAN & LITTLEFIELD PUBLISHERS, INC.

Lanham • Boulder • New York • Toronto • Plymouth, UK

Published by Rowman & Littlefield Publishers, Inc.
A wholly owned subsidiary of The Rowman & Littlefield Publishing Group, Inc.
4501 Forbes Boulevard, Suite 200, Lanham, Maryland 20706
www.rowman.com

10 Thornbury Road, Plymouth PL6 7PP, United Kingdom

British Library Cataloguing in Publication Information Available

Library of Congress Cataloging-in-Publication Data

Schachter-Shalomi, Zalman, 1924–
  My life in Jewish renewal : a memoir / Zalman M. Schachter-Shalomi with Edward Hoffman.
    p. cm.
  Includes index.
  ISBN 978-1-4422-1327-2 (cloth : alk. paper) — ISBN 978-1-4422-1329-6 (ebook)
  1. Schachter-Shalomi, Zalman, 1924– 2. Rabbis—United States—Biography.
  3. Jewish renewal—History. I. Hoffman, Edward II. Title.
  BM755.S2495A3 2012
  296.8'34—dc23
  [B]
                                                                              2012020627

∞ ™ The paper used in this publication meets the minimum requirements of American National Standard for Information Sciences—Permanence of Paper for Printed Library Materials, ANSI/NISO Z39.48-1992.

Printed in the United States of America

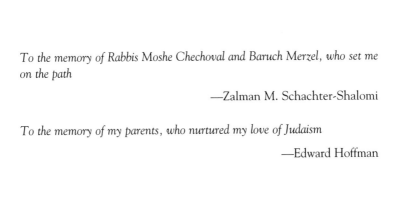

To the memory of Rabbis Moshe Chechoval and Baruch Merzel, who set me on the path

—Zalman M. Schachter-Shalomi

To the memory of my parents, who nurtured my love of Judaism

—Edward Hoffman

"All journeys have secret destinations of which the traveler is unaware."

—Martin Buber

Contents

~

Preface

Why should I bother to tell the story of my life? It is not because I have had vivid experiences that took me from the Ukraine, then to Poland, Austria, Belgium, and France, to the United States, Canada, and back to the United States. It is not because the story of my relationships and family situations is what I want to share with people. There are some things that are private. I made a conscious and deliberate choice not to include the parts of my personal private life and my family relationships that were intimately interwoven with the lives of others. I did not feel free to speak about them: they have not given permission to have their personal lives discussed in this book.

But there are some things that I would like to recount because they might make a difference to you and your life. Having been instrumental in birthing what is now known as Jewish Renewal, I would like you to understand where it came from and what brought about its special way of understanding Judaism—and all the other religions which are part-and-parcel of our world.

We all have undergone a paradigm shift. Many of us aren't yet aware that the shift has happened. And this is a reason why so much of my teaching has been to point out that there have been shifts in our awareness and the way in which we see ourselves in the universe. There have been shifts in the way in which we see our connection with the Infinite, with the spirit that guides life on this planet. Certainly, traditions have given us much worthwhile guidance. Sometimes, though, when people haven't had a chance to grow and find themselves in the new environment that life, politics, and technology have created for us, these traditions have become like straitjackets, not permitting us to live as citizens of the world as it is emerging at this time.

And this is the reason why my story is important, because it connects with a tradition like ours—that is over 4000 years old and that has produced offspring in the many Christianities and Islams, along with the variety of Judaisms, that exist today. It is important to see what this small group of renewal people in Judaism has produced. So come with me as I'm now in a retrospective of my life. This book describes the origins of the thoughts that shaped Jewish Renewal for me.

As a young man in the Lubavitch system of Hasidism, I married a woman who taught for Lubavitch and with whom I had five children in Winnipeg. We maintained the lifestyle of Lubavitch emissaries. This was yet quite far from my later life, in which I engendered Jewish Renewal.

Many people outside of what we narrowly call Jewish Renewal have taken from our well, and this development pleases me. However, it has also led some persons to dismiss Jewish Renewal as basically "Judaism lite." Therefore, by describing how I came to update Judaism together with my early students—who all had a traditional Jewish education—the process of renewal from the inside out becomes more clear. Otherwise, people would look at Jewish Renewal wholly from the outside—and then see only what has been removed from the tradition.

After the Holocaust (I arrived in the United States in 1941) with European Jewry destroyed, my Rebbe having escaped to America shortly before I did—was intent on not only restoring Jewish practice and spiritual life, but also on re-invigorating whatever manifested of Jewish culture within the United States. Years before I even thought about renewal, I was heart-and-soul given over to the restoration of the Judaism that existed before the Second World War. As I was working rabbinically not in Hebrew—nor in Yiddish—but in English, with American Jews, I had to find the approach and the vocabulary by which I could inspire those who had been highly acculturated to America.

This effort produced a reciprocal impact, for I began to see that there was much historical debris blocking the paths of those I dealt with—and it had to be removed. I had to find different ways to reach their spiritual center.

When the Dead Sea Scrolls were described, I found that they emphasized spirituality in a more fundamental way than Jewish aspects originating in Eastern Europe.

Nevertheless, the Hasidic "toolkit" provided me with many means for bringing people through story and music—as well as meditative and contemplative techniques—to experience with more immediacy a Judaism that they could embrace. In working in various summer camps for young American Jews in the 1950s and 1960s, I was able to hone these tools to greater effectiveness. Much of what happened during that era is what this book is about.

The University of Manitoba and my overall stay in Winnipeg were like a hothouse for my spirit. Ultimately, though, the Jewish community there was too small for my scope and Canadian Jewry lagged culturally behind its American counterpart with a correspondingly limited scale of activity. I was overjoyed when I was offered the position at the Department of Religious Studies at Temple University. As a result, a new phase began for me and for the students I had attracted.

By the time of my move to Philadelphia in 1975, Jewish Renewal already had a shape. What has occurred since that time is the subject for another treatment—in which I would describe the liturgical innovations, the *halachic* reasoning behind our religious practice, and the philosophical/theological dimensions that Jewish Renewal thought integrated. Eco-feminism, *gaian* theology, ecumenical understanding—all need to be amplified, and have already been featured in other volumes of my own and my students' writings.

Recently, I spoke to the rabbis we have ordained. It was my valedictory, completing my work as Rabbi, a guide to the spirits of many people. Growing old, I look at what I leave behind and hope that somehow you will find a way to gain direction for your own life and your own relationship with Heaven, Earth, and all the beings between them.

~

Acknowledgments

If I were to mention all the people whose collaboration and insights shaped my life, it would make for a book by itself. Honor with me all the individuals whose names and events are mentioned in this book because I honor them, too. However, several persons deserve special recognition for bringing my memoir to fruition:

First, of course, my parents and sister Ada Tamar, of blessed memory, and my beloved siblings, Rabbi Joseph Chayyim and Devorah Kieffer. Their impact on my life has been immeasurable.

Next, the people in Antwerp who set me on the track of service to God and the Jewish people. I have them in mind in my dedication of this book to Rabbi Moshe Chechoval and Reb Baruch Merzel.

Roger Kamenetz: I worked with Roger on several important projects. Most of all, I appreciate the way he reported on our visit to the Dalai Lama in Dharamsala. His eyes and his writing are true and harmonious. We had begun to work together on a biography, but alas, we could not agree with the editor on how to continue.

Netanel Miles Yepez: Much of what people are able to study of my writings is due to the loyalties and intellectual acumen of this man. When I read how he has brought my material together I am astonished to become his disciple.

Edward Hoffman: Ever since we collaborated on *Sparks of Light: Counseling in the Hasidic Tradition* nearly thirty years ago, I have felt that Edward really understood me at the level of the range of my personal experiences. Besides his ongoing psychological practice and college teaching, he has written bi-ographies of Alfred Adler, Abraham Maslow, and others. Edward not only heard my stories and recollections, but he also carefully researched the times and places I recounted in producing this memoir. His extraordinary precision will make our book a joy for the reader.

Mary Fulton is my faithful secretary. At times I feel that she could write an entire text on Jewish Renewal all by herself. It is due to her excellent archiving and memory that we were able to bring the material together for this book.

Eve Ilsen is my partner in life and work. She shares with me her incisive mind and sensitive, esthetic genius, and inspires me constantly to live up to my values. That I am still able to function is due to her kindness and care.

Zalman M. Schachter-Shalomi
—Boulder, Colorado

It has been an honor and a literary challenge these past few years to collabo-rate with Reb Zalman in writing his memoir. His life of eight-seven years has been so rich with wide-ranging experiences, prolific writing, and accumu-lated wisdom for our contemporary world that I initially found it difficult to shape this book effectively.

Indeed, only when this memoir was nearly completed in entirety has it crystallized into its present form. In assisting Reb Zalman on this auto-biographical project, my knowledge of Jewish—and especially Hasidic—philosophy, prayer, and history has been amplified. In some ways, too, my work here represents a complementary volume to my earlier study of Chabad Hadisim entitled *Despite All Odds: The Story of Lubavitch.* For Reb Zalman's memoir offers fascinating, first-person accounts of both the Sixth and Sev-enth Lubavitcher Rebbes, who did so much to safeguard and expand Jewish life in the twentieth century.

I am grateful to our acquisitions editor, Sarah Stanton, at Rowman & Littlefield, whose unflagging enthusiasm is much appreciated; her assistant, Jin Yu, has consistently been reliable and responsive.

Throughout my interviewing of Reb Zalman and editorial activities related to this book, I have been blessed with colleagues and friends who helped bring it to fruition. Their viewpoints, suggestions, and critical com-ments have been invaluable from start to finish. In alphabetic order, I there-fore wish to thank my son Rabbi Jeremy Hoffman and his wife Ortal Vaknin Hoffman, Aaron Hostyk, Rabbi Neal Kaunfer, Arthur Kurzweil, Paul Palnik,

Howard Schwartz, and Marcela Bakur Weiner. I am especially grateful to my wife, Elaine, for her emotional support, encouragement, and patience throughout this exciting project.

Edward Hoffman
—New York City

~

A Visionary Introduction to My Life Quest

About twenty-five years ago, I was working with Professor Howard Schwartz, among the world's leading interpreters of traditional Jewish folklore and legend. He is also a prize-winning author of children's books and poetry. It was our bold idea to take events from my life and recast them in the form of Hasidic parables and tales. We collaborated for about a year and a half and finished it working together every day in Jerusalem for a month. Published in 1983 as the *Dream Assembly*, it expanded popular interest in the mystical and intuitive features of Hasidism. Although I wrote the story with Howard Schwartz as part of a larger tapestry, it well serves as a relevant, dreamlike introduction to the story of my life—and my quest to be an authentic Hasidic rebbe in a world incredibly different from when Hasidism originated in the late eighteenth century.

A *Tzaddik* in Search of a Script

For Esperanza

Reb Zalman called Reb Shmuel Leib and Feivel the Dark and Feivel the Light and asked them to form a *Beit Din*, a court of law. Reb Sholem and Reb Hayim Elya were to serve as the scribes of the court.

Here, then, were the proceedings, as Reb Hayim Elya recalled them: Reb Zalman sighed with a heavy heart and said that he wished the *Beit Din* to meet after the morning prayer to hear a dream of his and to perform the ritual of *Hatavat Halom*, in which a dream is interpreted.

1

Once the *Beit Din* had been constituted, Reb Zalman stood before them, and Shmuel Leib, speaking for the court, said, "All interpretations are of God. Please tell us your dream." Then Reb Zalman said three times, "I saw a dream, may it be for good." And Shmuel Leib replied, "The dream you have seen is good, and for good may it be. May the merciful one make it turn out for good. Seven times may it be decreed from heaven that it is good and shall be."

Then Reb Zalman began to recite the words of the psalm: *You have turned my sackcloth into dancing.* And after this he related his dream. He said,

I felt my time had come and the *Hevra Kadisha* was surrounding my bed. I had said the *Viduy*, the confession, and was ready to invite the *Malach Hamaves*, the Angel of Death, to do his work . . . quickly. Utilizing every Name of God I had learned, I effected the Unification and saw myself plunged into a torrent of white light before Duma, the Angel of the Grave, even before he had a chance to intercept me and ask me his questions, for I wished nothing else but to be drawn into the very body of the One who is the source of all blessings. Like a drop merging with the ocean, I wished to be assimilated into *Ein Sof.*

Wave after wave of swirls interrupted the *mikveh* of the River of Light. Each time my head bobbed up from that river, I saw another image. Sometimes it seemed to be that all mankind was actually connected. And what seems to us to be the upper part of a person, that which stands out and makes him look separate, was only an appendage of that one being that we all are underneath the surface.

I saw myself from time to time rousing the somnolent parts of myself. Some of them woke up with smiles, some woke up startled, and others were angry and cursed for having been woken up from their long sleep and because they wished to stay in their separateness. And responding to their anger, I found myself getting angry as well. And only the next wave of the River of Light washed away my anger and carried it out to sea.

Then another wave came, and as I emerged from the river, every good deed I had ever done in my life surrounded me, tempting me with pride, and I did not know what to do with them. But suddenly I saw Meichizedek, the King of Salem and the High Priest on high. I said to him, "Please, take my *mitzvot* and offer them up. They are not for me but for the Holy One, blessed be He." And Meichizedek lifted up the *mitzvot*, and as he did, he lifted me up as well. And there, as he lifted me very high, the River of Light bathed my soul once more.

All during that time I heard the surging sound of a *bat kol*, a heavenly voice, although I could not make the words out. But this time, as I was about to plunge again into the next wave of the River of Light, I heard it but not very clearly. The voice said, "Whom shall I send?" and "Who shall go for us?" This time my mind did not merge with the River of Light, so painful was the cry of the *Shekhinah* with those words. And before I knew it, I cried out hoarsely, "I will go."

I followed the sound I heard, trying to reach its source, and before long I found myself before a Vale of Tears, smokestacks with blue smoke curling up to heaven in my father's town of Oswiecim. Countless people were crying out *Shema Yisrael* as their last outcry. And all the while the *Shekhinah* was wailing and wailing, but the Omnipotent One did not give Her any power to stop what was happening. Again I cried out, "I will go," thinking I was to join the martyrs.

In the next wave, the *Shekhinah* repeated Her question with urgent clarity, and this time I responded with a clear voice. I was carried still further into the future and saw a country in which many Jews made their home. And in that country there were Jews who, if they received any Torah at all, received only the outer trappings of *Yiddishkite* and none of its inner joys. And my soul was attracted to go there. And there I saw myself studying in a yeshiva where the joy and power of the Torah had not been lost and with others who had responded to the call and kept looking for that which was lacking in all of that country.

And then I found myself faced with an awakening in which I saw the River of Light once more and my path, to which I had become pledged, running beside it. And I started to look for a way in which I could fulfill the task that I had undertaken. And that path led me to a *Beit Midrash*, and when I entered there I saw that the shelves were lined with books. And I opened those books and saw that each one contained a script for a *tzaddik* who lived in a different time. There was a wonderful script about how to be a *tzaddik* in the time of Rabbi Akiba and Rabbi Shimon bar Yohai; a wonderful one about how to be a *tzaddik* in Medieval Spain, such as Yehuda Halevi; another that spoke of how to be a *tzaddik* in early Germany, such as Judah the Pious. The volume of the script of the Ari still had the letters dancing in it. And there was one about how to be a *tzaddik* in the time of the Baal Shem, but when I came to the book of how to be a *tzaddik* in my own time and opened it, I found, to my horror, that it was blank. There was no script.

Then I called out, and I said, "*Ribbono Shel Olam*, I have volunteered and said that I would come and serve. But I do not know how to serve you in this century. So much has changed. So few of the things that were guidelines in the past can be of help to me today." But there was only silence. And at that I fell into great terror, and I began to cry.

Then I began to count all the books on the shelves. And when I had counted them all, I found that there were 620 books, one for each of the 613 *mitzvot* and one for each of the 7 *mitzvot* of the *rabbanim*. And I opened up each and every one of those books and searched each of those ways, but none of them held the script I was searching for. At last I came back to the blank book, and I studied it more closely. And so I discovered that one thing had been written on it—my name. Then I realized that I myself would have to inscribe the pages of the book open before me. I looked for quill and ink but learned that each page had to be written by a mixture of tears, sweat, and blood, mixed with black bile—melancholia. Then I began to cry and sweat and pierced my finger for blood and began to write. But I discovered that if the ingredient of joy was missing, the letters would soon fade, and the page would become blank again. That is how I learned I had to add joy to that mixture, for only then would the ink be permanent.

Just then Reb Zalman stopped speaking and looked up and found himself standing before the *Beit Din*. And he was silent for a long time, but at last he said, "Now tell me, will the letters that I write in that book lead me to *Gan Eden* or will they bring me to *Gehenna*? Will I be able to fulfill that for which I offered my soul, or will I in my eagerness drag myself and those who follow me into the abyss?"

And when Reb Zalman had said this, the members of the *Beit Din* realized how complex was the matter and how heavy the weight of their decision. And they consulted together in whispers for a very long time, but they could not reach a conclusion. Therefore they asked the two scribes, Reb Hayim Elya and Reb Sholem, to join them. And they continued to consult for another two hours, until three hours had passed, and all that time Reb Zalman stood before them, his head sunk on his chest, and it seemed to him that his soul hung in the balance by a slender thread.

At last the *Beit Din* reached a decision, and Reb Shmuel Leib spoke for the court and said, "As to where the path you have taken will lead you, we are unable to say. All we can tell you is this: It is clearly destined that you will live until you have finished inscribing every page of that book. May He who gives peace to those who are far and near guard you well until that day and guard your soul in the days that follow."

At that point they all started to chant the *Hatavat Halom*, and Reb Zalman went to *daven* singing "Halleluiah" with a strange melody and a strange rhythm that none of the Hasidim had ever heard.

PART ONE

MY BOYHOOD AND YOUTH
BEFORE THE HOLOCAUST

CHAPTER ONE

~

Origins

On both my maternal and paternal sides, I am a descendant of Galicia. Home to one of the world's largest Jewish concentrations for several centuries, the region was long officially a royal province within the Austro-Hungarian Empire. However, following the Treaty of Versailles that ended World War I—and several additional years of fierce battle between Polish and Ukrainian forces—Galicia was annexed by Poland in 1920. My mother, Genia Ettinger, was born in 1905 Zholkiew, in eastern Galicia, whereas Papa was born in a small town named Krakowietz.

Their respective families were both affiliated with the Belzer Hasidim—an influential dynasty with thousands of devoted adherents—and the two were introduced to each other by a matchmaker. When they married in 1922, Papa was twenty-four and Mamma was seventeen. Soon after, they moved to the town of Zholkiew, where I was born two years later; back then it was Polish, but today it is part of rural Ukraine and known as Zholkova.

My parents named me Zalman after my maternal grandfather, who was tragically killed in World War I as an Austro-Hungarian conscript. While growing up, I heard he was a good man who unfortunately left behind a struggling widow, Chassiah, and three young daughters, the oldest of whom was my mother. Papa was the oldest male of seven children born to my grandfather, Shiye Yehoshua Dov Graf, a prominent *shochet* (ritual slaughterer), and his wife, Lifshe.

Poland had not existed as an independent nation for more than 120 years, but it lost little time in instituting anti-Semitic policies in Galicia, including the prohibition of Jews from all civil service occupations. To many young Jewish men like Papa, it seemed absurd to risk their lives fighting for a country that denied them rights equal to their Christian neighbors. Particularly for Orthodox Jews, who were unable as soldiers to obtain kosher food, military service was something to be shunned.

So in early 1925, Mamma, Papa, and I journeyed across Europe to bustling Vienna. Our little family was among some sixty thousand Galician Jews who had left the former Austro-Hungarian Empire's eastern flank to find security in the troubled postwar years. Soon after, my grandmother Chassiah and her two daughters likewise immigrated to Vienna, as did Papa's younger brother Akiva.

The city was divided into twenty-one different districts, and my family settled in the second, known as the Leopoldstadt. Situated between the Danube Canal and the Danube River, it housed Vienna's largest Jewish population. During the Renaissance centuries before, Leopoldstadt had been mandated the Jewish ghetto, where all Jews on penalty of imprisonment or death were obliged to return at nightfall. Although such repressive restrictions had long since been abolished, by the late nineteenth century so many working-class Jews had settled in the Leopoldstadt that it had become a de facto ghetto. Throughout Austria, it was sarcastically dubbed "Matzoh Island" for its strongly Judaic atmosphere. Among its famous longtime residents was Sigmund Freud, who, like his medical colleague Alfred Adler and the renowned composer Arnold Schoenberg, had also been raised there.

We initially resided with my mother's relatives before moving into a dilapidated ghetto house with primitive plumbing and toilet facilities. To bring in much-needed income, Papa invested his marriage dowry in a factory that manufactured soap and candles. Not altogether naively, he reasoned that the venture would surely be successful because "everyone always needs soap and candles." Then came 1928, and the factory went out of business. Papa was completely bankrupt; for years afterward, my mother used candle wicking to tie bundles.

After this financial debacle, my parents decided to open a textile remnants shop, and this proved more profitable. It occupied the storefront of a building about fifteen blocks away from our fifth-floor apartment in a walk-up tenement. Vienna had little public transportation in those days, and we hiked each way to and from home.

Stationed all day long at the shop's front counter, Mamma handled customers while Papa toiled in the back in a separate work area, making pickled herring for wholesale distribution. The shop was open five days per week, but in *shabbos* (Sabbath) observance they closed early on Friday afternoons and then all day on Saturdays. On Sundays, retail commercial activity in Austria was prohibited.

Their days were very long, for after closing the store at 8 or 9 p.m., Mamma and Papa would then cut raw onions on a special machine to prepare the pickled herring appetizers. The onions irritated my eyes, and often while I lay on bundles of cloth in the back area, I would cry and call out for attention. Mamma's enterprise regularly produced more income than Papa's, for her textile remnant customers included non-Jews shopping for bargains on Matzoh Island, where fixed prices were nonexistent at many stores.

When my parents emigrated from Poland, they were eager for me to become fluent in German, so they rarely spoke Yiddish at home. When they did so, it was usually to prevent me from understanding their conversation. By adolescence, I understood Yiddish reasonably well, but while I was a young child, it was alien to me. As my parents later recounted, Mamma's great-grandmother once came to Vienna for medical treatment when I was starting school. She asked me in Yiddish, "Does your daddy hit you?" Not comprehending her words, I politely replied in Yiddish, "Would you please repeat this, my gracious, great-grandmother lady?"

As a child, I felt more emotionally attached to Papa than to any other adult. I had minimal contact with his many relatives, for he had broken Polish law by leaving the country to escape military conscription and would have been in serious legal trouble if apprehended. To avoid that possibility, he simply never returned. I never met Papa's mother, and only one of his sisters visited us—and that was on a single occasion.

My paternal grandfather and I met only once, and it was not a joyful occasion. By then, he was badly suffering from heart disease, and because our Viennese tenement lacked an elevator, he had to be carried up the five flights to our apartment. A devout Belzer Hasid, he quickly demanded to see if I was wearing *tzitzit* (ritual undershirt fringes), and I felt ashamed that I had not put them on that day. He thereupon glared at Papa and then glared at me.

The one grandparent with whom I had any real involvement was Mamma's mother, Chassiah, and she was not a warm person. I never received even a perfunctory kiss or the slightest hug when ushered into her presence. How much of her austere personality was shaped by early widowhood and economic struggle I cannot say, but Mamma too was rarely physically or verbally affectionate. For both women, displays of love were expressed purely in terms of food. So whenever I was physically hurt or troubled about something emotionally, I sought out Papa for a comforting hug and reassurance.

Though busy working at the shop and delivering pickled herring throughout the Leopoldstadt on his heavy tricycle, Papa loved to teach me things. One day he rented a bicycle and taught me how to ride it; I still recall rolling alarmingly down the street the first time I did so. On one of my early birthdays, Papa took me to Vienna's zoo—located on the grounds of the famous imperial palace of Schonbrunn—whose renowned gardens were later immortalized in a painting by Gustav Klimt.

Despite Papa's Belzer Hasidic origins, he did not join the Belzer synagogue in Vienna. Rather, he preferred to *daven* (pray) in a *shtibel* (one-room synagogue) filled with expatriates of various Hasidic groups who, like him, felt the need to assert their religious autonomy; I often accompanied him there. Papa also became an active member of the local *Hevra Kadisha* (honorary burial society). Because *kohanim* (descendants of the priestly tribe of Aaron) are forbidden by Jewish law to touch a corpse, he ably served as the organization's bookkeeper.

Nevertheless, I have no recollection of Papa's ever explaining to me the value of Jewish study or observance. Also, despite their keeping a kosher household and regularly attending *mikveh* (ritual bath), my parents initially enrolled me in public school instead of a yeshiva. It was their well-meaning attempt to help spur my successful assimilation into wider Austrian society.

Papa certainly could have taught me Hebrew but was much too busy trying to support our family. One day he took pity on a poor, unskilled middle-aged man at *shul* and hired him as a home tutor. He forced me to learn the Hebrew alphabet—*Bo-Ba-Beh*—through joyless, rote repetition and would curse me in Polish when I erred. I cannot recall his name, but I still remember how he reeked of onions and that I despised him.

Much more adept and kindly were the two Hebrew teachers I had while attending public school, for Vienna authorized all pupils to receive one hour per week of religious "release time" instruction. Both men attended rabbinic programs and provided such tutoring as part of their training. They recounted Judaic Bible stories and helped me to master the Hebrew alphabet in a primer called *Kol Yakov* (*The Voice of Jacob*). Alas, its unadorned black-and-white design was much less attractive to me than the brightly colorful catechism book used by my Catholic classmates under priestly tutelage.

By then, I had already gained a little exposure to Catholicism, for my parents hired a Catholic babysitter after my brother Joseph was born in 1930. One day, without asking Mamma or Papa for permission, she took me to church, and I was awed by the fragrance. As a preschooler, I had sometimes noticed ladies with kerchiefs entering the building as they held candles; I had also observed that when Papa and I attended *shul*, only males were present.

At the tender age of three, I therefore reasoned that women were Catholic and men were Jewish.

Undoubtedly, religiosity in my childhood milieu was wrapped up with elements bound to confuse an impressionable youngster. In an illustrative anecdote that still remains vivid, I was once babysitting little Joseph alone in our apartment while my parents went to a *bar mitzvah*. It was *shabbos* afternoon, and I had been firmly warned by grandmother Chassiah never to touch the kitchen stove on the shabbos because a venomous snake lived inside and might lethally strike if someone came close. It was her way of preventing the possibility that I might desecrate *shabbos* by lighting the stove, and I believed her tale completely.

Suddenly, I had to relieve myself, but I was afraid to expose Joseph for even a minute to a possible snake attack. I grabbed a chopping knife and a broom and stood guard over the stove to protect him. Papa walked in and saw me standing in a puddle of urine and shivering as I clutched the knife and broom. When I explained about the snake warning, Papa first cleaned and re-dressed me, then immediately took us over to grandmother's apartment several blocks away. Right there and then, on the shabbos, he angrily berated her for filling my head with pernicious nonsense. "Tell him the truth," he thundered. "Tell him the truth!"

Papa rarely talked in my presence about faith, but one particular incident made a big impression on me. One day when I must have been about three years old, I saw him vigorously *davening* (praying with ecstatic movement) in his room.

"Papa, what are you doing?" I asked.

"I'm talking to God," he replied.

Coming closer, I noticed that beneath Papa's *tallit* (prayer shawl), his face was streaked with tears. So I innocently asked, "Does it hurt to talk to God?"

Papa smiled wanly and said, "No, it's just been a long time since I had such a nice talk with God. And it feels really good."

CHAPTER TWO

~

A Viennese Boyhood

My intellectual life really began when I started fifth grade at the esteemed Dr. Rabbiner Chajes Gymnasium, for my parents had gained enough financial security to rescue me from public schooling. Founded in 1919 in honor of Vienna's erudite chief rabbi, Hirsch (Zvi) Perez Chajes, it presented both a Jewish and a secular curriculum within a socialist-Zionist framework. A former professor at the University of Florence, Rabbi Chajes was also a celebrated Zionist leader until his death in 1927. The *gymnasium* reflected well his cosmopolitan perspective on Judaism. A progressive coeducational institution, it had a formidable curriculum that included mathematics and science, Latin and Germanic literature, and modern Hebrew.

Most of my classmates were Jewish by ethnicity but came from nonobservant families. An exception was my friend Pappenheim, whose father was involved in Agudat Yisroel, an Orthodox association for political action. A printer by trade, he published a German translation of a letter recently composed by Rabbi Yosef Yitzchak Schneersohn—Rebbe of the Lubavitcher Hasidim—in response to a query on what Hasidism had to offer German Jewish intellectuals. I knew little about Hasidism, but the inspiring pamphlet made a strong impression on me.

Wanting to have the best of both worlds—secular and religious—my parents also enrolled me in an Orthodox afternoon Hebrew school. My first teacher there was Mr. Rosenfeld, who usually spoke in a regular voice. One day he carefully began instructing the class in the traditional singsong melody used for absorbing the Talmud. Sitting in the back of the room, I loudly mocked his cadence and inflection. Immediately summoning me before the class, Mr. Rosenfeld sat me on his lap and slapped my face. I instantly burst into tears, and then he started to cry too.

"It was for the sake of this *niggun* (melody)," he sobbed, "that your great-grandfather and my great-grandfather were both burned at the stake for their devoted study of the Talmud. This *niggun* sustained them through such hard times for Jews, and you laugh at it? Now do you understand what you did wrong?" Ashamed for my immature behavior, I unhesitatingly nodded, and Mr. Rosenfeld motioned that I should return to my seat. From that sobering episode, I gained an increasing interest in Jewish melody and its importance for both study and liturgy. In particular, I began to observe more closely the prayer melodies that Papa chanted at home.

Jewish music began to occupy an increasingly important part of my life when I joined the highly regarded choir of the Polnischer Tempel. It was a big, architecturally attractive synagogue frequented by those who followed Polish ritual—and stood close to the *shtibel* where Papa often worshipped. The Polnischer Tempel's chief cantor was the renowned Herr Frankel. For a youngster my age to be a choir member was a real honor, and when at age twelve I was finally permitted to sing a solo, I felt a tremendous sense of pride and accomplishment.

Eventually, it came time for my *bar mitzvah*. Though I would like to recall otherwise, the whole process of study and the synagogue service itself harbored little inspiration or joy. Nor did it even have substantial emotional significance for my family. Unfortunately, this situation was probably true for the vast majority of European Jewish boys at the time; only since the rise of affluent, suburban Judaism in the United States have *bar* and *bat mitzvot* become a tremendous focus of family energy and money.

Among Hasidic Jews of the time, the ritual was celebrated mostly after the Torah reading, when the boy would present a *p'shettl*—a clever Talmudic interpretation often culled from the writings of a great rabbi. So here's what transpired. First, Papa taught me how to say the *musaf* prayer of Shabbat. That I mastered easily enough. Next, in order for me to learn the *maftir* (the final section of the weekly Torah portion), my parents hired a special tutor. That too I mastered dutifully but without inspiration.

As for my *haftorah* (designated selections from the Prophets related to the weekly Torah portion), at the time, it was not chanted melodically in accordance with the Lithuanian Jewish style known as *trope*. Rather, my expected style of Torah reading—associated with Papa's Galician background—was known as *yecke* and involved no appealing chanting.

And my speech? It was written entirely by an old Hebrew teacher and composed of stock expressions of filial piety and other clichés. He lived in the resort town of Bad-Voeslau—where we spent our summers and where my *bar mitzvah* took place in August 1937.

Shortly before the actual synagogue event, Papa bought me a good pair of *t'fillin* in a town called Tismenitz; years later, I learned that it had been the birthplace of Sigmund Freud's own religious father, Jakob Freud. Papa explained that every day after my *bar mitzvah* I was to put these on—and then demonstrated how to wind the twin black-boxed straps until I could do so easily. And that was about it. Though today I certainly try to make *bar* and *bat mitzvah* events a deeply spiritual initiation for Jewish boys and girls, my own possessed almost no transcendent or mystical power.

Following my *bar mitzvah*, my education in retrospect continued to be somewhat schizophrenic. My parents enrolled me in the Israelite Hauptschule on the Maltzgasse, a relatively religious middle school. My favorite subject was definitely chemistry, taught by Mr. Lehrer Loewy. I dreamed of becoming a professional chemist. My mother would often say that she wanted me to become a professor doktor, rabbiner. Alas, what she had in mind was not the shape in which she received all those achievements from me.

At the same time, I attended Yesoday HaTorah, a strictly Orthodox yeshiva, every afternoon. I learned important skills for mastering Talmudic content and language, which well complemented the modern Hebrew I was eagerly absorbing at the Israelite Hauptschule. Unfortunately, the teaching approach at Yesoday HaTorah was cold, joyless, and authoritarian. Not surprisingly, I found it almost completely repugnant. Lacking awareness of how little I was actually gaining from Yesoday HaTorah, my parents happily believed that they were providing me with an excellent Jewish background. Less than a decade later, as a fledgling Jewish educator in the United States, I would seek to innovate creatively from the dismal pedagogy represented by Yesoday HaTorah—and all institutions like it—as fully as possible.

Undoubtedly, my most satisfying Jewish communal involvement as a Viennese teenager occurred with Brit BILU—a Zionist youth organization whose name was an acronym of the verse from Isaiah 2:5: "Beit Ya'akov Lekhu Venelhka" (House of Jacob, come, let us go up!). Decades before Theodor Herzl made history with his Zionist writing and activism, BILU had been founded in Russia after a horrific pogrom in 1881. Inspired by Karl Marx's writings as well as the Bible, the small group mobilized idealistic secular young Jews to establish farm cooperatives throughout the Holy Land. In Austria, Brit BILU had competed with the better-organized Zionist movement known as Hashomer

Hatzair (Youth Guard), which had originated in 1913 Galicia-Hungary. For nearly twenty years, its activists had been pioneering settlements in the Land of Israel and, by the mid- to late 1930s, numbered nearly seventy thousand members worldwide.

However, Hashomer Hatzair in 1934 had been banned as subversive by Austria's fascist chancellor, Engelhart Dollfuss. As a result of an unsuccessful left-wing coup against his increasingly authoritarian government that year, Dollfuss had imprisoned or exiled thousands of socialists and communists and officially shut down many political and social organizations—including the avowedly Marxist Hashomer Hatzair. Thus, taking its place among Viennese youth like myself was the politically acceptable Brit BILU. Basically, it was the same old bride wearing a new veil.

Every shabbos afternoon after synagogue service and lunch, I would join with other Jewish teenagers to sing new Hebrew pioneer songs, dance the *horra*, and listen to impassioned speeches and upbeat reports from the Land of Israel. Socialist-Zionist pioneers had already established schools, cultural facilities, a publishing house, and a daily newspaper—and had recently founded the first kibbutz of American émigrés, at Ein Hashofet. I enjoyed the idealistic excitement and socializing at Brit BILU a great deal.

But such secular festivity did not fully satisfy my soul. For after several hours of singing and dancing at Brit BILU, I would then walk to shabbos-ending services held by Tzerei Agudas Yisroel (Youth of Agudas Yisroel), an Orthodox European organization that condemned Zionism as a mocking betrayal of traditional Jewish faith. None of my friends seemed able, or even willing for that matter, to involve themselves in both—seemingly contradictory—manifestations of Judaism. But for me, I felt a liberating inner unity that ultimately transcended all such apparent contradictions.

Shortly before my *bar mitzvah*, I became an avid reader of adolescent fiction, especially mystery and detective novels. My favorite writer was a man almost completely unknown today in the United States: Karl Friedrich May. Born into poverty, he had been arrested several times for petty theft, then imprisoned for counterfeiting, before turning to pulp fiction writing as a far more lucrative career. Beginning in the 1870s, until his death in 1912, May churned out action stories with vivid titles like *Winnetou, the Apache Knight* and *The Treasure of Nugget Mountain*, set mainly in the American West. Among his immensely popular characters was "Old Shatterhand," a German supercowboy who made his American counterparts look like bumbling fools or thugs.

Ironically, May never actually visited the United States until 1908 and never even ventured west of Buffalo, New York. But that meant nothing to me or millions of his other ardent fans, who included Albert Einstein, serious novelists like Herman Hesse and Herman Mann, and Adolf Hitler—who reputedly reread May's tales eagerly as an adult. At times, his pulp fiction was set in the Middle East and likewise filled with shoot-'em-up melodrama that pitted heroic goodness against dastardly evil. Sometimes I was so captivated by May's vivid books, which I borrowed from the local public library, that I pretended to be sick. That way, I could stay home on school days and immerse myself in exciting adventures occurring in far-off, exotic lands.

CHAPTER THREE

~

Austria under Hitler

Throughout the 1930s, as Austria's economic woes steadily worsened, anti-Semitism had certainly been on the rise. But under Chancellor Kurt von Schuschnigg, it was rarely overtly violent. Though as a youth back then I could not have articulated it, our general sensibility was that as long as one metaphorically kissed the cross, one could live adequately as a Jew.

Then in March 1938 Hitler annexed Austria in what was called the Anschluss (linkup). All governmental power was quickly transferred to the Nazis, as German Wehrmacht troops established military control throughout the country. News filled the air of elderly Jews at gunpoint being forced to clean streets using toothbrushes as crowds mocked and jeered. Sometimes in broad daylight, Jews were gunned down by Gestapo as onlookers hurried by.

At the Israelite Hauptschule on the Maltzgasse, all education quickly deteriorated. Within a week of the Nazi annexation, my beloved chemistry teacher, Mr. Loewy, escaped to Prague to avoid arrest as a socialist. As other instructors left too, the administration was required to hire retired, non-Jewish teachers called *Schulrath* (educational emeriti; privy counselors). Some were competent, but others were openly anti-Semitic, including a literature teacher who extolled German poetry for its "master race" outlook and denigrated anything Jewish.

My religious education at Yesoday HaTorah also quickly worsened. Enraged that my haircut failed to conform to super-Orthodox standards of piety, one teacher took a blunt knife to my scalp and began hacking away the offending tufts of hair. I came home to my parents and demanded that they notify the police. Papa and Mamma were disturbed but vigorously advised against it—for by then, the Nazis already controlled the penal system and would have relished torturing my Hebrew teacher to death.

Throughout the spring and summer, our family would meet at grandmother's house and peruse various atlases in hopes of finding a national refuge. There was a poignant Jewish song popular at the time; its title was "Where Can I Go, for Every Door Is Locked to Me?" ("Vu ahin kenn ikh geyn az farshpart far mir iz a yede tiyr?".)

For centuries, Jews have used humor to cope with life's vicissitudes, and this was true for us in Austria after Hitler took over. In particular, gallows humor abounded. One joke went like this: A man walks into an Austrian travel agency and hurriedly says, "Can you sell me a ticket someplace?" The travel agent spins the globe and asks, "Maybe to Paraguay?" Leaning forward, the man nods quickly, and the agent replies, "Wait. Do you have a baptismal certificate?" The man answers, "No, I'm Jewish." Shrugging, the agent spins the globe further, looks for British Guyana—for here or there—and finally says, "Sorry, there isn't a place on this globe to where I can sell you a ticket." So, the Jew thinks for a moment, then asks hopefully, "Maybe you got another globe?"

As the months progressed, it became increasingly clear that Jewish life in Austria was doomed. The Nazis had a joke too: "Are you Aryan, or are you learning English?" It was their way of saying that Jews no longer had a future in Austria—or perhaps outside the United States and Canada.

By June 1938, academic education was over for me. I had wanted to be a chemist, but that vocational goal no longer made sense. Under the Third Reich, Jews were no longer permitted to work as lawyers, physicians, scientists, and other educated professionals. By that time, we also knew about the gas murders being performed by Nazis at Dachau against the mentally retarded: Was this the future of Germanic science? What made sense was to learn a trade, but what kind? I soon decided to become a weaver and enrolled in a weaving school instead of returning to classes at the Dr. Rabbiner Chajes Gymnasium.

Then, in early November, I suddenly developed appendicitis. My parents rushed me to Vienna's renowned Rothschild Hospital. Because it was a Jewish institution, the Nazis still permitted Jews to work there medically. Its well-regarded staff included a young psychiatrist named Viktor Frankl, who would later become famous for his inspirational Holocaust memoir, *Man's Search for Meaning*, and his innovative treatment method of existential psychiatry.

My appendix operation on November 7 was successful, and I was convalescing in a large postsurgical unit with many beds. Just a few weeks past my fourteenth birthday, I was among the youngest patients there. Time was passing slowly, and I found myself impatiently waiting to resume weaving classes. Then came the night of November 9.

Known as Kristallnacht (Night of Broken Glass), it took its name from the myriad shards of broken glass that littered grounds the next morning. Historians today identify that night, and the night of November 10, as the actual start of the Holocaust, for the Nazi leadership orchestrated the worst pogrom in modern Jewish history. Rampaging mobs throughout Germany and its newly annexed territories of Austria and the Sudetenland attacked Jews on the street, demolished hundreds of synagogues with explosives, and pillaged thousands of shops and homes. Cemeteries and schools were vandalized. Falsely attributing these carefully planned actions to spontaneous local fervor, Nazi officials simultaneously arrested over thirty thousand Jews, including prominent journalists and writers, socialist politicians, and others, and sent them without trial to newly built concentration camps.

The pretext for this mass arrest was the assassination earlier that week of a minor Nazi diplomat in Paris by Herszel Grynszpan, a vengeful Polish Jewish teenager. Joseph Goebbels, Hitler's chief of propaganda, seized upon this isolated act—which he blamed on a conspiracy of "international Jewry"—as justification for launching the sweeping arrests and concentration camp internments linked to Kristallnacht.

The events of Kristallnacht included an atrocity I witnessed from my hospital bed. Among the patients in our postsurgical unit was a young man patched up from bayonet wounds who had been recovering for the past few days. Suddenly that evening, a Gestapo police officer entered our unit and began screaming. He insisted that the man was a Bolshevik agent pretending to be injured in order to evade the authorities. Before all our horrified eyes, the officer attacked the prostrate man and ripped off all his bandages. He bled to death in front of us. It was a horrifying moment, and right then and there, at the age of fourteen, I stared at my own mortality.

Adding to my misery, I was initially unable to reach my parents and siblings to learn if they were all right. Anything now seemed possible. Thank God, they were not harmed. Several days later, I was medically released from Rothschild Hospital and my father brought me home by taxi. We passed the Polnischer Tempel—a beautiful synagogue, ornamented with twin Turkish-style turrets— where I had happily sung in the choir. To my shock, the entire building was destroyed. Its pillars and entrance were nothing but rubble.

Fearful of being shot by Gestapo agents, my parents did not dare to search for the Torah scrolls amid the debris, but a few other congregants bravely did so.

On Vienna's streets, it was now open season on Jews. One of my elementary school friends had been a boy named Hans. He had no father and was poorer than me. His mother took in laundry to support them. Looking back, I think Hans's mother had worked in the world's oldest profession when younger but no longer did so. As a child, I had felt sorry for Hans and persuaded my mother to give me a cheesecake bun for him every morning at snack time. Jew and Christian, we were buddies.

But now things were different. Hans had become a surly teenager. Right after I was released from appendix surgery, he sadistically demanded that I perform deep knee bends to his satisfaction. He also made me wear a sign that read, "Aryans don't buy from Jews." What if I had refused his commands? Jews were being shot openly on Vienna's streets. Refusing a command cost too much for oneself and one's family.

Soon after Kristallnacht, I experienced another incident with a former public school classmate, Ernst. Confronting my friend Moses Eisenberg and me on the street, Ernst ordered us to accompany him to the river, where we came to a site under a bridge. As a Nazi storm trooper stood nearby watching amusedly and playing with his Luger pistol, Ernst proceeded to beat both of us until we were bruised and bloody. I am sure either of us could have defended ourselves adequately, but to strike Ernst back might risk terrible consequences for our entire families.

Less than a week after Kristallnacht, while my family lay sleeping late at night, we were suddenly awakened by the sound of heavy boot steps on the stairway. On orders from the Gestapo, the Austrian police had come to arrest Papa. Like thousands of other Polish Jews, he had been living in Austria for years with an expired visa. This had never mattered before, but the Nazis were determined to eliminate all such persons from the Third Reich.

Papa was first taken to a detention center, then placed on a train to deport him back to Poland. Only a few weeks before in Germany, the Nazis had arrested seventeen thousand Jews of Polish citizenship—many of whom had been living in Germany for decades—and initiated their forced return to Poland. When the Polish government refused their admittance, the Nazis placed these Jews in horrendous "relocation camps" situated on the Polish frontier.

To avoid this fate, Papa cleverly got off the train as it reached Zbonzhin on the German-Polish border. He then boarded a train to Dresden, Germany, and from there took a third train back to Vienna. But now he was in real trouble if caught, for the city of Vienna had become a police state.

Without official papers authorizing Austrian residency, Papa would be immediately identified as a Jewish relocation escapee and sent to a full-scale concentration camp. Afraid to return home, he lived clandestinely among relatives and friends for a night at a time.

Our family had to flee Austria in any way possible. It was only a matter of time before Papa would be discovered by the Gestapo. By December, my parents had decided on escaping to Belgium, but plotting the logistics was not easy for we were under close scrutiny. The Nazis had instituted a program of taking unemployed non-Jews and assigning them to run Jewish-owned shops and businesses like my parents' clothing remnant store. As compensation for their "management work," these Komissars were entitled to a percentage of the enterprise's gross income as their take-home pay. So my parents' escape plans had to be undertaken with great secrecy.

Rumors circulated that every so often the Dutch border would be open to entering Germans for twenty-four hours at a time. With high hopes, my family surreptitiously traveled to Emmerich, but we were not permitted to enter the Netherlands. So back to Vienna we went. Time was running out. If the Nazis found Papa, he and everyone who had harbored him would undoubtedly be sent to concentration camps. Finally, our plan was ready. With the aid of professional smugglers, my immediate family would escape from Cologne, Germany, into Belgium. Accompanying us would be Papa's brother-in-law and sister-in-law (Yankele and Peppi) and their son Sam, also known as Zalman. The fee would be immense, but we had no other remaining options.

Unfortunately, Papa could not persuade his brother Akiva to join us. A poor man, he owned a small grocery in an outlying Viennese district. He and his wife had three children. When Hitler took over Austria, Akiva asked Papa to lend him money so he could return with his family to Poland. He believed that Jewish life would be easier there.

Papa begged Akiva not to go. "We need to go West, not East!" Papa had urged. "I'll share with you every penny I have, but please don't go back to Poland."

But Akiva was stubborn and afraid for his life in Nazi-ruled Austria. So Papa gave him the money, and Akiva and his family relocated back to Oswiecim, Poland. It was a terrible mistake. Today, that town is much better known by the infamous German name it acquired after the Nazi takeover: Auschwitz. Its concentration camp opened in June 1940. My brother Rabbi Joseph Chayim has been a historian for the Yad Vashem Holocaust Memorial in Israel, and he learned that Akiva Schachter, his wife, and their three children were among the very first Jews to be murdered there.

CHAPTER FOUR

~

Diamond Cutting and Hasidism in Antwerp

Our escape into Belgium was a harrowing experience. After paying the smugglers a huge sum in advance, Papa, my brother, and I, and Uncle Yankele, Aunt Peppi, and their young son Sam were instructed to cross at a particular checkpoint, and there, at the German border, we were allowed entry. We anxiously proceeded on foot to the prearranged meeting point and waited for several hours. Suddenly, a single smuggler appeared as our guide to help us cross over to Belgium.

We were then obliged to walk through mine-laden fields and hills. Belgian searchlights brightened everything every few minutes so that we were often forced to crawl on hands and knees. It had been only a few weeks since my appendix operation, and I was in physical agony as the long night progressed. Finally, after six or seven hours, we reached the town of Eupen-Malmedie, on the Belgian side.

There we waited, hidden in a barn, while the smuggler went first into the farmhouse, then talked with taxi drivers in a nearby garage, to find someone willing to take the risky trip to Antwerp. After turning over our jewelry and rings as collateral payment, we managed to convince a driver to take us.

We arrived just before dawn. The taxi driver had dropped us off in the Jewish district, and as we eagerly walked toward an open bakery, a Belgian gendarme suddenly blocked our way. Demanding to see our documents, he began to interrogate us right there on the street. Uncle Yankele suddenly pleaded, "Don't send us back, I beg you." The man's heart opened; it was amazing to see.

"Well, you can't go walking around without papers," he said, then immediately directed us to Antwerp's city hall, where we could obtain temporary identification cards. And so, that morning we became official Austrian refugees and gained lodging from the Jewish Joint Distribution Committee.

Initially upon settling in Antwerp, I wanted to continue with my schooling. Instead of resuming training as a weaver, I decided to become an electrician. That seemed like a more useful, financially stable occupation in those unsettled times. In keeping with our family tradition, Papa was now studying to become a *shochet* (ritual slaughterer). But more than ancestral honor was at stake: he had immigrant relatives in far-off New Castle, New Brunswick, who could get him a Canadian work visa as a kosher animal slaughterer once he gained rabbinic certification. Of course, our whole family would then be granted visas as well. The Third Reich clearly aimed to take control of Europe, and this might be only our chance for safety.

Attending electrician school, I passably learned Flemish. But when school ended for the summer, I decided not to register for any more instruction. Electrical work just wasn't for me. Instead, I decided to apprentice myself to my mother's *landsman*, fellow Zholkover Yoshke Shapira, who had come to settle in Antwerp from my birthplace and owned a small fur shop. Yoshke was warm and friendly to me. I began by learning to sew snippets of Persian lamb into plates, then to fashion plates into whole coats. There I learned to match and sew Persian paws. Despite Yoshke's encouragement, my early enthusiasm quickly gave way to boredom, for the work was tedious and uncreative. As my fifteenth birthday passed in July 1939, I began to feel increasingly resentful and angry about my life. My dreams of becoming a scientist— a professional chemist—were just as much rubble now as the beautiful stone masonry of our former synagogue in Vienna. Both had been destroyed by the Nazis, and God had let it happen. In retrospect, I see that my wounded sense of religious piety, my weakening faith in divine justice, fueled my anger.

I wanted to pick a fight with somebody about all this, and so I went to Tz-irey Agudat Yisroel, the local hangout for Orthodox Jewish youth in Antwerp. I had been there a few times, and I knew that there would be a Shabbat afternoon class on *Pirkey Avot* (*Ethics of the Fathers*), the second-century foundational text of Jewish ethics. Seething inwardly at the naïveté of the earnest faces around me, I stood by the doorway and listened.

Sure enough, a student began to read the famous dictum "Every Jew Has a Share in the World to Come," and I suddenly burst into an angry retort. "Pie in the sky!" I shouted. "Has anybody ever come back from there? No, because it's all *narishkeit*, rubbish. Karl Marx was right: religion is the opiate of the masses!" I poured it all out. Enraged by my disruption, all the students seemed ready to pounce on me. I wanted them to disagree, to try tearing me apart verbally, just so I could enjoy the satisfaction of triumphing over their feeble insults and denials.

But the teacher suddenly quieted them. "Sh-sh-sh," he intoned softly while extending his hands in a calming gesture. "What else?" he asked me gently. Startled by his mildness, I halted for a moment, then continued pouring out the rage in my soul. Finally, I had nothing more to say.

Smiling empathically, the teacher asked, "Would you like to hear from someone who agrees with you?" My anger completely dissipated, I nodded wordlessly. He asked for someone to bring *Tractate Sanhedrin* of the Talmud, then slowly read aloud a statement that I found incredibly liberating and inspiring:

As I see it, there is a necessity to speak out concerning the cardinal principles of our faith, which are of the utmost importance. Know that the Masters of Torah differ in their opinion concerning the good that will accrue to man through the fulfillment of the Commandments which His blessed Name has commanded us through our Master Moses, peace be upon him. So also do their opinions conflict concerning the evil that will be found in transgressing these. The differences of opinion are many, due to the great diversity of minds. Also, due to this, a great number of errors have crept into their thinking, so that it is nearly impossible to find anyone who will have a clear answer for you in this area, with the exception of those opinions which are contaminated by fallacy.

There is one group which thinks that the *good* is the "Garden of Eden," a place where one eats and drinks without having to work and expend effort. In this Garden, there are houses built of gems and beds covered with silk, rivers of wine, brooks flowing with fragrant essences, and many things of that kind. The *evil* is the *Gehenna*, a place wherein fire rages, bodies are being burned, and all kinds of pain are inflicted on man. Their tales of the ingenuity of the infliction of the pain on the suffering sinners are limited only by their imaginations. This group adduces proof for their ideas from the words of our sages of blessed memory and from sentences in the Bible whose simple meaning would seem to agree with their idea, either partially or fully.

The *second* group thinks that the hoped for *good* is the "Days of the Messiah"—may He soon be revealed to us—for in that time, men will be angels, all of them living and existing for eternity, of tall stature, increasing in number and in strength, until the whole world will be settled for eternity. According to their thought, this Messiah will, with the help of His blessed Name, live forever. In those days, the earth will give forth ready-woven garments, ready-baked bread, and many other things that are, as we know, impossible. The *evil* that we will find then will be that some people shall have to be absent at that time and will not merit seeing it. This group also adduces proof from many things that are found in the sayings of our sages and in the statements of the Bible, whose simple meaning seems to coincide with what they say, either partially or completely.

The *third* group thinks that the hoped for good is the "Resurrection of the dead," that man will live again after his death and return to live with relatives and members of his family. In those days, they will eat and drink and never die. The *evil* that we will find then is that some will not be resurrected after their death in order to live with their relatives and friends. They too adduce proof for this from many sayings that are found in the words of the sages and verses of the Bible whose ample meaning would tend to imply all this, either partially or fully.

The *fourth* group holds that the intention of fulfilling the Commandments is peace of mind and bodily relaxation and the fulfillment of all bodily appetites in *this* world. They hold that the fat of the land and many possessions, a large number of children, health of the body, as well as peace and security will be their reward. They believe that there will be a Jewish king, whose rule will be firmly against those who have previously oppressed us. The *evil* that will reach us if we deny the Torah is the very opposite of these things. They point out that this evil is reaching us today, since we are in exile. They too adduce proof to their thinking from statements to be found in the Torah, from the *admonitions* and other things that are plainly written in the Scriptures.

A *fifth* group—and it includes many—combine all these things together and says the hoped for thing is that the Messiah will come and resurrect the dead, and we will enter into the Garden of Eden, eat, drink, and be healthy for the rest of our days, and never die.

But concerning the wondrous point, the *World to Come*, you will find very few who will have paid attention to it and will have taken this as one of the fundamental beliefs of our faith. And so you can see that there reigns a great deal of confusion concerning what constitutes the "end" good and the "means" good; for they would make it seem that the *good* they promise is an end and *final good*. There are many people among the masses who ask how the dead shall rise again, whether they will be naked or dressed. They want to know whether they will rise in the same shrouds in which they were buried: whether the same embroidery, image, and straightness of seam will be on their garments. Or else they wish to know if, at the time of the Messiah, there will still be rich and poor, weak and strong, and have all sorts of questions of this kind.

You who read this book will, I hope, understand this analogy, which I will draw for you; then you may prepare your heart and understand what I mean to tell you.

Imagine that there is a small child whom they have brought to the teacher that he may be taught the Torah—for the acquisition of Torah is the *real* and great *good*, for it will bring him to the attainment of perfection. However, due to his youth and the weakness of his mind, he does not yet understand the true value of the good and the meaning of the acquisition of perfection, and therefore, by necessity, the teacher, who has acquired greater perfection than the child, must spur it on in its studies by means of sweets which are beloved by this child according to his youth. Thus the teacher may say, "Read and I will give you nuts or figs; I will give you a bit of honey," and due to this, the child reads and expends effort. This the child does not do because of the content of the reading—for he does not understand its value—but only in order to gain the delight of the food which he has been promised. For the child sees a greater value in the food than in the reading. Therefore the child reckons that the reading and learning are effort and work, which he does not mind, providing that it will gain for him the end of his desire. As the child grows and his mind becomes stronger and that which was valuable to him before loses its value, while other things rise in value for him, at the time when the child turns to others for attention, then the teacher may tell the child, "Read and I will give you nice shoes or desirable garments." For this, the child will put his effort into reading. This he will do not for the content of the reading but for the sake of the garment, which is more valuable to him in his eyes than the Torah. As he rises to greater perfection even these things will have lost their value for him, and he will then turn his attention to that which is greater and of more importance. Then his teacher will tell him, "Study this portion of the chapter, and I will give you one dinar, or two dinars." For the sake of the dinars, the child reads and puts in effort so that he may gain the money, for that money is of greater value to him than the reading. At this moment, the end of his learning is that he shall be able to gain the money promised to him. Then, when he has grown further and even this will have lost its value in his eyes, his teacher will motivate him with honors, telling him, "Study in order to become a head of court, a magistrate, and so that people may honor you and rise before you just as they do for so and so." Then the child reads in order to gain this rung, and the receiving of honor will then be the highest value that he knows, so that for this he will expend his effort.

Yet all this ought to be despised, although it is necessary for the lack of intelligence of men at first. For in the beginning he sets as the *end* of wisdom something which is extrinsic to it, since always the aim is other than the content of his study proper and extrinsic to it. This is a folly covering the truth, and concerning such a study our sages have said that it is study "not for its own sake." They meant, in other words, he who does the *mitzvot* and studies the Torah not for its own sake but for the sake of something else. Concerning this, our sages have said, "Do not turn the Torah into a crown for thy greatness, nor into a spade with which to dig." Their intention is to point out what I have already explained to you: namely, that it is not the purpose of wisdom to become a means for honor or for the earning of money. How can one busy oneself with the Torah of His blessed Name when one does this in order to make a living by it? For the entire purpose and end of the study of Torah is to know it. There is no other end to the truth but knowing that it is truth, and the Torah is truth. Consequently, the end of its knowledge is to obey it. Therefore, it is forbidden to the man of perfection to say, "If I will obey these Commandments—which are the gaining of the virtues—and if I will abstain from sins—which are the vices—thus following the Commands with which His blessed Name has commanded us, what reward shall I get for this?" For this is precisely what the child does when it asks, "What will you give me if I read?" The child is answered that he will gain this or that, depending on his state of insight, since the child must still be extrinsically motivated. Therefore we answer the child according to his folly; as it is said in Proverbs, "Answer the fool according to his folly." Concerning this, our sages have already warned us, saying that a man should not take anything from the world of things as his reward for the service of His blessed Name. This is what the man of perfection, who had reached the understanding of the truth of things, Antigonos, the man of Socho, said: "Do not be like the servants who serve their master for the sake of receiving a bonus, but be like the servants who serve their master without expecting a bonus." He meant by this that a person must believe the truth for its own sake and that a person who does so, we call a "servant of love." Concerning such a one, the sages have quoted the verse "His utter desire is in his Commands," and Rabbi Eliezer said, "In His Commandments, but not in the reward of His Commandments, is his desire."

"So, you see the *Rambam* (Maimonides) agrees with you," the teacher said. "And we don't believe in the same God that you don't believe in. Maybe you should join us, and we'll all study Torah together?" I slowly took a seat, and he proceeded to review Maimonides's Thirteen Articles of Faith. They radiated such purity that my soul felt uplifted, but I felt even more uplifted by this gentle, warm teacher of Judaism, who had let me say what I needed to say.

Over time, I learned that his name was Baruch Merzl and that he was associated with Chabad Hasidism based in White Russia. Their local yeshiva was in Heide, near Antwerp, and their mentor was Moshe Tchechoval. He was originally from Kishniev in Bessarabia and had studied Hasidism with Kishniev's chief rabbi, Rav Tzirelson. Not a professional rabbinic scholar, Tchechoval earned his living as a *diamonteur*, someone dealing in diamonds. He spent most of each week at the Heide yeshiva as dean of students (*mashgiach* of the *Beyt Hamidrash*), assisting them with difficult Talmudic texts. He also taught Rabbi Moses Chaim Luzzatto's principles of spiritual management in *The Path of the Upright* (*Mesillat Yesharim*), Chabad Hasidism, and related topics to motivated students. Their chief text was the *Tanya*, a dazzling philosophical-mystical treatise composed by Chabad's founder, Rabbi Schneur Zalman of Liady, in the late eighteenth century.

I suddenly realized that this was the Hasidic group whose current leader, Rabbi Yosef Yitzchak Schneersohn, had written a Torah pamphlet that one of my friends had shown me and that had inspired me back in Vienna several years before. When Baruch Merzl invited me to join their diamond-cutting enterprise and learn Hasidism, I leaped at the opportunity. My old friend from Vienna, Avram Weingarten, soon joined our group.

The next few months in Antwerp were among the happiest of my youth. Nazi Vienna had receded into the background. Every morning except for Shabbat, of course, I would join a group of young men in a large workroom filled with special lathes. Diamond cutting is noisy work, and we would sit around a large table and often sing Hasidic melodies at the tops of our voices. At other times, one fellow would sit with a microphone and teach the Talmud while we all wore earphones and cut diamonds together. If someone had a question, he would give a signal, and the speaker would shut off the machines temporarily. The question would be answered, and then we would all continue with our work.

Although resembling a high-spirited yeshiva, it was also an ecumenical group. We listened to inspiring secular works, such as *Jean Christoff* by Romain Rolland, and those by Anker Larsen, a Danish playwright and novelist. It was a marvelous school and workplace for me, and I enjoyed both the physical and spiritual aspects. Baruch Merzl, who would later survive incarceration in Auschwitz, settle in Israel, and write profound Jewish philosophy, was a superb teacher. Sometimes, I came to pray with Moshe Tchechoval's group at his home, and those too were wonderful moments.

One shabbos afternoon, I went outdoors with the Chabad group. I felt something stirring within me and strolled off to be alone. In recent weeks, one key question had challenged and perplexed me: Why is God hiding in the world? I was filled with a mood of exaltation. It was strange at the time, but since then, I have experienced it is as a preparation for spiritual disclosure. Everything around seemed connected.

A luminous brightness surrounded me, and now the answer became totally clear: God bestowed free will to us so that we might grow spiritually, and therefore this is how human life had to be. I felt exhilarated and suffused with a wonderful sense of wholeness and unshakable faith. At that moment, I prayed with all my soul that God should not let me lose this insight. In a real sense, that epiphany in Antwerp has stayed with me ever since.

Later, I would often think about these moments of epiphany. The rabbis of the Talmud and Midrash would describe how totally unusual and difficult it is to split the sea, and yet, it did not require any special preparation; the theophany allows of the character of unearned grace and came almost unbidden to the people. The rabbis expressed it by saying that the hand-maiden witnessing the splitting of the sea saw more of the divine than did the Prophet Ezekiel in his vision of the celestial chariot. The language of the rabbis translates itself in a way that I would colloquially express as a moment in which God was a "flasher."

My intuition tells me that such moments occur much more frequently than we think. For example, I think of the period known as the Axial Age: the epoch of Socrates, Plato, and Aristotle; the Hebrew prophets Isaiah, Ezekiel, and Jeremiah; Zoroaster; the Buddha and Mahavira; Lao Tze and Confucius. What was happening at that time? Apparently, a great, powerful flash of insight came to the whole world. However, these were gifted people who recounted to us how they received that flash. Each one had vessels that were prepared by profound meditation, by their humanitarian concern, and by the way in which they puzzled over the great questions of the universe.

I too had puzzled over the question of the freedom of choice and predestination: the question of whether revelation is a true possibility and whether God communicates with us. So it was that *shabbos* afternoon. The moment of theophany did not pass me by.

Intellectually, I was bolstered by the works of Isaac Breuer, a brilliant Hungarian-born rabbi who lived most of his years in Frankfurt before settling in late 1930s Jerusalem; his maternal grandfather was Samson Raphael Hirsch, the founder of Modern Orthodox Judaism, but Breuer was a brilliant innovator in his own right. I had begun exploring his novels and philosophical works back in Vienna and now delved more deeply into his stimulating ideas. I was especially influenced by his apologia titled *The World as Creation and as Nature*, for it successfully seemed to defend traditional faith against the onslaught of science. Breuer's multifaceted writings remain relevant today, but unfortunately few have ever been translated from German into English.

My only complaint at the time was that I was not yet permitted to learn *Tanya*, as Baruch Merzl's group insisted I was not yet ready to understand it beyond its literal meaning and to absorb its abstruse insights into human existence. I felt very frustrated in reaction. One shabbos afternoon, while they were meeting to study this exalted text, I locked myself in the bathroom so I could overhear the discussion. They discovered me and gave me a scolding that I had deliberately ignored their admonition. On another occasion, someone found me reading the *Tanya* alone. He firmly closed the book, took it from my hands, and exclaimed, "This is not yet for you!" Nearly heartbroken, I waited for Baruch Merzl. He took me for a walk and consoled me by explaining, "All your longing for Hasidism will be rewarded by *Hashem* (God) in due time. Just wait until you are ready."

Soon after, the group gave me a copy of the *Tanya* for my upcoming sixteenth birthday later that summer. However, they made it clear that I was to begin study only after their go-ahead, and this time I sincerely agreed.

By now, it was spring 1940. I had learned something of the furrier trade, and I had learned some of the diamond business. My father's *shochet* certification had been approved, and after traveling to Brussels to obtain special League of Nations passports (known as "Nansen passports" in reference to their 1922 designer Fridtjof Nansen) for stateless persons, we were ready to get our U.S. visas. Within a matter of weeks, it seemed, our family would safely be living in New York City.

On Thursday, May 9, we went to the American embassy in Antwerp and brought our Nansen passports for immediate processing. After passing the health examination and personal interview and paying for the visa stamps, we were told to return the following day to pick up the validated visas. But that Friday morning, the Germans began their simultaneous attack on Belgium and the Netherlands, beginning with a ferocious air assault. We stood in a long, growing line waiting to enter the American embassy. No one was being admitted. Suddenly, an official came out and announced to the restless crowd, "We have strict orders from Washington: no more visas will be handed out until the international situation clears." Guards immediately ordered everyone to disperse.

We were stunned. We could not get our Nansen passports back, and we had no visas. Then, over the weekend, thousands of refugees started coming into Antwerp. As Germany intensified its bombardment of the Low Countries, rumors flourished that the Dutch would flood the dykes in order to stop the Nazi advance. For reasons that historians still debate, that potentially successful defensive maneuver never occurred. On Monday, most Jews began to flee Antwerp and head for the French border at La Panne; they were later overtaken by German forces, transported back to Antwerp, and then deported to death camps.

It was obvious that Belgium and the Netherlands would soon be under Third Reich domination. We tried the American embassy that day and the next, and it remained closed for business. It was time to leave the country before the Nazis arrived.

Unable to reach France directly from Antwerp, we first went to Brussels, then from there boarded a coal train comprising fifty or sixty big steel wagons hitched together and open to the sky. We loaded up and slowly headed west. Suddenly, as the train arrived at the French border town of Mons (Bergen in Flemish), the station fell under attack by German *Stukas*. Strafing and bombing with something resembling napalm, they set the station ablaze. At one point, we had to hide below the train for shelter from the *Stukas'* whizzing bullets and exploding shells.

All was chaos. Somehow, though, our train's engineer managed to get us through the bombardment, and we were now inside France. But instead of going to Paris that night, our train was switched to sidetracks that avoided Paris, and the engineer had no choice but to take us south. Like all other Jews aboard, we were completely disheartened. Paris seemed an unbreachable refuge from the Nazis; nobody could conceive that it would fall from French hands.

Finally the train stopped in a town near Montlucon. We were dismayed to be so far from Paris in southern France, but it was probably our salvation, for the town lay in the Department Alier, where Vichy, the region's capital, was situated. Just a little bit north of the Department Alier was the line of demarcation separating Nazi-occupied from unoccupied France. But the demarcation agreement still lay several weeks ahead; that night, and for the next few days, the battle was still raging between France and Germany.

For several days, we lodged with a hospitable farmer. On our first shabbos evening in France, my family enjoyed a memorable dinner consisting of a French baguette, a can of sardines, and some olives. My step-grandfather (he had married my widowed paternal grandmother), Yisroel Eltes, was with us, and he stimulated our imagination by pretending we were savoring gourmet victuals. We sang shabbos songs together, and for a little while, the war seemed far away. The next day, I learned that a tar factory situated near the farm needed manual laborers. I quickly found employment, commuting each way by bicycle.

CHAPTER FIVE

~

French Internment Camps

I had been working at the tar factory near Montlucon for only two days, when I came back to the farm in the afternoon to find a Black Maria parked outside the house. From conversations with men at the factory, it seemed that the Nazis were defeating the French everywhere in their homeland. Casualties were high. My grandparents, parents, and siblings were already sitting inside the official vehicle. Everyone looked worried.

The French security police (Sûreté Générale) had been waiting for my return. My few belongings were already packed away. Too surprised to speak, I quickly got into the Maria, and we sped off to Chateau Fremont several hours away. It was the headquarters of a newly created internment camp for Jewish refugees and would be a harrowing home for the next three months.

Chateau Fremont was a lavish estate, originally owned by a prominent Jewish businessman named Alexandre "Sasha" Stavisky. He had died mysteriously in 1934, in the midst of a huge corruption scandal involving high French officials and bankers. Now it housed the administrative office and residence for the internment camp's officials and guards, while the inmates were housed in a compound enclosed by barbed wire. All were Jews, an absurdity because the official explanation for our arrest and incarceration was that we had entered France from enemy Austria or Germany and were therefore spies. The very idea that thousands of bedraggled Jews would be spying on France as secret agents for the Third Reich was ridiculous, but it was the French government's way of saying it didn't want Jewish refugees to be settling in France's countryside, or cities for that matter.

The camp commander was a French lieutenant and a former high school principal. I pity his students, for he was a horrible, sadistic person and would strut around wearing jodhpurs, riding boots, and a pillbox hat. With a Hitlerian mustache, his face was mean and sullen. I wish I could remember his name, but I've blotted it from memory. "Pierre" serves as well as any. He typically held a steel whip in his hand and fondled a loaded revolver whenever entering our compound. Pierre would bark orders, and every day he made us go and work.

Along with hundreds of other Jewish refugees, we slept in a vacated area of barns and stables. The guards had placed some straw on the stable floor, and our family of eight occupied a single stable, with barely enough breathing space for one horse. Sanitary conditions were appalling, and many inmates developed dysentery and other infectious diseases.

Seven days a week, there was a morning *appell*, which meant that all the inmates had to line up, while Pierre called out each name and waited for an immediate reply. If you weren't present when your name was called, you were really in for trouble.

Pierre, of course, had assistants, who were French soldiers. Actually, many were friendly and fraternized with us. Whenever I'd report for duty to wash dishes at the officers' kitchen in the castle, they'd give me some extra food to share with my family back in the compound. Sometimes, too, I'd sneak up to the officers' kitchen and take the coffee grounds they'd thrown into the garbage. By recooking the coffee grounds in an old tin can, we made our coffee, because the guards didn't give us any.

We wore no special clothing to identify us as inmates, just what we had brought from Belgium on our own. Sometimes when we labored in the fields, the guards gave us work clothes. We never received any mail. At the time of the Nazi invasion of France, the Jewish community was in such turmoil that it hadn't even addressed the emergency needs of its own members, let alone refugees like us from Belgium, Austria, or the Netherlands.

Papa made sure that we prayed every day and maintained Jewish observance. It certainly wasn't easy. On shabbos eve, he'd make jokes about the stale bread we had to make the blessing. Then, on shabbos morning, we'd get up extra early for services, as we had to report for work at the usual time. During the day, when we'd go on work detail, the men who had *t'fillin* (phylacteries) would share them readily with the others—that too was part of our religious routine. There was no Torah. We had a handful of little prayer books, but not for the High Holy Days approaching in a couple of months.

Our awareness of what was happening outside the internment camp was minimal. The Sûreté Générale deliberately kept us as isolated as possible from the rest of the country. Though denied access to radio and news-papers, somehow we knew that Hitler's armies were decisively defeating French forces. We had been incarcerated at Chateau Fremont for about five weeks when France surrendered on June 14, 1940. There was an old rabbi in the camp who had been serving unofficially as our spiritual leader. On that day, he directed a memorial service for the French soldiers who had died and for the fall of France to Nazi Germany. We were all in tears as we participated.

After that, things at Chateau Fremont steadily got worse for us. Outside the area of barns and stables was a large field. I had often enjoyed going there to cut down trees and make firewood for our family. Chopping wood was a delight for me because the useful activity always called on ingenuity: Would I hit the tree trunk accurately with a good, solid blow? Would I successfully avoid the knotholes? I think it was one of the only things that gave me a sense of self-esteem in that horrid place.

One torrid day soon after the French surrender, Pierre marched us all into that field. His demeanor was more vicious than usual as he barked, "This field can't be worked! There are too many rocks here. Now dig 'em up!"

So we set to digging up those rocks, and they weren't easy to move around. We had to use a wedge as a lever to create a rolling motion, and this required a lot of pushing and heaving. It was exhausting physical labor, but after two days, we succeeded in removing all the rocks from the field. We massed them together in a huge pile.

At that moment, we felt really proud of our group's accomplishment. We figured that now we would be asked to smooth the earth to prepare it for planting. Some of us thought that we'd be growing mainly potatoes; others anticipated a crop of onions. Nutrition at the camp was wretched, so we expected to be eating better with potatoes and fresh vegetables before long. We were all excited.

Suddenly, Pierre appeared before us. He held his steel whip firmly in hand, and his face was filled with rage.

"Who gave you permission to remove these stones?" he screamed at us. "I want them put back as they were. Now!"

I've rarely lost my temper in life, but at that instant something within me snapped. The fieldwork had been so exhausting in the scorching sun, and clearly we'd actually been naïve enough to believe that, as Jewish inmates, we'd be able to achieve some useful goal as a result of our efforts. It was obvi-ous that Pierre was giving us tasks only to wear us out.

Upon hearing his taunting words, I seized a pickax and furiously struck one of those rocks. The last thing I saw before collapsing was a spark hurtling from that spot, perhaps a metallic shard that splintered from the old axe blade and ricocheted into my head.

From what I later learned, Pierre brandished his revolver and forbade anyone to help me as I lay unconscious and bleeding in the heat. Not even Papa was permitted to bring me any water. Finally, after a few minutes, a stray dog ambled over and licked my face. I groggily awakened and dragged myself back to the stables. For months after that episode, I experienced painful migraine headaches due to my physical trauma.

Despite our suffering at Chateau Fremont, I managed to fall in love. I had just turned sixteen, and it was certainly the first time in my life I felt romantic stirrings. Her name was Fernande Goodkin, and her family was originally from the Ukraine. Her father, who seemed to have held a professional position in Belgium, had been born in Antwerp. Like us, the Goodkins had fled during the Nazi invasion several weeks earlier—only to be arrested as spies and imprisoned in this camp. Fernande was my age and had large, dark eyes and lustrous black hair. We talked occasionally, but I was much too shy to do anything more. She was shy too. On many nights, I dreamed of caressing and kissing her in my arms.

Perhaps if my family had stayed longer at Chateau Fremont, something more would have developed between us. In an inexplicable way, my longing for Fernande was heightened, or intensified, precisely by the brutality and squalor of that internment camp.

I don't think people ever really forget their first love, and I've often wondered what happened to Fernande. Did she survive the Holocaust, as did my immediate family? Or did she perish in the gas chambers with so many other innocent children and teens?

One July afternoon, we heard through the grapevine that the Gestapo would be coming the next day to inspect the camp at Chateau Fremont. Daily life was harsh under Pierre, but at least we were surviving. There were even a few friendly guards who gave us extra food from time to time. Nobody knew what the Gestapo would do, and that uncertainty provoked a palpable fear. We all knew countless stories of men and women who had been tortured and killed in cases of mistaken identity—or just randomly, to serve as a warning to other Jews who might think about resisting. My sleep was fitful, sporadic that night. I worried especially about Papa and Mamma.

Early the next morning, I was awakened in our barracks by cries and agitated shouts. During the night, three men in our compound had hanged themselves, using their neckties and belts. Their dangling bodies had just been discovered, and the French guards hadn't yet arrived on the scene. I saw their lifeless bodies, their faces turning blue, tongues swollen. It was the most horrifying sight of my life. Papa thought that the Gestapo had been coming specifically to take these men away for interrogation by torture. They might have been socialists. Having no chance of escape, they deemed the act of group suicide their only option. The reality of our powerlessness really hit me hard. I didn't know these men well, but I was sure that they hadn't deserved to die like this.

Later that morning, the Gestapo arrived in several military vehicles. There were about a dozen agents. Dressed impeccably in crisp uniforms and shining black boots, they made the obsequious French guards look like schoolboys with their grey coats and hats. The French first showed them the three dangling bodies. After carefully examining the corpses, the Gestapo proceeded to inspect our compound methodically for contraband and security features.

Then they came to the latrines, which, as always, stank with a fetid odor. They comprised enclosed ditches, covered with planks smeared with feces and blood. As the French guards stood impassively, the Germans kicked in the wooden walls. Then, in words that I'll never forget, the Gestapo chief turned to Pierre and said curtly in French, "If you're going to kill Jews, do it sanitarily. I want these torn down and rebuilt completely. Do it immediately."

Instantly, the French guards ordered us to pour containers of kerosene over the latrines and set them ablaze. We were made to dig up the earth, pouring lye over the fetid human wastes, and erect new wooden structures. It was a definite improvement.

Two weeks after the French surrender, armistice terms were actualized. France was rigidly divided in two: an occupied zone based in Paris and ruled by Nazi Germany and an unoccupied zone in the south headed by a puppet government at Vichy. Its eighty-three-year-old leader was doddering Marshal Henri Phillipe Pétain. As part of the armistice agreement, all of France's Jews were ceded to German control.

Shortly thereafter, a Vichy government commission came to our camp. Its purpose was to begin sorting stateless Jews from those like our family, who were waiting for legitimate visas out of the country. Our documentation must have sufficed, for we were authorized to leave Chateau Fremont and wait in Marseille for steerage to the United States. At the time, it was the safe haven for all Jewish refugees in France.

Unfortunately, we were given refugee vouchers rather than regular tickets to take us to Marseille. As the train neared the city, French gendarmes refused to let us enter with those vouchers and took us to another internment camp called Rivesaltes. You can imagine our dismay. It was located near

Carcasonne, a city famous for its ancient Roman aqueduct. From the internment camp, we could see it plainly.

On one side of the sprawling Rivesaltes camp were housed Jewish refugees such as our family. Each family had a few straw bags in a designated
part of a large, open-walled barracks. We hardly saw the commander, but
he was much gentler than Pierre, and the atmosphere was considerably
calmer. On the other side of the barbed wire lay the compound for socialist
and communist prisoners from the Spanish Civil War. Some had already
been incarcerated there for several years and were treated even worse than
the Jewish inmates. Over the ensuing weeks, we made some interesting
connections with those inmates and learned some of their battle songs. I
remember that Papa became the cook during that time, so we'd at least have
something to eat.

One day, a representative from the Joint Distribution Committee came to
visit our compound. His name was Henri, and he was warm and friendly. He
became the unofficial ombudsman for families like ours, anxiously waiting
for their visas to leave France. We begged Henri to help provide us with at
least one High Holy Day prayer book while we waited endlessly for our visa
to the United States. Henri made no promise but definitely seemed to be on
our side.

As the September weather turned to autumn, I began to think about the
upcoming holy days of Rosh Hashanah and Yom Kippur. I think that one
of Papa's friends had a small Hebrew calendar so we could keep track of the
dates. But as in the first internment camp at Chateau Fremont, we had no
Torah or High Holy Day prayer books.

One day late in the month, I sneaked out of the camp and hiked into
town. Having just turned sixteen, I had a crazy plan borne of adolescent
bravado: to make a shofar for the Jewish community. But the strange thing
is that it succeeded. Reaching Carcasonne in the early morning, I quickly
found a butcher shop. The proprietor could see that I was a refugee and
asked if I wanted some meat. And I replied in halting French, "No, thank
you, Monsieur, I don't want meat. But I would like a horn—either of a sheep
or goat."

I'm sure the butcher was baffled, but he agreeably gave me a couple of
horns. I thanked him and left, then quickly returned to Rivesaltes. Remarkably, nobody seemed to have even noticed that I had been gone.

Spurred by my success in town, I set to work on making the shofar. Of
course, I had no tools. The butcher shop horns still contained flesh adhering
to the bone, so first I boiled the horns. The meat soon melted off. Next, by

taking a strand of wire and sharpening it on a stone, I created a makeshift drill. And I drilled, and I drilled, and I drilled.

While I worked on the first horn, my drill broke through the bone, and the shofar-in-making was destroyed. But with the second horn, I succeeded in carving a workable shofar. I was elated.

That year, Rosh Hashanah began on the evening of October 2. All the observant Jews in the camp gathered together for services. We had no High Holy Day prayer book, as Henri had failed to find us one. And so, as a group, we reconstructed from memory the evening prayer service. The following morning, we awoke very early for Rosh Hashanah services as we would be obligated to attend work detail at our usual time. We wanted to complete all the prayers before work.

Word about my shofar reached everyone. It generated tremendous excitement and, on many faces, even the long-forgotten feeling of hope. Pushing and jostling, several men loudly demanded the privilege of blowing the shofar, but I was assertive and filled with a sense of righteous purpose. "I made it," I insisted, "I'm past bar mitzvah age, and it's my shofar. I'm going to blow it!" In front of the assembled Jewish community of inmates, I placed the shofar to my lips and blew the time-honored sequence of notes. My tone was clear and surprisingly powerful.

Suddenly, the Rivesaltes commander appeared in our midst. In our frenzy, nobody had seen him approaching. "What's that noise?" he demanded to know. "What's going on?"

And proudly displaying my shofar, I answered poetically in French, "Monsieur, this is the trumpet of our liberation."

With a stunned expression, the commander stared at us all for a moment, then slowly replied, "How amazing this is! How remarkable!" He seemed truly shaken for an instant, as he lifted an official-looking document in the air and motioned for us to listen attentively. The commander anxiously cleared his throat; then, before reading from the document, he suddenly said to me, "Blow it again! Blow it again!" Sensing that something important was about to happen, I blew the shofar once more, even more heartily.

And then the camp commander slowly began announcing the names of those whose foreign visas were now ready to be picked up in Marseille. All whose names were called were free to leave immediately. Our family's name was among them! We embraced each other over and over. We were overjoyed, and Mamma and Papa were both weeping.

I felt sure that in some mystical way, my impassioned act of making that shofar had sparked divine merit for my family and our whole Jewish community incarcerated during Rosh Hashanah in that camp. In a way that I certainly couldn't have articulated as a sixteen-year-old, I had an unforgettable epiphany about faith and right action, blessing and redemption.

Do you know, I still have that shofar? It sits near my desk at home, and every day it reminds me of God's mysterious workings in the world.

CHAPTER SIX

~

Revelations at Marseille

We spent only a few months at Marseille, but they constituted an important period in my life. My family had arrived by train subsequent to Rosh Hashanah. After the detention camp commandant had announced the names of the visa recipients and departed from the barracks, some Jewish detainees decided to leave immediately—despite the holy day—before he changed his mind on a bureaucratic pretext. This had certainly happened before, though never with such potentially irreparable consequences.

Others, including my parents, however, felt that God had finally given us this life-saving blessing, and more than ever it was essential to observe Judaism precisely. Desecrating Rosh Hashanah by train travel now was unthinkable. So we waited the two days, and the commandment did not rescind his decision after all.

This time at the local train station, we bought regular tickets to Marseille, instead of using Joint Distribution Committee vouchers. We were taking no chances. Sure enough, the French officials let us pass unhindered, and at last we made it to our destination.

At the time, about thirty-nine thousand Jews lived in Marseille. While some proudly traced their ancestry there back for centuries, many others were refugees from Nazi Germany—or like my own family, from other regions in France—desperately seeking shelter in the "free zone" established in the country's July 1940 partition a few months before. Nearly all such refugees were dependent for survival upon Jewish organizations and institutions. Along with Lyons, Marseille held the largest Jewish population in southern

France and would remain in the free zone until late 1942, when, following the Allied landing in North Africa, the Germans occupied the city. Not long afterward, they would arrest and deport its Jewish populace to concentration camps.

Together with thousands of other Jewish refugees, we were housed and fed by the Joint Distribution Committee. They placed us in an apartment building in a rundown section of town. Our neighbors included an Armenian family who cooked their meals on a charcoal grill standing in the hallway. About a half mile away—not far from Marseille's notorious red-light district—was the Joint Distribution Committee's own building on the Rue de Convalescents. It comprised a second-floor soup kitchen above a small synagogue—a *shtibel*—where we passed the time while waiting for our original visas to be shipped from the U.S. embassy back in Antwerp.

Fortunately for my grandparents, their Canadian visas—authorizing five-year work permits as "farmers"—came through quickly. Uncle Yankele had already immigrated to Canada from Belgium and submitted the necessary paperwork for my mother's mother and her husband. An old ship brought them to Portugal, which was still politically neutral in 1940, and from there, they made it to Montreal.

For us, the bureaucratic wait proved much longer. Ever resourceful, Papa created a position for himself to teach Hebrew to some of the Jewish refugee children. It was unpaid, of course, but the work gave him something meaningful to do each day. One of the mothers coldly told Papa, "You can teach my son Hebrew, but nothing religious, I warn you!" Papa mildly replied, "It's good to have something to eat, isn't it?" The mother agreed. "So, when your son has something to eat, he'll know how to say the blessing over food: *Hamotzi' lechem min ha' aretz.* I'll teach him that. Is that all right with you?" The mother assented, and then Papa suggested another ritual observance her son might learn. By the time the conversation was over, Papa had convinced her to agree to his whole curriculum.

As for myself, I soon found other teenage boys with equally little to do, and we became friends. We would go for long walks through Marseille's picturesque, winding streets. In the Old Port, I discovered some fish markets that were throwing away fish heads, fins, and similar parts. I would bring them back to Mamma, who would make delicious soup from such seeming discards. The Old Port was an exotic place—from the shore we could see the island of the Chateau d'If, where the Count of Monte Cristo had been imprisoned in Alexander Dumas's famous novel—and I would dream of leading my family to safety from the war. At the time, Syria was under French colonial rule, and I reasoned that if we managed to board a ship to Syria, we could soon establish a permanent home in the Holy Land. My bold plan might have worked except for one detail: there were no boats to Syria.

One bright shabbos morning, I took a long walk to the beautiful Sephardic synagogue near the Old Port. Built in 1864 by the French architect Nathan Saloman, Temple Breteuil had fashionable Oriental motifs. As I returned to our *shtibel*, I noticed an unfamiliar man with a red beard and black porkpie hat. He was teaching Hasidic philosophy, and it sounded intriguingly similar to what I had learned with Reb Moshe Tchechoval's diamond-cutting group in Antwerp.

During a break, I learned that he was a Parisian refugee, and his name was Reb Shneur Zalman Chneurson. So I asked him, "When *shabbos* is over, may I walk you back to your hotel?" He nodded amiably. As we walked slowly, for he limped, to the Hotel Deux Mondes, I asked if he could provide us with a teacher because we had so much empty time on our hands. Reb Chneurson immediately agreed and set us up with someone who had studied at the same yeshiva in Heide, Belgium.

Several years our senior, young Rabbi Chaim Meir Zilberstein was an effective pedagogue. On a half-day basis, he directed our Talmudic learning. Our group of teenage boys was highly motivated, and suddenly my days seemed to pass much faster and more enjoyably.

Inspired by the class, I managed to obtain a badly worn Polish-Hebrew edition of the *Tanya*, the foundation book of Chabad Hasidism. My teachers in Antwerp had kept me from reading the *Tanya* because they felt I was not yet prepared, and I now reveled in the freedom to study it intensively. Published in my Polish hometown in the mid-nineteenth century, the dog-eared book held tremendous meaning for me. I was especially moved by the advice on how to emulate God's ten ways of manifesting in the world. For me, at age sixteen, this profound text provided a new vista by which to understand the challenges of daily life. More than seventy years later, I still treasure this book among my possessions.

During those months, I often noticed a youthful, middle-aged man whose dignified bearing greatly impressed me. He wore a traditional Hasidic beard, yet his clothes were contemporary, even stylish: a grey suit and a fedora hat. At the time, this was quite unusual, for Hasidic men with full beards invariably wore black hats and long black coats. He spoke impeccable French. As I sometimes saw him in our little *shul* studying Torah with an acclaimed Moroccan rabbi, I naively assumed that he was Moroccan too. His noble demeanor intrigued me to the point of religious fantasies.

One day in midwinter 1941, Reb Chneurson stopped by our *shtibel* and said to our group, "On *Tu B'Shevat* [the New Year of the Trees] unfortunately

I won't be able to join you. I'll be in Vichy on some personal business. But I'll send you a guest who will *fabrengen* [celebrate] with you." That seemed fine with us.

Tu B'Shevat arrived. With money given to us by Reb Chneurson, we had purchased several bottles of schnapps and fruit to celebrate the holiday. Suddenly that evening, as we sat and sang together in *fabrengen*, there entered the dignified man whom I had thought of as "the Moroccan." He was dressed in his usual suit and fedora. To my growing amazement, he sat down at the head of our table, close to me, and in Yiddish warmly greeted our group.

I learned forward to get a good look at him. Not until I reached New York several months later did I learn his identity: Rabbi Menachem Mendel Schneerson. Within a decade, this erudite son-in-law of the Sixth Lubavitcher Rebbe (Rabbi Yosef Yitzchak Schneersohn) would become the charismatic, world-famous leader of the Lubavitchers for more than forty years.

"What are you studying?" he gently asked, and we replied, "The Talmudic tractate of *Ketubot*." Pronouncing "*L'chayim!*" (to life!) over a small glass of schnapps, he began an extemporaneous discourse, without even a self-introduction, on a specific verse in that Talmudic portion: a virgin is betrothed (has her *Nissu'in*) on the fourth day (Thursday). This discourse remains one of the most memorable religious presentations I have ever heard. To the best of my recollection, this is how it went:

> Why do the sages say that she is married only on the fourth day (Thursday)? Because if it's discovered that she's not a virgin, her husband can approach the *Beit Din* (Jewish court), which meets on the fifth day, and make his claim that she is not a virgin. Why is it that one does not marry on Sunday, given that the *Beit Din* also sits in judgment on the second day (Monday)? This is because a woman must have three days to prepare for the wedding.
>
> Now, who is the virgin? The nation of Israel is the virgin. Who is the husband? God is the husband.
>
> There are numerous dimensions of the Jewish marriage ceremony that require consideration here. The first is the engagement (*t'na'im*), the commitment of the intent to marry. The second is the *Kiddushim*, betrothal, enacted with the offering of the ring from the bridegroom to the bride. The third and final phase is the *Nissu'in*, marital ceremony, including the recitation of the *ketubah* (marriage contract) and the seven blessings.
>
> The woman whom this *mishnah* describes is in the final stage of the marital process—the *Nissu'in* marital ceremony—and it represents here the coming of the Messiah. Hence, it occurs on the fourth day because the sages said, "There are three periods of history: the first two thousand years consist of confusion

(*tohu*), the second two thousand consist of Torah, and third two thousand are the era of the Messiah."

The culmination of the first four thousand years (the first two bimillennial periods of history) on the fourth day should be the beginning of the messianic era. The marital engagement was the moment of creation; as we learned, "God set a condition (*t'naiy hitnah Haqadosh Baruch Hu*) with creation: If Israel accepts the Torah then the world can be sustained. If not, it would revert to the void."

That oath, that contract, was the Torah. If Israel keeps the Torah, the world will continue to exist. But if Israel rejects the Torah, the purpose for existence becomes void.

The conditions preparing for the Messiah were thus instituted at creation. This moment represents the *tena'im*, or the first stage of the marriage process: expressing the intent to marry. When was the *Kiddushin*, the sanctification, the betrothal, the second stage? This occurred at Mount Sinai. At that time, God gave the wedding ring to the nation of Israel. And what was it? The ring was the *mitzvot*, for we say traditionally that "God sanctified us, Israel, through the *mitzvot*."

So, now we can understand why the sages teach that the bride must have three days in order to prepare herself for the wedding. We understand this by employing the Kabbalistic notion that sets the conditions for creation. Before the beginning of creation, Kabbalists explain, there was "a rupture of the vessels," and the sparks that were dispersed through that rupture were lodged in all dimensions of material and spiritual existence. When one does something good in the world, some of these lost sparks are raised and returned to their origin. For Kabbalists, this process of "raising the sparks" is the foundation for all redemptive activity.

It is written that before Israel left Egypt, 288 sparks were lost: 202 were elevated to their source when we departed Egypt, leaving 86 sparks still lodged in creation. The *gematria* of *elohim* (God) is 86. Thus, the remainder of the lost sparks involves divine judgment, the *sefirah* of *Gevurah*.

If we had merited divine action through our behavior, we would have been redeemed by the Messiah after the completion of the two bi-millennia of chaos and Torah. But, as you know, Israel sinned.

Now, there are sins that are unintentional, likened to a widow who has no control over the fact that her husband dies. What if Israel had been like a widow? The Talmud teaches that a widow can marry on the fifth day of the week. This would have been the Hebrew year 5000. Why can the widow marry on the fifth day? Because on that day, all the fishes were created, and God blessed them, saying, "Be fertile, increase, and fill the waters of the seas" (Genesis 1:22). That blessing would have been our blessing if we had deserved it.

However, intentional sins are likened to a divorce (Isaiah 50:1). "For your rebellions, your Mother was divorced." In our metaphor, this is the case where the husband, God, found a blemish in His bride, Israel. When does a divorcee get married? She marries on the sixth day, Friday, so she can merit the blessing of human beings: "Be fruitful and multiply" (Genesis 1:28).

It is already so late on Friday afternoon. When will the wedding take place?

Upon reaching the end of his discourse, our speaker suddenly began to cough. To me, it seemed to be masking spontaneous sobbing, and I was awestruck. This brilliant "Moroccan" had touched on sensitive issues that were palpable in our presence. He had spoken about raising the sparks of holiness buried in our shells of ignorance as a prelude to the Messiah—and lamented, as we all did, that the Messiah had not yet come. Not one of us was unaffected. We were displaced refugee children, not knowing what our fate would be and dreaming of redemption. As never before, I saw the travails and challenges of Jewish history in a meaningful light.

It was quiet for several moments. Then our speaker recovered his full composure and led us in lively Hasidic songs (niggunim). Finally, he provided a brief lesson about the meaning of Tu B'Shevat for our lives, then warmly departed. His discourse has inspired and exhilarated me to this day.

~

CHAPTER SEVEN

Freedom Voyage to America

My family's visas to the United States finally came through, and in early March 1941 we boarded the *Ipanema*. A big old French tub that carried cargo, it was among the last boats to get out of Marseille before Vichy leader Marshal Phillipe Pétain stopped all such maritime activity. We were housed in steerage lacking privacy, but the *Ipanema* was clean and free from both rats and vermin.

Our first leg was to Alicante, Spain. From there we voyaged on to Africa: Algeria, with ports in both Oran and Algiers, then Casablanca, Morocco, and Dakar, Senegal. After leaving Africa, it was a long trip across the Atlantic Ocean to the French island of Martinique in the Caribbean. Finally, in early April, we reached St. Thomas in the U.S. Virgin Islands, where we disembarked and, after clearing customs, became official residents of the United States of America. That was an ecstatic moment for us all!

During my six or seven weeks aboard the *Ipanema*, I became friendly with a French Jewish youth named André two years my senior. He came from an assimilated family, which, like mine, was fleeing the Nazis, and he was avidly reading Descartes. Andre was a proud atheist, and we engaged in many interesting debates about God and religion—frequently with an attentive audience of other adolescents. Bristling with teenage fervor, I urged them not to become atheists but instead to accept religious teachings for their ultimate truth. During these discussions, I sometimes recalled my own, antireligious stance of only two summers before—until Reb Moshe Tchechoval's Chabad group in Antwerp bolstered my precarious Jewish faith. Andre once asked me, "What would make you the happiest in the world?" At the age of sixteen, I found this a difficult question, but I still remember my spontaneous answer: "To be beside the woman I love and to pray."

Though Germany and the United States were not yet at war in early 1941, German U-boats had been unrelentingly attacking civilian Allied ships since the fall of France in June 1940. Between September and December, more than 150 Allied merchant ships had been sunk. Though some were now being armed with makeshift deck guns, this was not true for the *Ipanema*. At night, the threat of a sudden torpedo attack was especially real, and the *Ipanema* crew anxiously led several safety drills for all aboard.

Our family kept kosher by consuming a diet of bread and sardines, alternating with more bread and sardines. I must admit I came to enjoy the taste of sardines because there was no other source of protein available. Papa would persistently remind me, "Ask for lemon!" in order to have an adequate supply of vitamin C. Sometimes we ate bananas too, as vendors came aboard with their fruit cargo and sold some to passengers like us in steerage.

As soon as we had joyfully cleared immigration at St. Thomas, we began looking for local Jews and a synagogue, if one existed there. Walking down one street in the small business district, we noticed a store whose awning announced, "Hannah Levin Christensen, Proprietor." With my family standing at the door, I entered and asked the friendly black woman standing behind the counter, "Possibly, can we speak with Mr. Levin?" She replied in a warm Caribbean accent, "Honey, Mr. Levin has gone to his rewards. I'm Hannah Levin Christensen. How can I help you?"

We learned that Mrs. Christensen had converted to Judaism and, after her husband's demise, remained active in the island's sole synagogue. She immediately gave us walking directions to it. As we continued our stroll, we noticed another store with an awning that proclaimed, "David Sasso, Proprietor." I said to Papa, "That's a Sephardic Jewish name. Let's go in and talk to him!"

Mr. Sasso was the congregation's lay leader, and he soon invited us to Friday evening services. Wary about the congregation's degree of traditional observance, Papa advised us to pray at our hotel room beforehand and then attend. That's what we did. Hannah Levin Christensen had a beautiful contralto voice and led a stirring choir, whose repertoire included "Lecha Dodi." I had never experienced a Sephardic service before, and it came as a wonderful shock to me.

The St. Thomas Synagogue itself was amazing, for inside the attractive, gated masonry building, a powdery sand was strewn all over the sanctuary floor. I had never seen anything like it in my life. David Sasso explained to us that the current structure, built by an unknown French architect, was over a century old—replacing two older buildings dating back to 1792. Among its famous congregants was the impressionist painter Jacob "Camille" Pissarro, who was born and raised on St. Thomas before settling in Paris to pursue painting as a career.

As for the sand, David Sasso explained, the custom derived from the biblical tale of a man who was cured of leprosy and wanted to convert to Judaism. To best express his gratitude to God, he requested that his servant gather sand from the Holy Land and bring it to his prayer room in Damascus so that he could stand on holy ground. Mindful of this story, the Sephardic merchants who stopped at St. Thomas occasionally brought sand from the Holy Land so that its synagogue members could all stand on holy soil too. However, Sassoon confided, whenever someone in the congregation died, the synagogue staff took some of the Holy Land sand and buried it with the deceased. So the sand beneath our feet included both Holy Land and local sand.

We were close to New York City but not yet there. From St. Thomas we took a tramp ship to San Juan, Puerto Rico, which slowly made its way from island to island. When we finally reached San Juan, Passover was just a few days away. After checking our family into a hotel, Papa immediately began looking for *matzos*. The local "official Jew" gave us only one small box that contained all of six *matzos*; the rest were needed for a USO Passover *seder* for soldiers, which the bishop would be attending. Papa seemed resigned to the situation that for six days we would eat only bananas and pineapples and that single box of six *matzos*.

While my parents looked for passage to New York City, I walked with my little sister Ada to a nearby park. Suddenly, she needed to use the lavatory. Not knowing where to go, I stopped at an information office. An amicable, strongly built man of about sixty asked what we needed. Balding, with a reddish complexion and a hearty manner, he directed Ada to the bathroom. Introducing himself as Mr. Frank Richardson, he was a retired army officer and now served as information officer for the park. He began peppering me with friendly questions. When I explained that my family was marooned in San Juan and desperately trying to get passage to our relatives in New York City, he immediately took up our cause.

To my surprise, Richardson went to a safe behind his desk and opened it. Inside was a smaller safe from which he gently withdrew three cigars. Placing them in his pocket, he said to us, "Come!" and headed over to the Alcoa Steamship offices several blocks away, as Ada and I trailed after him. Exchanging friendly greetings with the secretarial staff, Richardson strode straight into the vice president's office and said, "I need six passengers to be put on the next boat to New York." The immediate reply was, "But, Frank, we haven't got the berths for them."

Offering his cigars in an encouraging gesture, Richardson answered, "Then you're going to have to fix them up. We're going to stay in this office until you find them places." Sure enough, the vice president succeeded in finding six cabin couches for us to sleep on. My parents were dumbfounded by how Ada and I had succeeded in gaining us passage, and we happily arrived in New York the day before Passover.

CHAPTER EIGHT

~

Encountering the Sixth Lubavitcher Rebbe

We joyfully arrived in New York City on April 21, the day before Passover. Meeting us at the dock, Uncle Abbie soon escorted us to the Hebrew Immigrant Assistance Service (HIAS) building situated on Lafayette Street in lower Manhattan. It had originally been the opulent Jacob Astor Library, but HIAS had taken over the building in 1921 to serve as a shelter and caregiving center for families like ours. Offices on the first two floors gave way to housing on the third and fourth; the elegant former library also held kosher kitchens and a small synagogue, classrooms for job training and civics education, and an attractive playground. We were lodged in a nearby apartment building on Third Avenue, close to Cooper Union and the skid row section known then as the Bowery.

As we celebrated our first Passover in the United States, I eagerly contacted Avram Weingarten, my good friend from Vienna and then Antwerp. His family had emigrated from Belgium several months before, and he was now actively studying in the Lubavitch yeshiva. Enjoying his classes, Avram spoke at length about the Lubavitchers and their distinct Hasidic outlook. He was effusive in praising their leader, Rabbi Yosef Yitzchak Schneersohn. As early as my yeshiva days in Vienna, I had known something about him, and then in Antwerp and Marseille, I had learned somewhat more. Now, Avram began to provide me with a much fuller picture of this extraordinary man.

Rabbi Schneersohn had become the Sixth Lubavitcher Rebbe in 1920. By then, the Bolsheviks had ruthlessly begun crushing all religious activity throughout Russia, and at the age of forty, he had quickly emerged as the unofficial head of the nation's observant Jews. In order to protect Jewish religious rights to worship and education, he had mobilized remaining Jewish communal leaders and spearheaded legal battles within the new Soviet courts. In this way, Rabbi Schneersohn had been able to safeguard at least a modicum of Jewish religious freedom.

By 1927, though, the Bolsheviks had had enough. Rabbi Schneersohn was arrested as a counterrevolutionary and taken for interrogation in Leningrad's dreaded Spalerna prison. Initially, the NKVD (secret police) planned to execute him for fostering clandestine observance of Judaism, but an international protest group that included President Calvin Coolidge and governmental leaders in France, Germany, and Latvia succeeded in winning Rabbi Schneersohn's release and gained permission for him to leave Russia with his immediate family and aides.

Over the next twelve years, Rabbi Schneersohn lived first in Latvia, then in Poland, where he successfully developed a network of yeshivas. The main Torah academy, based in Warsaw, had produced a scholarly journal with the part-time assistance of his energetic son-in-law and distant cousin, Rabbi Menachem Mendel Schneerson. Though suffering from multiple sclerosis, the Lubavitcher Rebbe traveled widely and become its first leader to visit the Holy Land as well as the United States.

Besides promoting the establishment of Jewish schools and synagogues, Rabbi Schneersohn was a prolific writer who maintained a voluminous correspondence with his followers and Jewish communal leaders around the globe. Due to the upheaval of World War I and the Bolshevik takeover in Russia, many of these were now scattered in unfamiliar countries and desperate for guidance on both secular and religious matters.

When the Germans invaded Poland in September 1939, Rabbi Schneersohn succeeded in avoiding capture until international diplomacy arranged for his safe departure from Poland—through neutral Latvia and Sweden—before he hastily boarded an ocean liner for New York in March 1940.

Avram excitedly recounted stories about Rabbi Schneersohn's miraculous survival in Warsaw during its intense bombardment. These eyewitness accounts seemed amazing to me too. The Rebbe was now living in Crown Heights, a comfortable section of Brooklyn, and vigorously organizing Jewish religious activity in his new homeland. Though confined to a wheelchair because of severe health problems, Rabbi Yosef Yitzchak Schneersohn radiated a holy charisma.

I could not wait to meet this remarkable person, but the Rebbe was surely too busy for casual meetings with teenagers, I reasoned; I therefore needed an "excuse" for my visit. Serendipitously, Avram supplied it when he asked if I had ever met the Rebbe's son-in-law during my months in Marseille. I didn't think so. But when Avram carefully described him to me, I realized that this was indeed the seemingly Moroccan Jew whose noble bearing and *Tu B'Shevat* sermon had affected me so deeply. Now, I had my "excuse": I would bring personal regards from Rabbi Menachem Mendel Schneerson to the Rebbe!

After copying onto a pad the address of Lubavitcher headquarters, I began my hike to Brooklyn. The spring day was pleasantly mild, and from our apartment building at Eighth Street and Third Avenue, it was probably a two- to three-hour trek. Upon crossing the Brooklyn Bridge, I immediately asked a police officer, "How do I get to Eastern Parkway and Kingston Avenue?" Eyeing me closely, he answered, "What number Eastern Parkway do you want?" I gazed at my little paper and said, "770," and to my amazement, he replied in perfect Yiddish, "Du vilst geyn tzum Lubavitcher Rebben?" (Do you want to see the Lubavitcher Rebbe?). I nodded vigorously, and smiling, he explained the directions. I resumed my pace but gave up exhaustedly at St. John's Place—which, I later discovered, was only two blocks away from Eastern Parkway. Then I walked all the way back home, though the police officer had given me trolley directions from Tompkins Avenue in Brooklyn to lower Manhattan.

But I was not deterred. The next week, I more wisely traveled to Brooklyn by trolley. I entered Lubavitch headquarters, a large, attractive, crosshatched building on a tree-lined parkway. When the Rebbe's secretary asked me, "What are you bringing the Rebbe?" I assuredly answered, "Regards from his son-in-law!" At the time, Rabbi Menachem Mendel Schneerson was still an ocean away in Marseille, preparing with his family to reach the United States.

I was ushered into the Rebbe's office, and there I saw a portly man with piercing dark eyes and a long white beard. He was outwardly frail, but an indefinable strength was immediately apparent in his demeanor. I felt nervous but excited, as he asked me in Yiddish to repeat exactly what his son-in-law had said. His physical condition caused his speech to be halting and frequently even labored. I tried my best to present the sermon I had heard, as occasionally the Rebbe gently shook his head to show I was missing accuracy.

Then he slowly asked me questions about myself, my family, and my Jewish background. I felt he was giving me his full attention and gazing at me with unfettered kindness. During our conversation, I experienced a growing sense of awe, certainly influenced by my knowledge of the Rebbe's heroic and seemingly miraculous life. As the conversation came to a close, it became clear that he had already decided on specific aid for my entire family. My brother would be enrolled in the Lubavitch yeshiva and my two sisters at the new Shulamith Hebrew day school for girls, and my parents and I would be set up as furriers and given our first business contract.

As I left the Rebbe's office, I began to sob uncontrollably. Someone standing nearby asked, "Why are you crying?" and I replied, "Because look what those damned Bolsheviks did to this wonderful person!" But in retrospect that was only a partial and ultimately shallow answer, for at the age of sixteen, I had only meager awareness of and insight into how my encounter with the Lubavitcher Rebbe was transforming me spiritually. Though this may sound sacrilegious, however, I had the unspoken feeling that if God had taken human form, He would be like Rabbi Yosef Yitzchak Schneersohn. I wanted to learn from this holy man and to be whatever he wanted me to be. I remember thinking very clearly at that moment, other rabbis are not of his caliber. For who else stood before the Living God and advocated for the Jewish people?

CHAPTER NINE

~

The Making of a Chabad Hasid

I soon moved with my family to the Borough Park section of Brooklyn, which remains to this day a bastion of traditional Jewish Orthodoxy. Occupying the corner of Fifty-third Street and Thirteenth Avenue, the small building in which we resided consisted of three levels: the first held a *shul* with the men's section, the second comprised the women's gallery, and our apartment was on the third.

With the Rebbe's materialized support, we set up a fur business in one of the rooms, and my parents and I became partners together. Thanks to my training with Yoshke Shapira in Antwerp, I already knew how to cut fur professionally and taught both of them. As I succeeded in gaining several contracts for cutting Persian paws into coats, income began coming in. Since Mamma had earned money as a dressmaker and Papa had no other vocational skills, this was certainly a welcome development.

Nevertheless, I felt furrier work to be no more fulfilling in Brooklyn than it had been in Belgium. Rather, what exhilarated my soul was an increasing involvement with Lubavitcher Hasidism. My friend Avram Weingarten was already enrolled in their Crown Heights yeshiva, and we soon became so inseparable that my mother sarcastically began to identify him as my "wife."

Every shabbos afternoon under Lubavitch auspices, Avram and I would sponsor a party for neighborhood Jewish youngsters. Our goal was to encourage synagogue and Hebrew school attendance by using candy, cake, and soda as our initial bait. Of course, we had to escort all the children from their various apartments to the party—and then back again. I felt honored to carry out such noble religious work that emulated the Baal Shem Tov, founder of Hasidism. But Papa considered it menial and an embarrassment to his entire family.

During my first months in Brooklyn, I experienced an unexpected delight when I encountered Rabbi Menachem Mendel Schneerson, my "Moroccan" from Marseille, visiting colleagues and friends at Lubavitch headquarters. He had arrived in June with his wife, on what may have been the last passenger ship allowed out of Vichy France. Striding over, he returned my greeting and said, "*Tu B'Shevat* in Marseille, and you sat to the right of me." I introduced myself and expressed my gratitude for his *Tu B'Shevat fabrengen* several months before. Smiling, Rabbi Schneerson asked what I recalled from his discourse and nodded with satisfaction as I repeated it; in the places where I erred, he carefully corrected me. I saw him often at 770 Eastern Parkway, especially after the Rebbe appointed him to direct several key Lubavitch educational and charitable organizations. I found Rabbi Schneerson an inspiring figure, though we had little day-to-day involvement.

Meanwhile, neighbors increasingly teased Papa that his oldest child was a lowly *belfer* (Yiddish slang for *behelfer*, teacher's aide), akin in status to a deliveryman. Papa repeatedly asked me to find another activity to occupy my leisure time, but I politely ignored his requests. Eventually Papa gave me an ultimatum: "Either stop doing this, or get out of my home." At the age of seventeen, I was ready for a showdown. "Okay, great," I answered, "I'm out!"

Gathering my worldly possessions, including several orange crates that held my books, I carried everything on the subway to Lubavitch headquarters. Announcing myself to the Rebbe's *gabbai*, Rabbi Elye Simpson of blessed memory, I was ushered in after the Rebbe completed his other appointments.

I related that Papa had thrown me out of the house for being a *belfer*. Surprised, the Rebbe said to me, "But why is that? He's an observant man. You've got to go back home and apologize to your father."

"What about next *shabbos*?" I exclaimed. "Should I still go around with the kids?" And the Lubavitcher Rebbe gently answered, "Yes, that you continue."

By the time I arrived back in Borough Park, it was nearly 2 a.m. I knocked on our apartment door, and as Papa opened it, I immediately said, "The Rebbe said that I should apologize to you." He warmly chuckled and replied, "A smart Jew, that Lubavitcher!" and allowed me back with the family. He considered the matter settled.

Several days passed, and then on the next shabbos, I again spent several hours escorting neighborhood children back and forth for the enticement party. When Papa confronted me as I had expected, I recounted the Rebbe's words, and Papa replied, "That he told you also? Oh, that sly Litvak!"

In early 1942, my parents finally permitted me to study full time in the Lubavitch yeshiva. I could not have been more delighted to end my career as a furrier, though for years to come Mamma and Papa supported themselves well financially from that trade.

Initially, I was not at all interested in becoming a rabbi as a profession. Instead, my goal was to learn how to *daven* (pray) more effectively and access the mystical, innermost part of the Torah. Studying the laws of Orthodox Judaism was important to me, but more potent was the issue of how one gets close to God. In my life, the only Jews who truly seemed focused on this question were the Chabad Hasidism I had known in Antwerp. They had raised my expectations of what prayer could be. By comparison, the prayer of all others appeared to me as little more than just reciting and repeating time-worn words, although they did so with accustomed melodies and swaying.

During the next few years, my two most important rabbinic teachers were Shmuel Levitan and Yisroel Jacobson, my *mashpia* (prayer coach). Both inspired me greatly; I was less influenced by my Talmudic teacher, Rabbi Mordechai Mentlick, who also served as yeshiva director. Born and raised in Russia, Rabbi Levitan had been arrested by the Bolshevik *yevketzia* for spearheading "underground" Torah study after all such religious activity had been officially banned. He had been exiled to Siberia as severe punishment, but this had only increased his determination. Allowed to accompany the Lubavitcher Rebbe into exile, Rabbi Levitan had emigrated with him to Lithuania before settling in the United States.

Devoting his life to the Rebbe's service, Rabbi Yisroel Jacobson would become one of the Lubavitchers' most beloved teachers. Some twenty years after I came under his wing, he founded Hadar Hatorah, one of the world's first yeshivas for *baal teshuvah* (returnee) Jewish boys.

Motivated by such wonderful mentors, one day I serendipitously uncovered an out-of-print Hasidic treatise on how to conduct deep *teshuvah* (repentance). By hand, I eagerly copied ten chapters in order to learn it closely, and this became my personal "manual" for inner work. Perhaps more than today, back then Lubavitcher Hasidism strongly emphasized soul development among its students and not just the performance of traditional rituals. Rabbi Jacobson often explained the nature and techniques of inner work; he also directed group discussions that resembled "gestalt therapy" sessions later pioneered by the German psychiatrist Fritz Perls, in which an individual sits on a chair within a circle and lets groups members offer "no-holds-barred" feedback about his attitude and conduct.

Although Rabbi Jacobson never singled out individuals, we all knew "when the shoe fit." We would also sing songs and cry together. During those years, my main study partner was Avram Weingarten, though I had others too.

I must have made a good impression with my energy and zeal, for soon I was allocated a small room at Lubavitch headquarters for my lodging, along with the job of opening and locking the doors to the building. Before long, I felt that I knew all the nooks and crannies of 770 Eastern Parkway.

The Lubavitcher Rebbe not only stressed inner work for yeshiva students like myself but also encouraged outreach or apostolic activity among his Hasidim to help American Jews become more observant. He advised us to memorize certain phrases from the *mishnah* and utter them aloud on the streets in order to cleanse the spiritual atmosphere around us. "The air of America is polluted!" he memorably declared; it was up to us to change that situation for the better with holy speech and deeds.

Certainly, I was eager to follow the Rebbe's guidance. My classmates and I would knock on doors wherever we saw a *mezuzah*, ask the adults if they had any children, and offer brochures about our day school classes. Because New York State public schools in that era allowed one hour of "release time" daily for religious instruction, I would also stand in front of Brooklyn school buildings and distribute flyers to Jewish students as they left in mid-afternoon. Once they enrolled in "release time" instruction, we encouraged them to attend Hebrew afternoon school as well.

I was very happy in those years. I knew that no other Jewish organization could remotely match what we were accomplishing. I believed that all other rabbis—Reform, Conservative, and even Modern Orthodox—were "selling out" to widespread and ever-increasing assimilation.

In this light, the Rebbe was my role model, for he spoke from the heart and not only from sacred texts. On Rosh Hashanah of 1943 (5703), for example, he openly wept as he led evening prayers. It was amazing to everyone assembled. One Hasid kept as a treasure the handkerchief with which Rabbi Schneersohn had dabbed at his tears—tears particularly for the suffering of European Jewry under Hitler. These tears were also personal, for as we well knew, he had a daughter and son-in-law who had disappeared when war broke out.

I was passionate in my studies. My weekdays begin quite early in the morning, with *mikveh* immersion and prayer, and continued until well into the late evening. On Thursdays, I kept at it until 3 a.m. First I would study two hours of Talmud, then two hours of legal codes based on the Talmud, then several hours of Hasidic philosophy, and finally Chabad meditation. Sometimes I placed my feet in a basin of cold water to prevent my exhausted body from succumbing to sleep.

Undoubtedly, such religious dedication sometimes seemed strange—if not outright pathological—to outsiders. At the time, though, my classmates and I had little awareness of such social considerations. For example, one day, we were all called to the local draft board to present ourselves. We recounted our typical daily routine of prayer, Talmudic study, more prayer, Hasidic study, and then still more prayer. Of course, as yeshiva *bochers* (male youth), we were completely forbidden to go to movies, theaters, dance halls, and night-clubs or to socialize at all with members of the opposite sex.

Finally, a skeptical draft board psychiatrist demanded, "Well, then, what do you do for fun?" And one of my classmates memorably retorted, "We sit and study with Shalom Ber Gordon. He's a barrel of laughs!"

Heartfelt prayer was something I had greatly valued for several years, and it was an important part of my training at the Lubavitch yeshiva. To maximize the potency of my *davening*, I had somehow developed the habit of tensing my entire body and contorting my face into a huge grimace. From my adolescent perspective, this must have seemed like the best way to draw closer to God.

One day as I was praying with my usual intense pout, I noticed Rabbi Jacobson quietly passing near me. Suddenly I felt a whack on the side of my head. As I sharply looked upward, he said to me, "Have you already tried *davening* with a smile?" It was a Zen-like epiphany for me, and I instantly understood what he meant. From that day onward, I sought to pray in a mood of joy and affection, and grimness became a clear sign of what to avoid in all prayer life.

In 1943, I underwent another transformation, but one more painful, and it related to messianism. The Warsaw Ghetto Uprising had begun in April, and soon after, Rabbi Yosef Yitzchak Schneersohn issued four impassioned broadsides, published in the *Tag* and the *Morgan Journal* (both prominent Yiddish newspapers). "The walls of the Exile are burning down!" he poetically declared, "*Moshiach* [the Messiah] will soon be here!" At our yeshiva, students and teachers alike became increasingly optimistic that the Great Redemption was indeed close at hand.

Enthusiastically, we distributed everywhere little gummed stickers printed with the Hebrew phrase "*L'a'lter Lit'shuvah, l'alter Lig'ullah*" (Let us repent; we are on the verge of the Messiah). And I fervently believed it. When one of my classmates was jailed overnight for defacing public property by affixing these stickers to subway walls, we celebrated his martyrdom and even envied him. Why? Because every Lubavitch leader in history had been jailed and persecuted by governmental authorities.

I was particularly inspired by a relevant story told about our Rebbe. Arrested for counterrevolutionary religious activity, he was incarcerated in a

Bolshevik prison. A malicious guard pointed a loaded revolver at his head and demanded that he renounce Judaism or die. Wholly unperturbed, the Rebbe calmly ignored the guard. "Aren't you afraid of my words?" he asked in astonishment, for no inmate had ever reacted so tranquilly to impending death. "Only someone with many gods to serve and only one world is intimated by your threat," the Rebbe forcefully replied. "But I have only one God to serve and many worlds in which to serve Him, so I am not threatened."

Though never arrested for trying to hasten the Messiah, I became increasingly fervent in my belief about his imminent arrival. Otherwise, how could we make any sense at all of the horrors we were hearing about? (WEVD's newscaster Hershel Levin announced in mid-August that the Nazis in Poland had massacred twenty thousand Bialystock Jews in a matter of days.) How could our faith be justified or even meaningful? A big event was being planned at the Lubavitch yeshiva for September 18, less than two weeks before Rosh Hashanah; surely the Rebbe would announce something crucial, I reasoned. But Rabbi Schneersohn said nothing at all about *Moshiach* that afternoon, and I was crestfallen.

Less than a month later, my hopes for American governmental intervention to save Europe's Jews were lifted by plans surrounding the march on Washington organized by Orthodox rabbis. Naively, I felt sure that this historically unprecedented rally would help rouse political action, for more than four hundred Torah scholars and leaders were scheduled to demonstrate at the nation's capitol and then at the White House.

To my shock and disbelief, however, President Franklin D. Roosevelt refused to meet with the solemn group and instead sent Vice President Henry Wallace, who offered only noncommittal platitudes in response to its pleas. Fortunately, the rabbinic march was not entirely useless, for within days Roosevelt agreed to establish the War Refugee Board, later credited with saving a quarter million Jews in the war's final year. But both these events during that fall—religious and secular—left with me a bitter sense that European Jewry was essentially doomed.

Unfortunately, my premonition would soon be confirmed by the Hungarian Jewish refugee writer Arthur Koestler, living in London at the time. In a January 1944 *New York Times Magazine* article, which I read with crushing dismay as a *Reader's Digest* reprint, Koestler reported, "At present, we have the mania of trying to tell you about the killings, by hot steam, mass-electrocution and live burial, of the total Jewish population of Europe. So far three million have died. It is the greatest mass-killing in recorded history; and it goes on daily, hourly, as regularly as the ticking of your watch."

~

PART TWO

INITIATING JEWISH RESTORATION IN AMERICA

CHAPTER TEN

~

A Fledgling Rabbi:
Hasidic Outreach in New Haven

As World War II came to its horrendous finale, the Lubavitcher Rebbe and his staff immediately initiated a program of establishing Orthodox yeshivas outside New York City. This bold venture was not only historically unprecedented for American Jewry, but it also reflected a truly revolutionary mindset: that Hasidism could take root and flower beyond its narrow Brooklyn confines. To this end, Rabbi Yosef Yitzchak Schneersohn vigorously began appointing *shlichim* (emissaries) to create centers of Judaic learning and observance throughout his new homeland. In many speeches and letters, he emphasized that it was up to Hasidism to take on this crucial task, for not a single other organization—not Reform, Conservative, or even Orthodox—was doing so; sometimes in this context, the Rebbe contemptuously referred to "worm-eaten" rabbis, who did nothing to stem the massive tide of Jewish assimilation.

Rabbi Schneersohn made it clear that education was not about rote memorization or even factual knowledge of Torah; it encompassed character guidance. In a booklet titled *Principles of Education and Guidance* that I found empowering, he stressed that teachers must come to know the individual traits and qualities of each pupil, "for the inept [pedagogue] not only does not achieve [positive] results, but also wreaks destruction."

Having just turned twenty-one and still a rabbinic student, I felt greatly honored to be among the first of the Rebbe's emissaries. After serving several weekends as a "support person" for Lubavitch activity in Bridgeport, Connecticut, I was given the more permanent assignment of helping to establish a yeshiva in New Haven. The opportunity excited me tremendously, for in a very real way, this optimistic effort originated in the same messianic fervor that I had experienced during the war years. True enough, the Messiah had not come in response to Hitler's annihilation of European Jewry. But I was sure that under the Rebbe's impassioned directive, a resurgence of Jewish education would provide the necessary "tipping point" to bring down *Moshiach*. And what could be more important than that?

And so, in the summer of 1945, I eagerly moved to New Haven. Soon after getting acclimated (taking lodging in a rooming house near Orchard Street's *shul*), I got to work in actively recruiting unaffiliated Jewish boys to join our day school, or at least our afternoon program for those whose families were committed to public schooling. Both groups of youngsters shared my own background, for like their counterparts in dozens of American cities at the time, New Haven's Jewry comprised mostly first-generation East European immigrants and their offspring. While strongly identifying ethnically as Jews, relatively few were eager to increase their religious commitment.

Motivating my students successfully was my aim, and I knew it would not be easy. Certainly, I had no desire to emulate my authoritarian and punitive teachers back in Austria. Through listening to the radio, I developed the technique of using jingles—so prominent in advertising—to help my students learn *brachas* (blessings) enjoyably. I also created various quizzes with singsong ditties for such questions as, "Which *bracha* do we make for eating bread? Which do we make for lighting *shabbos* candles?" My days were full and satisfying. During mornings, I taught yeshiva classes, then supervised recreation (often stickball or punchball) and lunch, then took my own break. In the late afternoons, my Hebrew classes were geared toward those attending public school.

To be effective in my work, I had already decided, I needed to know as much about children's development as possible. For the Rebbe had emphasized that educators must be concerned with how students relate to one another, as well as to their instructors. In conversing on this subject with our yeshiva's English teachers, I learned that the world's leading authority on child psychology was Arnold Gesell at nearby Yale University. Gesell had pioneered the concept of developmental norms: the notion that youngsters develop various mental and social skills in a more or less predictable chronological sequence. For example, nearly all four-year-olds readily believe in Santa Claus, but very few children just a few years older do. Likewise, eight-year-olds find it much easier to share with peers than do their five-year-old counterparts.

One afternoon, I went to the main branch of the New Haven Public Library, situated on the city's attractive historic Green, to read some of Gesell's works. There, on a table of new acquisitions, I saw two books that immediately caught my attention. It is no exaggeration to say that both changed my life in ways that I could not possibly have foreseen at the time.

Difficulties in Mental Prayer was written by Eugene Boylan, a monk at the Cistercian Abbey of Mt. Joseph in Ireland. The small volume's title intrigued me, for outside of the Lubavitcher Hasidim, no Jews I had yet encountered even mentioned the reality and nature of "mental prayer." At the Lubavitch yeshiva in Brooklyn, I had eagerly learned both *hitbon'nut* (meditation) and *devekut* (cleaving to God) and found these techniques immensely appealing—and challenging.

Opening to Father Boylan's preface, I silently read these words: "The pursuit of [spiritual] perfection is utterly impossible without mental prayer—which, of course, may be made quite unconsciously. In fact, it may be said that if a man does not pray, he cannot save his soul." Several pages later, Boylan remarked, "Now, prayer, especially from the individual's point of view, can often be very indefinite and quite unclassifiable. Further, even if there does exist a well-marked ladder of prayer for each individual, it is by no means necessary, at least as a general rule, to know on which rung one is standing. The important thing is to avoid standing still, and to keep on climbing."

Such passages amazed me, for this Catholic priest was using concepts and even metaphors consistent with my lessons from Rabbi Yisroel Jacobson and other mentors. In a practical way, the book was clearly asking, What should we do with distracting thoughts during prayer? This was an important spiritual issue that Hasidism's founder, the Baal Shem Tov, had raised; his specific term was *machshavos zoros* (alien thoughts).

Over the next few weeks, *Difficulties in Mental Prayer* awakened my soul to the realization that other religions besides Judaism hold real wisdom and effective methods for drawing closer to God. Mostly from shyness, I suppose, I never contacted Father Boylan to thank him for his transformative book. However, I discussed it intensely with Thomas Merton, the influential Catholic theologian, when we became friends in the 1960s.

On that same memorable day in the New Haven Public Library, a second book caught my eye: *The Portable World Bible*, edited by Robert O. Ballou. This was a hefty anthology of sacred writings drawn from humanity's major religions. Today, hundreds of such works exist, but published on the cusp of the Holocaust at the time, such ecumenism was unusual and almost visionary. Its opening section was devoted to Hinduism, including selected writings of the Hindu sage Ramakrishna. As a teenager, I had heard Papa talk admiringly about the Indian writer Rabindranath Tagore, so I was not entirely ignorant about Hindu spirituality.

In taking *The Portable World Bible* home, I also learned that Ramakrishna was born in 1836 into a poor, uneducated Brahmin family near Calcutta. After being drawn at an early age to storytelling and acting, he became a Hindu priest in 1866. In a short lifetime of fifty years, he established his own Hindu order, emphasizing that all religions are paths to the same goal of union with the Divine. Ramakrishna called this "God realization"—and insisted, like my Hasidic teachers—that what really matters is how we live and worship day to day. After he died, Ramakrishna's followers published several books of his sayings and teachings, and Ballou had skillfully presented some of the most inspiring for general readers like myself.

"Many are the names of God," Ramakrishna declared, "and infinite the forms that lead us to know Him. In whatsoever name or form you desire to call Him—in that very form and name you will see Him." This Hindu sage also observed, "As the lamp does not burn without oil, so man cannot live without God."

Ballou's anthology included a particular Ramakrishna aphorism that I came to quote often in coming years as a rabbinic teacher: "Hast thou got, O preacher, the badge of authority? As the humblest subject wearing the badge of the King is heard with respect and awe—and can quell a riot by showing this badge—so must thou, O preacher, obtain first the order and inspiration from God. So long as thou hast not this inspiration, thou mayest preach all thy life, but that will be mere waste of breath." I have long liked to cite this maxim for it dovetails with my own conviction that seminary and university degrees ultimately mean very little in matters of *neshamah* (soul).

One of the more memorable people I met in New Haven was a Shinran Buddhist bishop named Kenmiyo Taira. At Yale University, he was teaching Japanese as a second language, and due to the city's acute housing shortage after the war, his family needed lodging. In exchange for his diligent custodial services, we provided free accommodations for Mr. Taira, his wife, and their two young children. I was intrigued by his odyssey in coming across the world to teach in New Haven, but due to language barriers, we unfortunately never had really deep, "soul-searching" conversations. Decades later, with the rise of the 1960s American counterculture, I would delve into the fascinating parallels between Zen Buddhism and Hasidism.

Despite my position as a Chabad yeshiva teacher, I retained a lively curiosity about religious activity among other Jewish groups, and one weekday afternoon, I had the opportunity to walk by New Haven's Reform temple. Peering inside, I noticed a pipe organ and asked the caretaker if I could try it. He agreed, and I found myself merrily producing Hasidic *niggunim* (melodies). I also met the rabbi, and we chatted briefly. From time to time during the next couple of years, I would play the organ, and we would converse together. Such activity was satisfying to me, but I knew that my Lubavitcher colleagues would have strongly disapproved of such mingling with non-Orthodox Judaism.

Yeshiva student recruitment was always challenging financially, and when Passover approached in early 1946, I had insufficient funds to prepare an adequate *seder*. In desperation, I wrote to the Rebbe for a blessing, and to my amazement, he sent me a check for $200—a sizable sum in those days. It was accompanied by a note that strongly inspired me: "Consider this money not as a donation, but rather, that I am entering into partnership with you."

During those years in New Haven, I was influenced intellectually by another Catholic theologian: Saint Tikhon of Zadonsk. I found it fascinating that he was a contemporary of the Baal Shem Tov and likewise lived in Eastern Europe. Born into an impoverished Russian family in 1724, Tikhon managed to secure a good education and eventually became a bishop in the Russian Orthodox Church. In this capacity, he energetically founded a seminary, instituted special sermons, and set up caregiving programs for the poor and sick.

Tikhon's main concern, however, was religious education. One of his first publications was therefore titled *On the Duty of Christian Parents to Their Children and of Children to Their Parents*. Expressing a higher perspective that I found inspiring, Tikhon sternly advised his upper-class readership, "God will not ask you whether you taught your children French, German, or Italian, or the politics of society life . . . but you will not escape divine reprobation for not having instilled goodness into them. I speak plainly but I tell you the truth: if your children are bad, your grandchildren will be worse . . . and the [world's] evil will increase. . . . The root of all this [harm] is our thoroughly bad education."

By the time I was ready to leave New Haven in 1947, I felt part of a noble tradition—including both Jews and non-Jews—that saw education as among the worthiest of all human endeavors. And I viewed modern psychology as a valuable contributor to this same sacred realm. In this regard, Arnold Gesell's two popular books about children (written with collaborators), *Infant and Child in the Culture of Today* and *The Child from Five to Ten Years*, definitely influenced my outlook, for unlike the teachings of Hasidic sages and non-Jewish theologians like Father Boylan, Saint Tikhon, and Ramakrishna, his ideas seemed solidly—and vitally—rooted in scientific study.

"Every generation rediscovers and re-evaluates the meaning of infancy and childhood," Gesell and Frances Ilg wrote in their *Infant and Child in the Culture of Today*. "The child's personality is a product of slow gradual growth. His nervous system matures by stages and natural sequences. He sits before he stands; he babbles before he talks; he fabricates before he is altruistic; he is dependent on others before he achieves dependence on self. All of his abilities, including his morals, are subject to laws of growth. The task of the teacher in guiding the child is not to force him into a predetermined pattern but to guide his growth."

This sentiment made perfect sense to me, and achieving it within the context of Jewish education was my goal.

CHAPTER ELEVEN

~

Raising the *Klippot*
in Rochester, New York

As the Lubavitchers energetically expanded their educational activities after the war, I was unexpectedly offered a promotion in 1947: to direct my own yeshiva in either Pittsburgh, Pennsylvania, or Rochester, New York. Though I knew little about either industrial northeastern city, the latter offered a decisively healthier lifestyle, for back then Pittsburgh ranked among the most industrially polluted areas in the United States.

In New Haven, I had gained tremendously in my knowledge of education and child development. I had also become acquainted with religious wisdom outside of Hasidism. Yet, ultimately, I had been just an ordinary classroom teacher with little control over my assignments; now, at the age of twenty-three and a newly ordained Orthodox rabbi, I would actually be principal. The opportunity to plan and implement my own educational institution was an enticing dream. But I quickly learned that dream and reality are not always the same.

Though Chabad's leadership certainly meant well, it was not until Rabbi Menachem Mendel Schneerson became the Seventh Lubavitcher Rebbe in 1951 and appointed Rabbi Chaim Mordechai Hodakov as his chief of staff that the rapidly growing organization really began to function smoothly. A brilliant executive who had headed a yeshiva in Latvia while still a teenager, Rabbi Hodakov was a master at crisis management and effective trouble-shooting while still keeping his eye on the big picture of Hasidic development throughout the United States and abroad. Unfortunately, his ascension lay several years in the future when I took the position in Rochester.

71

The city's Jewish community numbered about twenty-five thousand, mainly comprising families of East European background, which, like their counterparts in New Haven, were predominantly first- and second-generation Americans. Struggling to rise into the comfortable middle class after fifteen years of economic depression and world war, they focused their outlook sharply on assimilation, and trying to establish a Hasidic day school there proved to be among the most daunting tasks I have ever faced.

From day one, the fundamental problem was money, money, and money. Only after moving from Connecticut did I learn, to my shock, that the yeshiva's budget was so miniscule that I was expected not only to be a tireless principal and classroom teacher but also the chief fund-raiser, school bus driver, and janitor. Compounding the difficulty was that the yeshiva's previous director had operated the institution at a significant loss, and I was obligated to pay off these prior debts as part of my new job responsibility.

How big was our educational program? We had a full-day kindergarten of twenty children; another twenty in public school attendance comprised our afternoon Hebrew school. My one employee was a teacher my age: Yankele Smith. We had enjoyably studied together at the Lubavitch yeshiva in Brooklyn and shared many good times. But now times were not so good. I had no previous experience in fund-raising, and if my efforts from month to month were mediocre or poor, then the yeshiva had inadequate money for books and supplies. Matters got so bad that one *shabbos*, I was down to $5 cash in hand—not enough money to pay the cleaning woman and make *shabbos*. Because I felt religious obligation came first, the result was dismal.

Then came the winter. Situated on Lake Ontario not far from the Canadian border, Rochester is definitely a "frost belt" city, considerably colder than New York. Despite my most valiant efforts, I found myself unable to raise sufficient funds to meet the large building's colossal heating expenses. One afternoon that I well remember, I returned from lunchroom supervision to the yeshiva office. There on my desk sat an ominous registered letter from the local bank. We had not paid them in months. As Yankele Smith stood anxiously nearby, I tremblingly opened it and promptly fainted to the floor: the bank's officer was informing us that they were immediately foreclosing on the building because of overdue mortgage payments, plus charging additional fees in penalties and accrued interest.

It was a sad day when the yeshiva building closed. Not long afterward, it was purchased by Aimee Semple McPherson's Four Square Gospel Pentecostal movement; following her death several years earlier, its leadership had passed to her son Rolf. After the bank foreclosure, I managed to keep the yeshiva going for another couple of months by renting classroom space at a local synagogue. But the proverbial handwriting was on the wall, and by the late spring, I shut down the entire program. I felt demoralized but quickly needed a steady source of income.

During the next few months, I became certified as a *shochet* after first obtaining the Rebbe's approval for my intended career change. Working as a kosher butcher seemed like a respectable way to make a living, especially as it ran in my family: both Papa's father and father-in-law had conducted this profession as devout Belzer Hasidim. Indeed, as chief *shochet* for the town of Oswiecim, my paternal grandfather had been a Jewish communal leader and renowned for his exalted piety. And so, in an Upstate New York meat factory thousands of miles from my Belzer origins in Galicia, I continued family tradition by learning how to ritually slaughter chickens and receiving Orthodox certification for my training.

Back then, I embraced Chabad teaching about the whole matter of *kashrut*, that four classifications of beings exist: inanimate objects, plants, animals, and humans. As the Baal Shem Tov emphasized to his numerous followers, there are *klippot* (fallen sparks) in all things; whenever we raise the sparks upward, we bring them closer to God and thus help restore the primal unity of the cosmos. Therefore, when Jews eat food in the kosher way and with the right intention (*kavvannah*), they redeem its *klippot*—and the purpose of that animal's incarnation has been fulfilled. When I became a *shochet*, this outlook very much inspired my activity.

CHAPTER TWELVE

~

A Pulpit of My Own:
Fall River, Massachusetts

Though I was committed to earning a living as a *shochet*, business success was not to be my destiny. I entered into partnership with acquaintances who owned a kosher butcher shop in Brooklyn. The hours were long and involved frequent delivery treks to the Catskills to service clients. Suffice it to say that the venture utterly failed, and by the summer of 1949, I was looking for a new position. I answered a Yiddish newspaper ad placed by an Orthodox *shul* in Fall River, Massachusetts, seeking a rabbi/Talmud Torah schoolteacher, and soon enough I was hired. Of course, I had first requested and received the Lubavitcher Rebbe's approval before taking the position.

At the time, the small city had a respectably large and close-knit Jewish community, numbering about ten thousand residents. As a southern Massachusetts harbor town close to Providence, Rhode Island, Fall River had been one of several drop-off points for German and East European Jewish immigrants at the turn of the twentieth century. Initially many of the latter were peddlers who eventually established shops and stores.

My new venue—the Quarry Street Synagogue as it was known to locals— was nominally Orthodox. I jokingly called it the "Horowitz Family Chapel," for the *shul* had been founded by an extended family of Ukrainian Levites. Except for the presidency, all leadership positions were held by Horowitzes. Several blocks away stood the Lithuanian synagogue, and beyond it, a *shul* frequented mainly by Jews of Lithuanian and White Russian descent.

The congregation was small, and my duties were not particularly demanding. With little on a day-to-day basis to inspire my *neshamah* or provide a sense of religious camaraderie, I felt the need to maximize communication with my Lubavitcher colleagues back in Brooklyn. But how? Long-distance phone calls in those days cost a fortune. I had always been drawn to technology, and so I taught myself to operate a ham radio and, after securing a license, kept in frequent contact with my friends about the latest doings at Lubavitch headquarters.

From the outset, I was most inspired by Jewish activity with young people; certainly, this had been true when Yankele Smith and I had worked together in Rochester with high school and post–high school teenagers. Fortuitously for me, the rabbi at the larger Conservative synagogue in Fall River had meager interest in getting involved with his Young People's League affiliate and therefore allowed me to take on this responsibility. Eagerly doing so, I wrote English lyrics for traditional Hasidic *niggunim* and taught methods of Hasidic prayer and meditation. I called it the "Chapel Group" because we met in the Conservative synagogue's chapel on a regular basis. I also had time to talk with Jewish students at several nearby college campuses, including prestigious Brown University. Many had never met a bearded Hasid like me before in their lives, and I enjoyed dispelling the stereotypes they had absorbed.

During these months, I sent the Rebbe regular reports about my youth work. I found it inspiring and effective, but I wasn't sure of his own reaction until the Chabad holiday of 19 Kislev, celebrating the 1798 release of the First Lubavitcher Rebbe, Rabbi Schneur Zalman, from Czarist prison. On that day, I was visiting Lubavitch headquarters with hundreds of others to join in the festivities.

By that time, the Rebbe was extremely frail. His assistants did not allow everyone to join the *farbrengen*. We would stand outside his door and sing *niggunim*, and sometimes the Rebbe's personal secretary would open it and call for certain people to enter. My name and that of my friend Rabbi Shlomo Carlebach were suddenly called. Shlomo and I had known each other in Austria and later studied together at the Lubavitch yeshiva. We approached the Rebbe's table, and he warmly gave us a big "L'chayim" and said the time was right for us to begin Jewish outreach on college campuses.

We eagerly assented, and he asked that Shlomo and I make a specific agreement about time and place. After leaving the Rebbe's table, we decided on logistics: Shlomo would take the train from New York to Providence, I would arrive from Fall River and meet him at the station, and we would drive together to Brandeis University and then Boston University.

Undoubtedly, to most observers at the time, the idea of launching Hasidic emissaries, known as *shlichim*, to fortify Jewish observance seemed absurd, even laughable. In the aftermath of World War II and the Holocaust, the survival of Hasidism seemed tenuous at best. Yet today hundreds of Chabad houses involving thousands of staff span college campuses across North America and abroad. By whatever destiny was at work, Shlomo and I were the first of these emissaries.

What was our Hasidic toolkit? In recent speeches, the Rebbe had been stressing the importance of teaching nonobservant Jewish males to put on *t'fillin* daily. So, in preparation for my trip with Shlomo, I collected and rehabilitated thirteen pairs of damaged *t'fillin* that people had donated. I also brought English translations I had made of the Rebbe's varied teachings. Finally, I took a tape recorder—a big reel-to-reel contraption—together with several hours of Hasidic melodies I had played on a Hammond organ and recorded. With that gear and my accordion, Shlomo and I drove from Providence to fledgling Brandeis University's new location at Waltham.

Chanukah was occurring at midweek, and we arrived on campus at a building called "The Castle." We entered the cafeteria. The lights were off, and a man with spotlights was illuminating couples in the dark as a jukebox was playing. Shlomo began our debut by telling Hasidic stories. A bright young man commented, "That sounds like Hindu mysticism, right?" and I immediately engaged several students in a discussion about cosmology.

Then I opened my bag with the thirteen pairs of *t'fillin* and offered an enticing deal: anyone who learned to put on *t'fillin* and take them off three times could keep a pair. This proved a successful inducement, and we distributed all we had brought with us. Many students stayed until the wee hours, and at 4 a.m. Shlomo and I dragged ourselves to a hotel in Boston.

The next day, I met the B'nai B'rith Hillel director at Boston University. He talked about promoting Jewish life on campus and the intellectual and creative challenges it entailed. It was a life-changing conversation for me. I was so impressed with his work that I thought to myself, If I can do that and get paid for it, that would be my dream.

Shlomo and I returned to our respective communities, immensely pleased with our first *shlichim* work on college campuses. We made a good team and continued such outreach for the next six years, until I moved to distant Canadian Manitoba.

⌒

Only a few weeks later, on January 28, I received a phone call from Rabbi Moses Pinchas Katz at Lubavitch headquarters. *Shabbos* had just ended.

"The Rebbe is *nistallek gevoren* [has ascended]," he quietly said with grief and astonishment mixed in his voice.

"How could that be?" I asked, completely stunned. "The *Moshiach* hasn't come yet."

In a way, I should not have been so surprised. Earlier that week, the Rebbe's latest printed *ma'amar* (religious discourse) had come not by regular mail but by special delivery—to ensure that we would study it that exact *shabbos*. Moreover, the theme—a mystical interpretation of the Song of Solomon 5:1, "I have come to my garden, my sister, my bride"—had been provided by the Rebbe on the occasion of his grandmother's *yahrzeit* in a somewhat different form. The message concerned God's indwelling with the Jewish people, and the mood was one of yearning. Undoubtedly, the Rebbe knew of his imminent passing and wanted to give this final teaching.

I immediately headed to Providence, picked up a waiting Lubavitcher Hasid, and we drove all night to Brooklyn. After entering 770 Eastern Parkway, I stood in the hallway and recited psalms while, within an adjacent room, the Rebbe's body was being purified and prepared for burial. Every so often, one of those involved in this sacred duty came out and asked Rabbi Menachem Mendel Schneerson—and not Rabbi Schmaryahu Gourary, the Rebbe's older son-in-law—for advice. It was already clear who would be the Rebbe's successor.

On another visit from Fall River about two months later, I noticed Rabbi Menachem Mendel Schneerson standing in the hallway at Lubavitch headquarters. I had been at his father-in-law's gravesite at the Old Montefiore Cemetery in Queens and was washing my hands in accordance with Jewish law.

"You have just come from the *Ohel?*" he asked me.

"Yes," I replied, and he said, "May God help that what you prayed for should be accepted."

"I prayed that people shouldn't get in the way," I said.

"What do you mean?" he asked, surprised.

"I prayed for three things," I answered. "That we should have a rebbe, that you should be the rebbe, and that you should be blessed with children." As all Lubavitchers knew, Rabbi Schneerson and the Rebbe's daughter Chaya Mushka had been childless for more than twenty years—and were now in their late forties. Among Orthodox Jews in general, especially among Hasidism, infertility to this day is regarded as a tragedy.

As I uttered these words, I burst into tears. Rabbi Schneerson took my hand and began to cry too. "We *have* a rebbe," he said, "and what difference does it make if he is in this world or the next world?"

I fixed Rabbi Schneerson with my eyes and boldly replied, "Why is it that God buried Moses in a place where no one would know where his grave was? It's so that Joshua wouldn't send people to Moses's grave for advice, for Joshua was now the rebbe."

Rabbi Schneerson knew that I was rebuking him in a vibrant religious language we shared. Still tearful, he softly said, "It will be all right." Within the year, on the date of his father-in-law's *yahrzeit*, Rabbi Menachem Mendel Schneerson announced that he would assume the title and awesome responsibilities of Lubavitcher Rebbe.

My dual position as rabbi and Talmud Torah schoolteacher in Fall River didn't pay well at all. Back then, few jobs in America's Jewish community were available for bearded Orthodox rabbis like me. So to earn extra money, I found additional employment as a *shochet*—kosher-slaughtering chickens in a Providence, Rhode Island, meat factory. When I began to work there, I found myself badly upset by the obscene language of the factory's chicken pluckers. They tended to pass the time by boasting of their sexual exploits, and whether reality or fantasy, their comments harshly conflicted with the purified spiritual mind-set I was trying to cultivate as a *shochet*. For example, it was important for me to water and speak softly to each chicken before I dispatched it, affirming its goodness as a creature of God that would provide people with physical sustenance. I couldn't do this while the chicken pluckers whooped about their sexual triumphs, and so I would ask them temporarily to step outside. To them, I was an oddball "who talks to the chickens before he kills them."

Fortunately, I was able to hit on an effective solution by using song to alter their behavior. They all knew the gospel hymn "Joshua Fit the Battle of Jericho," and I led them in vigorously chanting it as they rhythmically plucked the chickens I had just slaughtered; in such work, the feathers have to be removed immediately, while the chicken is still warm, or the task becomes much more laborious. The men enjoyed the rhythmic singing and laughingly began calling me the "Bee-Bop Rabbi" as an affectionate moniker. And their obscene talk disappeared in my presence.

The prosaic town of Fall River, Massachusetts, might seem an unlikely place for a mystical experience, and yet this is what happened on a quiet Sunday in the fall of 1950. I was schmoozing with Dr. Ploni Rofe (not his real name), an internist who had acquired psychiatric board certification in order to better treat his patients, and we were looking for something interesting to do.

But what? Back then, Massachusetts, like virtually all other states, had tightly enforced blue laws that prohibited commercial activity on Sundays. Only churches would be open in our small city, so we perused the religious notices in the local newspaper. Nothing looked very enticing except for the Spiritualist church, scheduled to begin its service at 7 p.m. We hurriedly drove to the listed address, which proved to be a private house in a residential neighborhood.

A friendly woman with grey hair and deep blue eyes greeted us at the door. She motioned to a side entrance leading to the basement and asked that we "write a question for Spirit" on a little piece of paper and place it with a twenty-five cent donation into her basket. With a joking attitude, I tossed in a quarter and scribbled some semicomical lines, while Ploni wrote something more serious. Then we descended into a room filled with locals sitting on rickety folding chairs as a wheezy organ played "Nearer My God to Thee." The woman came down, introduced herself as Agnes Taylor, and briefly described her background. Then, she began talking about herself in the third person—as though a spirit were now speaking through her.

Reaching into the basket, Agnes began opening the billets individually and giving advice. She stated to one person, "There's someone standing behind you. He committed suicide, and he's having a hard time leaving this world because he's still tied to it." To another, Agnes commented, "Your case will come up, but not in Providence. It will be in Newport, Rhode Island." Those around us were clearly moved by her specific replies, and my edge of sarcasm had vanished.

Then Agnes came to my friend Ploni's paper. She said, "There's a young girl here. She's about ten years old. She has beautiful locks of hair—like Shirley Temple locks—and she was killed in an automobile car accident." I gasped and grabbed Ploni's hand, for he had left his daughter alone at home that afternoon. He softly assured me that I needn't worry; later Ploni explained that while growing up, he had lost his sister in a car accident, and she had looked just as the medium had described.

Agnes now looked carefully at Ploni's face and said, "Behind you stands a man. His name is . . . Frank. He is your father. And he has been wanting to be in touch with you ever since he passed over. Because he was babysitting for your children when you and your wife went to the movie. You came home and found him dead, slumped in his chair. Your boy was sitting on the floor and crying. And you have been blaming yourself ever since that had you been at home, you might have been able to save his life. He wants you to know that he had a massive heart attack. It was his time to go. He's been trying to tell you that all these years." I knew that Ploni's father had died about seven years earlier, but I had never heard about the circumstances.

Ploni sat there with tears streaming down his face. I was absolutely amazed. When we left the service and drove back, he told me that everything the medium had said was true.

I reacted very powerfully to this experience. I had read a little about mediumship and parapsychology, and of course I knew that Hasidism had a long tradition of seeking guidance from departed rebbes through dreams or at their *kevers* (gravesites). But the reality of what I had seen with my own eyes was much more potent—and unforgettable.

I decided to return for a private session, and Agnes asked me this time to play the organ. As I began performing a slow Hasidic *niggun*, she stood up suddenly and said, "There is a man here with a fur hat. He's coming from the twentieth plane, very high. Oh, I am in awe of him." She described Rabbi Yosef Yitzchak Schneersohn and transmitted his blessing.

Not long afterward, I met with Rabbi Menachem Mendel Schneerson at Lubavitch headquarters in Brooklyn. At the time, he was advising Hasidim to seek graveside guidance from the *neshamah* (soul) of his father-in-law emanating from the World to Come. I carefully described my experience in Fall River and asked, "Would it be worthwhile for me to learn mediumship so that we could channel the Rebbe?"

Rabbi Schneerson laughed and replied, "He doesn't need dancing tables. If he wants, he can come in through a window, the door, or your mind. So, no, we don't need that."

CHAPTER THIRTEEN

~

Caribbean Travels:
Voodoo and Mitzvah Missions

In the summer of 1952, I had my first opportunity for foreign travel since arriving in New York City more than a decade earlier as a wartime refugee. As I had hoped and expected, Rabbi Menachem Mendel Schneerson had become the Seventh Lubavitcher Rebbe. I was glad to follow his request to spend the summer raising funds and strengthening Jewish observance in the Caribbean and Central America. My suitcases included a *shochet*'s knife for kosher slaughtering and tools for fixing Torah scrolls, as I knew that in every town I visited, there would be a *sefer Torah* in need of a little repair. For two very different reasons, my trips to Haiti and Nicaragua were among the most intriguing—and exerted a lifetime impact.

That year, I had been excited to read Marcus Bach's new book *Strange Altars*. Based on the author's personal experience, it was a dramatic account of voodoo as practiced on the island of Haiti. I was needed for fund-raising in Panama City in a few days and had all of one weekend to connect with Haiti's voodoo subculture. It was definitely worth a try.

Haiti, then as now, had very few Jews. Arriving in Port-au-Prince on a Friday, I would fly to Panama on the following Monday. I knew that Saturday night was voodoo night, and once settled into my hotel room, I eagerly asked the staff, "Where's a good place to watch a voodoo ceremony?" Cautioned to stay away from Port-au-Prince's tourist traps, I was instead directed to a venue in the countryside. While checking into the hotel, I had become acquainted with a vacationing schoolteacher named John from Ohio, and he wanted to join me. A taxi was called, and before long, we arrived at the designated place.

The Haitian countryside was lush and dark. Even before stepping out of the cab, we could hear loud rhythmic drumming and catch glimpses of leaping flames. Of course, we were the only two foreigners there. Standing close together in the large crowd, John and I watched as a voodoo priest began slaughtering a chicken to feverish accompanying drumbeats. Whenever its spurting blood struck a dancing woman, the crowd cried out encouragingly, for the blood touching was believed a good omen for conception. All the women were dancing and dressed in white.

I began to focus on the drumming, trying to establish in my mind its compelling rhythm. I felt myself more and more absorbed by the beating drums, and they began to create a strange sense of opening within. I didn't want to lose consciousness, but multiple paths started looming and diverging in my mind's eye, and I felt myself becoming lost, lost, lost.

The next thing I knew, John was yanking me from the center of the group. I must have still been entranced for he looked frightened—and then suddenly I felt frightened too. I had apparently become hypnotized and was trance dancing for several minutes. As John later recounted, the excited crowd was murmuring that I was being "ridden by Legba." Why? Because how a person trance-dances during voodoo allegedly reveals the particular deity performing the riding. Still later, I learned that Legba is the voodoo god who acts as intermediary between humanity and the spirit world, opener of the celestial gateway.

While returning in the taxi with John back to the hotel, I still felt dazed and light-headed. The next morning, I felt like myself again. But I was convinced I had tasted something involving real powers in the universe and not at all mere superstition. With memories of the Fall River medium still fresh in my mind, I knew clearly that, as Shakespeare's Hamlet declares, there are "more things in heaven and earth" than most people are ever aware of.

In Managua, Nicaragua, I experienced another epiphany, this one decidedly more Judaic in content. Like other traveling Lubavitchers, I was accustomed to staying with an observant Jewish family in each foreign city, whether in Costa Rica, Panama, or Puerto Rico. In Managua, the Jews all recommended "the *meshuggeneh*" (crazyman) Almoni. Someone kindly carried my luggage and drove me to Almoni's store, a well-stocked and air-conditioned enterprise selling dry goods, machetes, and countless other commodities.

Introducing myself, I handed my calling card to his chief saleslady. She politely explained that Señor Almoni was studying holy books as usual in his office and ordinarily could not be disturbed for two hours. I told her that it was important, and she reluctantly heeded my request. After a few moments, Almoni emerged from his office: bearded with side locks and big *tzitzit* (fringe garments) hanging out, he warmly greeted me in Yiddish. And, then to my surprise, he added, "I'm studying Talmud with my son, and there's something we don't understand. Maybe you can help us a little?" I was filled with joy. All this authentic Jewishness in the back of the most successful dry goods store in Managua!

So why was Almoni called *meshuggeneh*? Because he was the only Jew in the entire city who insisted on closing his store on *shabbos*. Saturday was the big market day in Managua. People came from miles around to the central market; even Jews did most of their business on Saturday. But not Almoni. He had decided to maintain his observance.

For the first year or two, he really struggled. Then word of this strange man got out among the local Seventh-day Adventists, and the minister came to visit. Somehow they managed to bridge their language gap. Almoni needed honest, polite, well-trained employees, the minister pointed out, and his congregants also wanted to observe the shabbos. Did they have a deal?

The arrangement worked out wonderfully. Almoni had less employee pilferage than any other merchant in town. His Seventh-day Adventist staff got to rest on what was normally the busiest sales day of the week. And the store flourished. On Friday afternoons before they closed, Almoni and his employees would prepare Saturday night bargains. Customers would line up with their donkeys to carry home all the goods they had bought—waiting until nightfall, when Almoni and his Seventh-day Adventists would open their store for business.

So here was a person in far-off Nicaragua who sat and studied Torah for two hours in his store every day, observed *shabbos* on the busiest sales day of the week, and thrived financially. *Meshuggeneh* Almoni! What a crazy guy, and what an admirable Jew! In countless conversations I've had over the years, he has been my exemplar.

CHAPTER FOURTEEN

~

Widening Horizons:
From New Bedford to
Boston University

By 1953, I was delighted to take a full-time position with Ahavath Achim, a nominally Orthodox congregation twelve miles east of Fall River in New Bedford, Massachusetts. The salary was more substantial, and my days as a chicken slaughterer were over. A much larger city than where I had resided the past few years, New Bedford had a correspondingly bigger Jewish population whose breadwinners were employed mainly as engineers and other professionals at several large companies.

Like Fall River, New Bedford was rich in New England history. It was first explored by the English in 1602, eighteen years before the Pilgrims arrived at Plymouth. Granted its town charter in 1787, it became famous for whaling. At the height of its whaling prosperity in the pre–Civil War years, New Bedford set out more whaling ships than all other U.S. ports combined. Textile manufacturing and fisheries were also prominent industries. During the nineteenth century, its most famous resident was the abolitionist and former slave Frederick Douglass.

Jews had been living in New Bedford for about a century, coming mostly from Germany, Poland, and Russia. Before a synagogue was built, worship services had been held in private homes. In 1899, Congregation Ahavath Achim had been completed and dedicated on Howland Street, and a new building was erected during World War II. The synagogue was officially Orthodox with mandated separate seating for men and women, but only about 15 percent of congregants were actually *shabbos* observant. The board's members were almost exclusively non-Orthodox men, who would have gladly joined a Reform congregation, except that New Bedford had none, and the Conservative *shul* charged a lot more for dues.

I never really fit in well there, though I tried my best. Some of the congregants came to the daily *minyan* (quorum) just to say *kaddish* (prayer for the dead) for a deceased parent. Sitting in the back and wearing miniscule *tallitot*, they were annoyed to discover that the *kaddish* prayer comes at the end of the services and would grumble that I was unnecessarily wasting their time. I would offer them *t'fillin* to wear, and they would typically reply, "I don't believe in that stuff, rabbi"—and back away. Then I began to wonder, Did they truly not believe, or were they simply too embarrassed to admit publicly that they did not know how to put *t'fillin* on?

Having joined the Ministerial Association in 1953, I began to make what I considered "pastoral calls"—visiting congregants in their homes and offering to put up *mezuzahs* and instruct them on *t'fillin* usage. I had some success in these ventures, but then several board members warned me to stop such "snooping" and "spying." I was aghast by their reaction.

Meanwhile, the concept and practice of personal prayer was becoming increasingly important to me, and I decided to innovate in this regard. I wanted to lead a late Friday night service for a whole group of congregants, but I didn't dare attempt that in the big *shul*—because I wanted to eliminate separate seating between men and women. So I offered a special service in the vestry with family seating. The cantor and I would have an introit, entering and singing "Shalom Aleichem" together, and then we all would *daven* from the Birnbaum *siddur*.

I also encouraged personal prayer in the vernacular and translated from the Hebrew to come more easily from the heart. This was unconventional, but it seemed to attract a serious crowd. I still remember how one Friday evening, an earnest young man came in and asked if he could pray near me.

I replied, "Yes, and I will say 'Amen!' to your prayers."

And he said, "Dear God, I have to make up my mind about whether to take the offer of buying into a trucking service. It's risky financially for me and my family, but it might be a good thing. Please help to clarify this for me."

And I answered "Amen!" It was a wonderful moment of spiritual union and unfortunately so rare in synagogues back then.

⌢

In the spring of 1955, I was finally ready to embark on educational training to become a B'nai B'rith Hillel rabbi. Ever since Rabbi Shlomo Carlebach and I visited Boston University in our first campus outreach for Chabad in the late forties, I had yearned to work in this capacity. It seemed to offer its staff wonderful, creative Jewish opportunities in an intellectual milieu. From Hillel's national headquarters in Washington, D.C., I learned that my *smicha* (rabbinic ordination) plus a master's degree would be my entry ticket for a campus position. So I enrolled in Boston University's pastoral counseling program. Its starting date lay a few months ahead in September, but I needed to complete several preparatory psychology courses during the summer. If all went well, I might eventually be able to earn my doctorate: that was my dream.

Boston University had an excellent academic reputation, but it certainly wasn't nearby: it was two hours each way from my home in New Bedford. Leaving that first day at 5 a.m., I arrived with enough time to *daven* morning prayers as I had planned. But where? At that hour, everything on the Charles River campus was closed, except for Marsh Chapel at 735 Commonwealth Avenue. An attractive new building, it was named for Daniel Marsh, the Methodist minister who had been the university's president for a quarter century.

I went inside expectantly, but the ornate main chapel featured wooden statues of Jesus and the four Evangelists. I didn't feel comfortable even thinking about *davening* there, so I headed downstairs to the smaller chapel. A cross was prominently displayed above the pulpit—again, not the place for me. Walking over to a small side room, the Daniel Marsh memorabilia room, I put on my *tallit* and *t'fillin*; facing east toward Jerusalem, I recited morning prayers and then I took my breakfast. Right after, at 8 a.m., I went to the first of my classes and drove back in the afternoon to New Bedford to teach Hebrew school.

I repeated this routine for several days, when one morning a middle-aged black man peeked inside the downstairs side room where I was *davening*. "Is there a reason why you don't pray in the chapel?" I mumbled something about the symbols. To my surprise, the man warmly replied, "When you come back tomorrow, see if you don't feel more comfortable," and smiled enigmatically.

The next day, I entered Marsh Chapel and was quite curious about what I would find. In the downstairs chapel, a large white candle was burning, and the Bible on the lectern was open to Psalm 139:7, which says, "Whither shall I flee from thy Presence?" The large cross was no longer where it was the day before but rested on its side against a wall. Feeling very grateful to the janitor, I did my *davening* right there. When I finished, I replaced the cross in its regular position and turned the Bible to Psalm 100, the thanksgiving psalm—"Enter His gates with thanksgiving and his courts with praise! Give thanks to Him, bless His name!" And so, the downstairs chapel became my prayer place from that morning onward.

My weekly schedule was grueling as I was taking a full load of courses plus working full time as a pulpit rabbi. But thanks to my mental training at Lubavitch, I had a way of dealing with the academic material I had to master. As I drove from New Bedford to Taunton, I would mentally review one course, then driving from Taunton to Stoughton a second course, and from Stoughton to Boston's Blue Hill Avenue a third course. And my grades were very good.

Soon it was time for me to plan my spring course schedule. A catalogue course titled "Spiritual Disciplines and Resources" caught my eye. Ever since my teenage years in Antwerp, I had been fascinated by the subject of inner growth and studied it avidly with my Hasidic mentors in Brooklyn. However, this time the instructor would be no Hasidic rabbi but Minister Howard Thurman, dean of Marsh Chapel. Although the topic certainly intrigued me, the catalogue indicated that the course would involve "labs," experiential class activities.

Deep down in my guts I felt anxious about entrusting my soul to a "Christian"—knowing that they all want to convert Jews. Was he open enough to allow me to learn spiritual disciplines and resources to make me a better Jew? As a pulpit rabbi for several years, I had learned enough to know that such methods require ample trust to be effective, and to do that, I wanted to make sure that Minister Thurman was trustworthy—that is, that he wouldn't try to convert me to Christianity.

At the time, his name meant nothing to me, though he was already famous as a leading theologian and descendent of southern slaves. He was also the first black man to be appointed dean at a major American university and would later exert a strong intellectual influence on Dr. Martin Luther King Jr. As I later learned, Thurman's course was truly innovative. He had developed it only two years earlier, upon becoming dean at Boston University in 1953, for the purpose of acquainting students "with their own inner life."

After making an appointment through Dean Thurman's secretary, I appeared at his office and knocked on the door. To my amazement, Minister Thurman was none other than the kindly black man whom I had misperceived as the building's janitor!

Talking over coffee with the dean, I explained that I really wanted to take his course and learn from his experiential methods. But I also confessed that "I'm not sure if my anchor chains are long enough" to relinquish self-control and allow him (as a non-Jew) to guide me spiritually. With a pensive expression, he put down his coffee mug. His graceful hands went back and forth, as though mirroring my dilemma. Finally, Howard Thurman looked right at me and said, "Don't you trust the *Ruach Hakodesh* [holy spirit]?"

To hear a non-Jew speak these Hebrew words so eloquently shattered my composure. As though yanked on an invisible chain, I immediately stood up and hurried out of the dean's office without offering even a word of thanks or a good-bye.

It was a profound challenge: Am I a Jew because God wants me to be a Jew, or am I a Jew without reference to God? I agonized over my decision for three weeks, and committing myself to be led by God, I registered for Dean Thurman's course.

"Spiritual Disciplines and Resources" was a tremendous learning experience for me. My classmates included many Christian clergy working on higher degrees and the young Walter Pahnke, who would later become famous as a psychiatrist for his "Good Friday" study involving psychedelics and religious ecstasy. I remained in touch for years with several of my peers. Under Howard Thurman's able tutelage, we experimented with a variety of spiritual techniques, including guided meditations. In one memorable exercise, our class was instructed to translate an experience of one sense into another: for example, we would read a biblical psalm several times and then listen to a beautiful meditative Bach composition—in order to "hear" the psalm's meaning in the sounds of the music. In this way, we refined our senses and became better able to experience the divine around us. Beginning the first lab with the reading of Psalm 139, we reflected on it to Bach's melody. When afterward Thurman played a recording of Max Bruch's orchestral composition of the ancient *Kol Nidre* prayer sung on Yom Kippur, I allowed myself to relax. During the course I visited Thurman frequently during office hours to discuss my practice.

Several years passed, and when one of my sons was close to *bar mitzvah*, I introduced him to Dean Thurman and asked the minister to bless us both. For an instant he seemed surprised, then wordlessly prayed while placing a hand on our shoulders. This profound experience has stayed with me intensely for over fifty years. Decades later, I was moved to learn that Thurman long remembered this soulful encounter between us. In an unpublished part of his autobiography titled *With Head and Heart*, he wrote, "I'd never been in a position like that before, where the fact of being the instrumentality of a blessing was so personal and intimate and exclusive. It was not like saying a blessing with a group at a moment of some sort of celebration, but here was the celebration of a common religious experience and a friendship and an affection that existed between two men, each of whom came from a radically different tradition but had met in that zone in which there is no name or label. And standing there I bowed and I prayed. I do not recall any words that were said, but what I do recall is the intensity of the religious experience in that moment, and the transcendent and yet penetrating look in his face when I opened my eyes and found that he from his kneeling position was looking up in my face."

~

During the summer of 1955, I was invited to present Hasidic stories at the annual conference for B'nai B'rith Hillel directors and student leaders. It was my first appearance at their annual meeting in the remote and poetically named setting of Starlight, Pennsylvania, nestled among the state's rural northeastern hills. My sponsor was Hillel's president, Rabbi Arthur Lelyveld, a Reform Judaic scholar whose wide-ranging works included the early history of Chabad Hasidism. We became good friends. Later, during the 1960s, Arthur gained national acclaim for his civil rights activism, which almost cost him his life in Hattiesburg, Mississippi.

His invitation could not have come at a better time for me, for pulpit work in New Bedford was wearing. Here was a different world of creative Jewish scholars and innovative educators. Though B'nai B'rith Hillel at the time had a decidedly Reform Judaic tilt, many rabbis were receptive to Hasidism. Though usually presented in a kitschy, Norman Rockwell–like form in popular media and synagogue programming, Hasidic dance and tales were beginning to reach a wide audience.

One morning a panel of theologians was discussing the "God idea in Judaism." Though obviously sincere and intelligent, they were making the topic needlessly abstruse. Then, unexpectedly, Rabbi Lelyveld invited me to take the microphone. I said, "These ideas are so complex. God is so simple. All it takes is—to meet the God that is seeking us. Period."

Was it brazen for me to speak this way? Perhaps. Certainly some there seemed close to my message. But several prominent Hillel rabbis, including Moshe Pekarsky of the University of Chicago, seemed delighted by my retort. He took me aside, and we chatted—the beginning of another long, wonderful friendship. Born in Poland some twenty years before me, he had come to the United States with his family as a teenager. Moshe perhaps became best known for launching the famous *Latke vs. Hamentashen Debate*, an annual exercise in Jewish satire that takes place every Purim before hundreds of University of Chicago faculty and students—and has featured such participants as Nobel laureate Leon Lederman.

Though Moshe certainly had a light side, he shared my growing conviction that American Judaism needed a major overhaul. "One does not need to be a university teacher or a student to sense the emptiness and hollowness, the superficiality and more than occasional vulgarity that dominates much of Jewish communal life," he eloquently insisted in a typical speech. "American Jews have settled down to a kind of Judaism that demands little and offers little in return."

Moshe envisioned B'nai B'rith Hillel on college campuses as a means to energize Jewish life, and I immediately understood his view. It could serve as a "hothouse" for breeding new forms of Jewish *davening*, liturgy, and learning in ways not possible in most synagogue settings. For example, the mixed seating of men and women favored by Hillel's services was already more consistent with my sensibility than the separate seating dictated by Orthodox *shuls*. Generally, too, young people were inherently more open to new methods of expression than their older counterparts. As a pulpit rabbi for the past five years, I had seen this plainly enough.

By the end of that week, I was pumped to the brim with enthusiasm. Everyone joined for a final celebration, and afterward I went into the field and cried out to God, "Look what wonderful material there is for soul work, for *Yiddishkeit*, in America! Please give me a chance to participate in doing it!"

Unfortunately, things were not going so well for me back in New Bedford. In retrospect, most of the difficulty was due to my lack of experience. As an active member of the Ministerial Association, I had begun visiting various local churches, partly to gain ideas for my own pulpit work: the notion of "ministering" vibrantly to my congregation had become increasingly important to me. I liked attending the Quaker meetings in my community: these always felt religiously "neutral" as I could wear my *kipah* and enjoy the ritual in which individuals said something brief and sat down, then everyone experienced a sacred silence together. I had also attended midweek Christian prayer meetings, in which participants would speak one at a time, and the group would reply "Amen!" I was impressed too with the testimonials in Christian Science services: there, members would stand up and relate God's healing presence in their lives.

One Friday night, therefore, I decided to dispense with prayer books and instead lead the congregation in a more intimate, soul-baring way. First, I informed the astonished cantor and *shammas* (sexton), "Tonight, no *siddurim* (prayer books)." Then, as our members took their seats as usual, I announced that we were doing something different: Did anyone want to say something about God or ask for a blessing? Something? Anything? Initially, there was a long, awkward silence that seemed interminable. Then one man got up and spoke about faith in his life; then, after another long silence, another person stood and contributed. Eventually, there was a surprising amount of personal religious sharing. I felt gratified and sensed at least a mixed reaction. But later that week, I received a terse note from the board's president: "We have 438 *siddurim*. They are meant to be used."

My final mistake at Ahavath Achim was likewise borne of good intentions. Soon after that Friday night innovation, I asked the congregation board for an evaluation of my rabbinic performance—a common procedure today, known of course as "asking for feedback," but rather unusual back then. The board members, thinking that I was asking for a raise in salary, quickly agreed and asked me to wait in my office while it deliberated. Three hours passed, and I began to feel uneasy. Finally, I was called in. I immediately sensed that their mood was far from cordial.

The board presented me with fifteen different "complaints," as they called them. I still remember their self-contradictions, as Complaint Number 7 was "not modern enough," whereas Complaint Number 8 was "too much English." I stood there speechless with dismay. Two months later I was informed that my contract would not be renewed. I would then no longer be their rabbi.

This was my learning time. I was so naive, for at Lubavitch yeshiva in Brooklyn, I had been given no training whatsoever in pastoral work. Nobody had told me that before conducting the kind of unexpected forms of liturgy I did that Friday night, it's necessary to prepare congregants slowly and gradually, that it's vital to gather group consent, confer several times with the ritual committee and senior board members, and build consensus painstakingly. All I knew from fifteen years of involvement with Chabad was that the rebbe is on top and calls the shots—and I was now on top, and I was going to call the shots. I had no inkling of how my actions would affect some of those board members at Congregation Ahavath Achim. Everything was a learning situation.

~

PART THREE

PLANTING SEEDS OF JEWISH RENEWAL

~

CHAPTER FIFTEEN

Jewish Innovation in Manitoba

In the summer of 1956, I arrived at the University of Manitoba to serve as Hillel director in Canada's prairie heartland and begin my new position as a part-time faculty member in the Department of Judaic Studies. I would have preferred continuing in Ahavath Achim for another year to complete my doctoral coursework in pastoral counseling—but without a job, that was financially impossible. Receiving my master's degree that spring had finally given me the credentials to become a Hillel campus rabbi—but one more hurdle remained to be overcome.

And what did it involve? My beard. Though it may seem incredible today, Hillel's national administrators had made it clear that until I removed my Hasidic beard, I would not be considered for any available opening. With my pulpit post terminated, I had no choice but to comply. And so, one bright June morning as my children watched with shocked expressions, I used clippers and scissors to reduce my full beard to something akin to a Vandyke. Then I traveled to Hillel headquarters in Washington, D.C., to confirm my compliance.

To cheer me up, my friend Moshe Pekarsky joked, "Zalman, beneath your bearded rabbinic visage is a clean-shaven rabbi," and I retorted, "Beneath your clean-shaven rabbinic visage is a bearded rabbi." We both laughed. Once I had safely passed my grooming inspection, I soon grew back much of my Hasidic beard.

Two B'nai B'rith Hillel openings existed at the time, in very different locations: Gainesville, Florida, and Winnipeg, Manitoba. Because Gainesville had neither a *mikveh* nor a Hebrew day school, my choice was clear. When I came to Manitoba, it was high summer, and I must admit that I had little inkling about Canadian winters; perhaps if I had come for a wintry visit, I would have chosen sunny Florida instead.

There was no doubt, however, that Manitoba had a well-established and vibrant Jewish community for its small size of twenty thousand souls. Jews had first arrived individually in the 1870s from both Eastern and Western Europe, steadily increasing in subsequent decades due to pogroms in Russia and Romania. Many Jews were peddlers or small businessmen with meager education. Beginning in 1905, though, a new wave of immigration from Eastern Europe brought a considerable number of Jewish intellectuals to Canadian shores, men and women who had been part of Yiddish and socialist-cultural movements in Russia. They helped contribute to Manitoba's culturally rich Jewish community, centered in the provincial capital of Winnipeg. In 1883, its first synagogue was built, and as early as 1921, an impressive Lubavitcher *shul* was opened on Magnus Street. Eventually, I came to serve as its rabbi, on top of my various teaching responsibilities.

The University of Manitoba's Hillel had gone through ups and downs since it was founded about a decade earlier. When I arrived, my first task was to whip up enthusiasm among Jewish students, for Hillel House had become rather moribund. Fortunately, I never lacked for energy or ideas. I created lunch-hour programs and then weekend events in which I led retreats with students. When the Soviet Union launched the world's first space satellite in October 1957, I launched my own luncheon program, "Sputnik and Matzoh Balls," which proved highly successful.

Before long, I also founded my first Jewish meditation group, which I called the "Chapel Group"—for lack of a better name, because we met in a chapel. My goal was to introduce students to various Hasidic methods of meditation, inner exploration, and awareness. My first lessons were on mind steering—that is, how to direct your mind instead of floating in its flotsam and jetsam of thoughts.

My years of Chabad training had taught me the importance of concentrating and focusing. So, I would tell students, "Take a single idea or sentence from our *davening*—for example, 'The soul of every living being praises thy name'—and ponder it. Consider it the way you enter a shop and consider a purchase. Or, if you're more visual, then visualize that sentence. See all the world's creatures breathing—how they live and give thanks to God." That was the beginning. I would also show students how to sing a Hasidic melody—and that's when I wrote words to *niggunim*, so the songs would also offer content for conscious reflection.

I showed ways of reciting psalms. Among my favorite labs was to select a chapter of the psalms, such as Psalm 23, "The Lord Is My Shepherd." Everyone knew that verse, so I could easily begin with it. I would advise students, "Recite the words in a loving, devotional way." And they would spend a few minutes doing that. Then I would say, "Now, recite the same words scornfully or sarcastically." And they would inject that attitude into their recitation. I taught my students a variety of melodic lines to instill feeling, for that's really what we do in *nusach*, chanting, and *davening*.

A decade earlier in Lubavitch yeshiva, Rabbi Yisroel Jacobson had clapped me Zen-like and suggested, "Can you *daven* with a smile next time?" I wanted young people to know how it feels to pray that way, to navigate their way around inner space while *davening*. If you don't know how to steer consciousness in there, then you don't really know how to perform Hasidic meditation. Howard Thurman's course also influenced me a lot. He gave me formats for group activities: before studying with him, I was teaching meditation by the seat of my pants, but after learning with this great technician of the spirit, I became far more effective.

Another lab I liked to do involved body movement. I would ask students to lie down on the floor while I played a recording of Bach's "The Art of the Fugue." And when the first movement came, they would dance it with their right hand, then with their left hand, then with their right leg, and finally with their left leg. Participants would become aware that instead of always taking predetermined dance steps, you can let the music take you places.

To teach body awareness, I played many kinds of music, from children's songs like "The Hokey Pokey," to classical and rock-and-roll pieces, to Lalo Schifrin's *Jazz Mass*, which involves distressing noises and sounds of people screaming. I would play Tibetan *bardo* (experiential dying) music followed by resurrection music, and then everyone would rise.

In still another lab, I asked participants to line chairs up like church or synagogue pews. I would say, "Now I want you to dance, but not in a visible way. In other words, it must be submuscular dancing. You can wiggle your toes or your eyes, or your tongue, but if I catch you make an outward movement, you're out of the group." In this way, students came to internalize their body movements, to enhance their subtlety. When reciting a psalm, they learned how to communicate its meaning bodily not just verbally. Masterful cantors do this—emphasizing words with their hands.

My students included non-Jews as well as Jews. Sometimes that led to fascinating results. Every year I would lead a lab investigating the subject of the first-, second-, and third-person experience. At the time, the University of Manitoba comprised various colleges, separated not only by departments like agriculture and engineering but also by religious affiliation. St. John's College was Anglican, St. Paul's was Jesuit, and United College was United Church of Canada. St. Paul's had extra space for my labs, but every classroom featured a crucifix.

So we met in the chapel, and one day I explained to my students, "First person is 'I,' second person is 'you/thou,' and third person is 'he.'" Then I said, "I'm going to ask you to close your eyes, and when you open them, I'm going to ask you to look at various objects and assign each one a number—1, 2, or 3." Then I pointed to the crucifix. What was the result?

Most of the Protestants assigned it the third person: that's *him*, Jesus on the cross. Most of the Catholics assigned it a 2: that's *you*, Jesus on the cross. And most of the Jewish students assigned it a 1: that's *me* hanging up there.

I was encouraging amazing things in those days. I required each student to attend different kinds of worship services and write reaction reports. When I began teaching the psychology of religion and assigning books like Aldous Huxley's *The Perennial Philosophy* and William James's *Varieties of Religious Experience*, they were just empty words for my students. To make these brilliant books come alive, I directed my students to attend a Quaker prayer meeting, a Russian Orthodox service, and other religious happenings. I wanted my students to gain direct experience of what Huxley and James were describing.

Not only the students in my psychology of religion classes but also the Jewish students involved with B'nai B'rith Hillel needed to become more acquainted with what was happening in various houses of worship. I had an arrangement with them. Each Sunday, they would come to Hillel House, and we'd *daven* together, eat bagels and lox, and then choose one of the many churches in Winnipeg to visit during their worship services. Afterward, we'd return to Hillel House to discuss what we had seen and learned.

Three of these visits stand out in my memory. On one, we went to the Roman Catholic cathedral. My students and I went up to the balcony where we could watch the priest at the altar. Each time he intoned one of the segments of the Mass, I whispered to the students what the Hebrew equivalent was. One of the students picked up a mimeographed handout given to visitors at the church, and it indicated the time when the purgatorial society would meet.

As my group left the church, I heard that student mock the Catholics for their beliefs. I didn't answer at the moment, but we went back into our cars and traveled to the Lubavitcher synagogue. Because I was active on their staff, I had a key and opened the building. We all went down to the *Beyt Hamidrash* on the lower floor, and I pointed to some plaques on the wall.

One of these mentioned the society of those who recite psalms. They listed the members and also the entitlements; among these was that the deceased member's surviving colleagues would recite the psalms for his soul's benefit to release him from purgatory. After seeing this, my students began seeing that we shared more spiritually when we kept our minds and hearts open.

There was also a Buddhist church in Winnipeg. I was curious, thinking that perhaps it would reveal intriguing Eastern meditative techniques to my students. It was a church for Japanese families belonging to the Shinran denomination, and the worship service was very close to Low Church Protestant. There I bought a little calendar that showed a picture of the Buddha inviting a group of little children to come to him. It was very similar to what one might find in a Catholic church with a picture of Jesus inviting small children to come to him.

Since I'd had a connection in Fall River with the local Spiritualist church, and there was also one in Winnipeg, I took my Hillel students there too. One time, the head of the church called me to attend a special session with a "prominent and excellent medium" from the southern United States. I asked that I be allowed to participate, as she claimed to do "direct voice"—which meant that everyone would sit in the dark. There would be a megaphone-like trumpet flying around, and we would hear the dearly departed in their original words and language. When the day came, our group sat in a circle, and we gave our first names. When I heard a ghostly sounding voice behind me say "Zaaalman," I responded with the formula "Welcome to God's blessing, who would you be?" With a rural southern voice, the swift answer came: "I am yo' grandpa!"

Of course, my grandfather never spoke a word of English. He had been a *shochet* his whole adult life in Galicia. Instantly amused, I asked, "And what are you doing in summer land?" The answer was, "The same thing I did on earth." Somehow, I could not imagine my grandfather slaughtering cattle in *Yenne Velt*.

Sometimes you hit a good one at a séance. That time I did not.

When living in Fall River, I had avidly read a book titled *The Pillar of Fire* by Dr. Karl Stern, a psychiatrist. In it, he powerfully described his personal journey from assimilated Jew in pre-Nazi Germany to Roman Catholic convert. The book was persuasively written, and at the time I felt half-torn between running to the nearest Roman Catholic priest and immediately burning it. A while later, someone wrote to ask me if I knew where Dr. Stern lived, and I replied that I thought he had passed on.

The years went by, and one day when I resided in Manitoba, I was watching an interview on television—and it was none other than Dr. Karl Stern, who was serving at the time at St. Mary's Hospital in Montreal. Although the interviewer kept interrupting Dr. Stern, he presented himself as both thoughtful and serious-minded, and I decided to write to him. I said, "As a psychiatrist, you'll understand why as a rabbi I had difficulties with your book, and why I thought unconsciously that you were dead. I'm glad you're not, and if you have the time, I'd love to meet you." He responded graciously, and I traveled to Montreal to see him at St. Mary's Hospital.

By this time, I had become acquainted through my Trappist friends at Our Lady of the Prairies with various liturgical Catholic texts, and we had a wonderful conversation about the need for spirituality and deeper prayer in contemporary life. At one point, Dr. Stern was called out of our meeting because of an emergency on one of the wards, and he genially handed me some books by Sigmund Freud to keep me occupied. But I was far more interested in the pictures of some illuminated manuscripts he had in his office, and when he returned, I showed him a picture accompanying the liturgy of the canonical hours and explained the Hebrew equivalent.

When my time was up, we were about to shake hands good-bye, and I asked, "And now, Dr. Stern, that the honeymoon is over, what does it feel like?" It wasn't a nice thing to say at the time. He looked at me seriously for a moment, and then said, "I forgive you, of course." He then picked up his phone and told the secretary he would need ten more minutes.

Then Dr. Stern began to teach me how the five stages of Freudian psychosexual development also apply to religion. For instance, the oral phase shows itself in religion as the way that new converts feel so happy receiving grace—the "milk and honey" of the new spirituality that they have embraced. There are also some people who get stuck in and fixated on the oral phase; these are the people who keep hopping from one religion to another because they can't get beyond their infantile need for nurturing.

The next phase is the anal period of religious involvement, when people feel the need for discipline, purity, and precision in religious observance. Every little detail is deemed important and cannot be ignored. Some people become fixated at that level; they're the ones who become literalist fundamentalists and even fanatical. Then there is a third period, which Freud called the phallic. In religion, it's the time when people experience everything as beautiful, inspiring, and glorious. There are persons who become fixated in the aesthetics of religion and cannot move from there. This is followed by the latency phase, in which religion is experienced as the great agape—a joyful sharing with other people of the same religion and glorious fellowship with them. A lot of what is being done in social gospel comes from that fourth phase. But still beyond that phase and the entire Freudian system is the genital period. This fifth one calls for one-on-one intimacy and is the aim of the true mystic, as best modeled by St. John of the Cross.

I thanked Dr. Stern for this illuminating teaching. It has been with me ever since, because it has been proven right in my own life and in the lives of the people I have served. Thank God, I had many more times to meet with Dr. Stern and to share our views on spiritual growth.

As a direct result of creating the Chapel Group, I authored my first work on Hasidic meditation, titled *The First Step* (not to be confused with my 1983 book by the same title). There was so much receptivity, among both Jewish and non-Jewish students, to what I had to offer, and I especially saw the need for a simple, practical guide on what was an immensely complex topic. Of course, it needed to be in English and written in direct, straightforward language.

The writing came extremely easily to me. It was as if the words and ideas were waiting to pour out from my *neshamah* and flowed effortlessly. What emerged was something unique in booklet length, and I was very pleased with what I had accomplished. But Manitoba's Hillel House had no budget to print it, and the topic was totally off the radar for B'nai B'rith's national headquarters. How the financial resources materialized make for an interesting story.

At the time, my friend Moshe Pekarsky at the University of Chicago was doing what he could to enhance Jewish spirituality on campus. As B'nai B'rith Hillel director, he had invited Gershom Scholem to speak about Kabbalah—quite an esoteric subject on the American college campus back in the late 1950s. Among the audience was a Jewish Irish businessman named David Jackson, who had apparently undergone an out-of-body experience and wanted to understand the Kabbalistic viewpoint about it. To those in the Orthodox rabbinic world, it was well known that Scholem, as an aloof scholar, found all such nitty-gritty questions abhorrent.

After the lecture, Jackson handed Scholem an envelope with some money and a request for a private interview. Scholem agreed, and when Jackson asked how to follow up Kabbalistically his mystical experience, he was curtly advised, "Study Hebrew grammar." It was Scholem's way of saying, "Buzz off." But, as Moshe Pekarsky admiringly told me, Jackson took the answer at face value and was now grappling with this subject matter through a private tutor.

When Pekarsky invited me to lecture at his Hillel chapter, he made sure that David Jackson and I got together. We hit it off well, and he generously provided all the funds needed for printing *The First Step*. So in 1958, it was published in Winnipeg.

What was its basic message? Long out of print, it presents what I now call a "restoration" approach to Hasidism and traditional Jewish spirituality. Perhaps these excerpts can best convey my viewpoint, which still holds although the text was written exactly fifty years ago:

> Let me explain to you the function of *kavvannah*. It means intention. Our intention is always free. There is nothing that can obstruct your intending. Even if the whole world coerces you into a pattern of actions, you can always "intend" whatever you want.
>
> Before going to sleep, start out by fully and completely forgiving anyone who wronged or hurt you, and pray for the welfare of that person. Continue by affirming the Oneness of God, and your longing to serve Him, and then read the *Shema*.
>
> Inspirational reading is of immense importance. Hold on to this time as something very important. Address God and ask Him that your reading may inspire your continued effort.
>
> One can really live a whole life with just one meditation. So you subdue the boredom and work until it breaks through. You will know that you have broken through by the fact that your subconscious has, in this area, become slightly reoriented. Life, filling the All, will have become a real factor in your living.

Were I writing today the same type of practical manual for spiritual growth, would I do it the same way since so much has been published on prayer and meditation? Of course not. But at the time, the Holocaust had happened little more than a decade earlier, and I fervently wanted to preserve aspects of prewar Jewish worship and meditation—especially among Hasidim—that I knew were nearing extinction. I saw that the result of the Holocaust would be so terrible: there would be so much forgetting, and all the previous nuances would be gone. I wanted to preserve the liturgy—the *nusach*—and the distinctiveness of the various Hasidic groups, for they differ: Chabad is not the same as Bobover, and so forth.

Besides working as a Hillel director and a Judaic professor at several colleges, I also served occasionally as a pulpit rabbi in Manitoba. Sometimes I presided in Yiddish and other times in English. One Orthodox *shul* was rather amusing. The building's longest side was its width. This meant that all the big shots would sit in the *mizrach*, and when I preached, I would be talking to them in front. There was a Mr. Garfinkle among the synagogue's leaders, and whenever I said anything in my sermons, they all looked to see his reaction. He was a *melammed* and regarded as the most learned person there. If Garfinkle nodded in agreement at what I was saying, then everyone smilingly nodded too. But if he didn't nod, then I was in trouble, for everyone immediately began thinking, Uh-oh, what's this man saying? Garfinkle doesn't agree with him!

Although I was steadily moving beyond traditional Orthodoxy in both my outlook and my Hillel activities, I continued to maintain close relations with Lubavitch. I corresponded often with Rabbi Schneerson about my activities, interests, and reflections on Judaism. Sometimes, though not always, he mailed back my letters with handwritten comments in the margins. I had elicited and obtained the Rebbe's approval for both my synagogue posts in Massachusetts and then for my job with Hillel in Manitoba. When Chabad asked me to serve as a rabbi at their well-established *shul* in Winnipeg, I gladly agreed, though the position carried no salary except for officiating at High Holy Day services. By the early to mid-1960s, I had become well known throughout Lubavitch circles as "the guy who can work with far-out people" drawn to the Hasidic world.

It must have been around 1961 when I brought a delegation of Hillel students to meet Rabbi Schneerson at 770 Eastern Parkway in Brooklyn. Having just concluded the annual B'nai B'rith Hillel conference in Starlight, Pennsylvania, everyone was fired up with Judaic fervor. After a warm greeting, he invited questions. There was a moment of silence. Then a young man who was president of my Hillel group raised his hand and sharply asked, "What is a rebbe *good* for?" I drew in my breath for a moment, but instead of being insulted, Rabbi Schneerson gently replied, "This is a very good question. Let me tell you. It is written in the Torah, 'You shall be unto me a land of desire.' Within the earth are all kinds of treasures, but you have to know where to dig to find them. If you don't, you'll hit either rock or mud. But if you ask the geologist of the soul where to dig, you might find silver—which is the love of God; gold—which is the fear of God; or diamonds—which is faith. All a rebbe can do is to show you where to dig. You must do the digging yourself."

I felt it was a beautiful answer.

Reb Zalman as a child in Vienna, about 1932. P'nai Or Religious Fellowship, which is now ALEPH: Alliance for Jewish Renewal; originally printed in *Worlds of Jewish Prayer: A Festschrift in Honor of Rabbi Zalman M. Schacter-Shalomi.* © 1993, P'nai Or Religious Fellowship

Reb Zalman's passport photo in Antwerp, about 1939. P'nai Or Religious Fellowship, which is now ALEPH: Alliance for Jewish Renewal; originally printed in *Worlds of Jewish Prayer: A Festschrift in Honor of Rabbi Zalman M. Schacter-Shalomi.* © 1993, P'nai Or Religious Fellowship

Reb Zalman and cantor at a wedding in New Bedford, Massachusetts, about 1952. Photo courtesy of Rabbi Zalman Schachter-Shalomi.

Reb Zalman in his Winnipeg office, 1957. Photo courtesy of Rabbi Zalman Schachter-Shalomi.

Rabbi Menachem Mendel Schneerson, the Seventh Lubavitcher Rebbe, 1961.

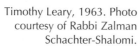

Timothy Leary, 1963. Photo courtesy of Rabbi Zalman Schachter-Shalomi.

Dr. Howard Thurman, 1965. Photo courtesy of Rabbi Zalman Schachter-Shalomi.

Rabbi Shlomo Carlebach and Reb Zalman at the Lama Foundation, 1965. Photo courtesy of Rabbi Zalman Schachter-Shalomi.

Father Thomas Merton, 1968. Photo courtesy of Rabbi Zalman Schachter-Shalomi.

Reb Zalman in the early 1970s. P'nai Or Religious Fellowship, which is now ALEPH: Alliance for Jewish Renewal; originally printed in *Worlds of Jewish Prayer: A Festschrift in Honor of Rabbi Zalman M. Schacter-Shalomi*. © 1993, P'nai Or Religious Fellowship

Reb Zalman at his daughter's baby-naming ceremony, 1978. Photo courtesy of Rabbi Zalman Schachter-Shalomi.

Polish Synagogue (Polnische Schul), Leopoldgasse 29, 2nd District in Vienna. Referred to in the *Jewish Encyclopedia* as "Exterior of the Leopoldstrasse Synagogue." Photo courtesy of *Jewish Encyclopedia*.

CHAPTER SIXTEEN

~

Adventures with Catholic Monasticism

Not long after I moved to Winnipeg as a B'nai B'rith Hillel director and professor of Judaic studies at the University of Manitoba, I became close with the monastic Catholic community in the area. It was a gradual process of friendship and learning catalyzed by a chance encounter on an airplane flight.

Call it serendipity. It must have been around 1960. I had just completed a stimulating ecumenical weekend at a college in Northridge, Minnesota, after visiting my friend Max Ticktin, the Hillel rabbi at the University of Wisconsin, Madison. Max had been there for more than five years after graduating as a Conservative rabbi from the Jewish Theological Seminary in New York, and I regarded him as a kindred spirit. A dynamic, creative figure who would later help spur the *chavurah* movement, Max shared my passion for bringing new energy to Jewish life on American college campuses.

As I was boarding my airplane, I noticed a nun getting on before me; back in that era, they typically traveled in pairs, but this one was alone. Once we were aboard the airplane, as the flight attendant ambled by my seat, I handed her my calling card and said, "Could you please ask the sister if I may talk with her?" The flight attendant agreeably did so, and after our takeoff, the sister invited me to come over—and we talked.

She was Mother Claudia of the Sisters of Our Lady of Sion, but I didn't know that yet. Looking closely at her garb, I respectfully asked, "Is this the original habit of your Order?" She answered that it was. I replied, "Well, it looks to me like it's from nineteenth-century France," and she immediately said, "That's correct—because we're the Ratsibonne Sisters." At that moment, if I could have pulled the ejector seat to escape, I would have. For I knew that her order had been founded by a Jewish convert to Catholicism, Theodor Ratisbonne, who became a priest, as did his younger brother Alphonse several years later. Although I had already made pleasant contact with Trappist monks in Manitoba, I was well aware that, in those years before the historic Vatican II Conference in Rome, the Catholic Church was still officially praying for the conversion of world Jewry to the "one true religion" of Catholicism. Theodor Ratisbonne had actively sought to convert Jewish children to Catholicism, an endeavor for which he received Pope Gregory XVI's enthusiastic support. To this end, Ratisbonne opened several Parisian houses staffed by Our Lady of Sion nuns for the purpose of imparting Christian education to Jewish boys and girls. Originally, Theodor and Alphonse had tried to join the Jesuits, but the Jesuits wouldn't take them. So they started their own order, whose main purpose was to convert Jews to Christianity. By the time of their deaths in the mid-1880s, the order they founded had spread to many countries in Europe and lands beyond—including Jerusalem.

Nevertheless, the sister and I began to chat amiably. After a while, it was time for her to perform her office (obligatory recitation of all 150 biblical psalms, divided into seven sections and completed weekly by all pious priests, monks, and nuns). I took out my Hebrew prayer book and recited t'hillim (psalms) as she was doing her office—and there and then, we became friends. When our airplane landed in Winnipeg, I finally asked the purpose of her trip. She introduced herself as Claudia—the superior of the Sisters of Our Lady of Sion—and explained that she was visiting their local foundation. It was situated on the way to Pembina, where my university was located, so I congenially met her colleagues too. Before long, several of the nuns enrolled in Judaic studies courses that I was teaching at the University of Manitoba. Most often, they took my course on the history of Jewish thought, which included the Bible and the writings of Abraham Heschel and Martin Buber, among other theologians. I remember being impressed with the excellent writing ability and intellectual understanding that the nuns demonstrated in my courses.

After I left Winnipeg for Temple University in 1976, the nuns remained close with my colleague Rabbi Neal Rose of the Jewish studies faculty. Like me, he has long emphasized an ecumenical view of religion, and though now retired academically, he codirects tours of the Holy Land and Italy with a Roman Catholic priest who shares his New York City origins.

As the 1960s progressed, I became increasingly friendly with the Trappist community in Manitoba. Ever since I had discovered Father Eugene Boylan's inspiring book *Difficulties in Mental Prayer* back in 1948 New Haven, I had been intrigued by Catholic spiritual insights into prayer. Many of the monks radiated a sense of selfless piety and devotion to God that resonated well with the rabbinic training I had received from Chabad-Lubavitch; participating with the monks in fervently reciting the psalms opened my heart.

By this time, I was also well acquainted with the writings of St. Ignatius of Loyola—especially the "Loyola method" for inner development, as presented in his classic book *Spiritual Exercises*, written in the mid-sixteenth century. I considered it eminently valid more than four hundred years later. The story that most impressed me about his life was this: A new pope was installed in Rome after Ignatius had founded the Jesuit Society in 1540, approved by the late Pope Paul III—and there was a danger that it might be disbanded. So someone asked him, "Ignatius, what will you do if they disband the Jesuit Society?" He swiftly replied, "Fifteen minutes in the oratory, and it's all the same to me."

This famous story, emphasizing the inspirational power of experiencing God's presence during prayer, reminded me of the Hebrew phrase "Shiviti ha-Shem K'neqdi Tamid" (I will place God before me always). That is to say, no matter what happens in this conflicted world, I will keep my balance through all events, and I need only be in God's presence.

The Abbey of Our Lady of the Prairies was a fascinating community. Founded in 1892 by five Cistercian monks from the far-off Abbey of Bellefontaine, France, it was the only Trappist monastery in western Canada. Located in the historic town of St. Norbert, it was a ten-minute drive from the University of Manitoba and perhaps a half hour by car from my home. I remember a cheerful young monk named Denis Bernadine, who recently died and who eventually did missionary work in Northern Rhodesia (now Zambia), Africa, for nearly a half century. Father Bernadine had spent time at Our Lady of the Prairies before I met him at Gethsemani Abbey in Kentucky, where Thomas Merton was also a monk. Denis had a warm, kindly demeanor and poetically once wrote, "Our silence and exercises are not an end in themselves, but rather a means to an end. . . . These [monks] have no reason for living other than to praise God for what he does."

At Our Lady of the Prairies, I was especially close with Abbot Dom Fulgence Fortier. As a gift, he gave me a cloth abbatial robe, which I sometimes still wear when conducting Yom Kippur services. Abbot Dom Fulgence and I had many stimulating conversations about prayer and monastic life, for by the early 1960s, I had become fascinated by newly emerging archaeological discoveries about the Essene community, which produced the Dead Sea Scrolls shortly before the Romans destroyed the Second Temple of Jerusalem.

Although the Trappists, of course, differed from the Essenes in many ways, both groups shared from my perspective an intense commitment to prayer as the foundation of spiritual life. I began to realize that mid-twentieth-century American Judaism had much to learn from the ancient community that produced the Dead Sea Scrolls. It seemed clear that something was truly lacking in American Judaism of all denominations from Reform through non-Hasidic Orthodox. What specifically? An attention to prayer. It was precisely this attention that the Trappists demonstrated so convincingly to me. Once I began writing my doctoral dissertation at the Hebrew Union College in Cincinnati a few years later, I sometimes went to the scriptorium of Our Lady of the Prairies for editing work. There, in that superbly quiet space, I was not bothered by phone calls.

During those years, my mentor Howard Thurman at Boston University once came to my campus for a visit. I asked what he wanted to see—perhaps the Canadian parliament? But he wasn't interested. Instead, to my surprise, Thurman asked me to show him around the Trappist community at St. Norbert. I called Abbot Dom Fulgence and asked for permission to come. When we arrived, I asked Thurman, "Do you want to meet the abbot?" He replied, "No, the abbot is just an administrator. I want to talk with the master of novices."

So Thurman and the master of novices began animatedly talking, and Thurman bluntly asked, "Tell me, what's the biggest complaint the novices have here?"

"They report," Thurman was told, "that all the great raptures come to them when they're outdoors, and nothing much happens when they're on the floor, praying, at 2:30 a.m., or at chapter, and so, they ask to be removed from those things. So I forbid them to attend anything except the obligatory masses, and I keep them outdoors in the field. A few weeks later, they say, "'Look, I didn't come here to be a farmhand.'"

Thurman and I both laughed aloud. Of course, I now know that the Trappist novices usually came to realize that what happened in the chapel—though it didn't seem so fruitful at the time—was vital to their spiritual growth. That is one of the wonderful things that a monastic life can bring about. In a broader sense, my experience with Catholic monasticism contributed to my view that prayer is the "work of the heart"; therefore, we must find the pathway.

Let me try the following simile: if I were to write the musical score for a violin and then ask the tympani to play it, that would be foolish. Similarly, it is foolish to try to use *head*-ing with abstract concepts to enter into prayer when we have not enough experience and practice in *heart*-ing.

When it is effective, theology is the afterthought of the believer (read: *be-live-er*, one who has lived an experience and then wants to tell the head something that it might possibly understand). When theology tries to make sense of God ideas without a basis in experience, it becomes a card house built from flimsy concepts. Here again, Catholicism provides a good example. Thomas Aquinas created the structure of Catholic theology, with all its myriad abstractions. At the end of his life, he had an immediate experience of God and declared that everything he had written before was like empty straw. Blaise Pascal ranked among the greatest mathematician-physicists of the seventeenth century. Yet, for all his genius, he wrote a note with his own blood about his mystical encounter at the age of thirty-one, not with the God of the philosophers but with the God of Abraham, Isaac, and Jacob.

Whenever we are seeking a relationship with God, we must recognize the cosmic "world" in which we want to relate. Let me recap: When we are in the world of sensation, *Assiyah*, we are dealing with God the Creator in an indirect way, because we are encountering only the effects of His creation. Prayer does not apply there. When we are dealing with God as the vast infinite intelligence and consciousness behind the universe, we are encountering the mind of God and the mode of reason. Prayer does not apply there either. When we are dealing with divine infinity extending infinitely—what the Kabbalah calls the *Ayn Sof*—we cannot connect with our sensation, feeling, or reason. In that infinity, we do not even really exist. Still, we can intuit at moments a flash of our identity with that dimension. That is a moment of rare grace. However, when we are dealing with the world of *Yetzirah*, the realm of feeling, there the means by which we access the other worlds do not apply.

For the heart, it is essential to have an "other." The world of *Yetzirah* is the world of feeling: it is the dialogical universe, and it is here that prayer does apply. Herein is the difficulty that the theologian experiences: in order to allow for a real "other," one must descend from the brain into the heart. There is no shortcut, and it is important that the reasoning mind is grounded enough in the four worlds to give assent to the reality of the heart. It is for this reason that the study of the writings of the praying mystics does allow the mind to consent to the work with the heart.

~

CHAPTER SEVENTEEN

My First Trip to the Holy Land

In 1959 I went with other college campus directors of the B'nai B'rith Hillel Foundations to Israel. It was in the summer and, of course, before the reunification of Jerusalem brought about by the momentous Six-Day War of June 1967. The border between Israel and Jordan was situated at the Mandelbaum Gate: when you came to the edge of Meah Sh'arim, you could see right into Jordan. I remember standing at Mount Zion and gazing into their country. Of course, the Kotel (Western Wall of the Temple) was held by Jordan, which refused Israeli access to the Jewish people's holiest site.

We flew to Israel on KLM Royal Dutch Airlines, which provided blankets with a tartan design that I liked a great deal. I decided to buy one from the airline and later on added *tzitzit* to it. It was the Anderson Clan Tartan, with a very lovely blue and all kinds of other colors, and in some ways it was the beginning for me of the multicolor *tallitot* that I later created. From the Tartan design, I graduated to Mexican serapes with their beautiful psychedelic colors, because if you've done psychedelics, you will recognize those hues and blendings. Later, when I asked myself, What would be a color scheme that I'd like to have for the best concept of a *tallit*? I began to think in terms of the spectrum.

Several years after this trip to Israel, I was invited to speak at Yale University, and I was offered the choice of payment in money or a *tallit* woven from reindeer wool according to my design. I chose the *tallit*. I began my first layout of the spectrum of what later became the B'nai Or *tallit*. In other words, since there are seven colors in the spectrum and seven lower *sefirot*, I paired them. So it begins with *Chesed* as the ultraviolet and ends with *Malkhut* the infrared and includes all the colors between. If you look at chemical spectra, you can also see black lines on the sides, and that's how it happened that I gave strong black lines to *Chesed* because it needed a good container. *Gevurah* didn't need any; *Tiferet* does, and in the green center, I left a series of white stripes indicating that *Keter* shines through *Tiferet*.

On this trip I met Professor Shmuel Hugo Bergmann of the Hebrew University in Jerusalem. It was one of the most wonderful things that happened to me during the entire trip, and I really fell so in love with this man. Born in Prague, he had been friendly with both Max Brod and Franz Kafka and emigrated to the Holy Land in 1920. A philosophy professor close with Martin Buber, Bergmann was both brilliant and gentle, but people would complain about him saying, "I tell you, he's not a good philosopher!" Why? "Because he always talks about the latest book that he's reading." Bergmann was nearly seventy-five years old at the time, but his mind was still open to new ideas. Known for his writings on the philosophical implications of quantum physics, he enjoyed meeting me because I was able to discuss meditation with him and relate Hasidic teachings in both philosophical and psychological language. He had been from the Marburg/Kantian school of philosophy.

On Friday night, the tour organizers decided to take us to the service of a Reconstructionist *minyan* in Jerusalem held at the *Beit Hachalutzot*. The service was conducted by a man named Ben Chorin-Freedman. He was a wonderful person. Unfortunately, the other campus Hillel directors didn't enjoy the service—which was all in Hebrew, as Mordechai Kaplan in his seminal Reconstructionist prayer book had made sure that every prayer he composed in English also had a Hebrew version. Then Ben Chorin gave a sermon on the Torah portion in which the Prophet Elijah goes to the mountain and hears the small still voice (1 Kings 19). I like to translate this phrase as the "sound of subtle stillness." As a finale, Ben Chorin asked those attending the service to meditate in silence.

As I left the building, some of my colleagues turned to me and said, "We saw that you were so absorbed, but we just couldn't relate to the service. What was going on for you?" I jokingly replied, "After about five minutes, I realized that this was going to be a Jewish Reconstructionist service in Hebrew with the flavor of a Protestant American liturgy." Everyone laughed.

Among the tours we received was an ascent of Mount Zion. There are many steps leading up the mountain and fifteen stations of ascent in ancient Jewish tradition. Our Israeli tour guide didn't have a single idea about how to make the tour into a true pilgrimage. I wanted to have a pilgrimage experience—to recite, on each of those fifteen steps, one of the psalms of ascent as per tradition in biblical times.

Then our tour guide wanted to bypass the historic Abbey of Dormition, a beautiful Benedictine church. I didn't want to bypass the abbey, so I quickly donned my Hasidic *gartel* and entered to recite some psalms with the other worshippers inside. Our tour guide was utterly shocked. For him, this was absolutely crazy: a religious Jew going into this *goyishe* (non-Jewish) place to pray!

At the time, the superior of that abbey was Abbot Leo Rudloff. A German-born monk who was a major figure in improving Christian-Jewish relations around the world, Father Leo was a remarkable man. I knew that he and Abraham Heschel had often shared correspondence with one another. Father Leo was also in charge of the Benedictine priory in pastoral Weston, Vermont. The monks there composed and sang many beautiful songs, such as one based on the biblical verse "Wherever you will go, I will go" (Ruth 1:16).

During this trip, the possibility existed that I might be able to obtain a position as associate or assistant to Rabbi Jack Cohen, then director of the Jerusalem University Hillel. I very much hoped for this position and felt that it would be productive to meet two important potential mentors if it materialized: Professor Gershom Scholem at the Hebrew University of Jerusalem, renowned scholar of Jewish mysticism, and Dr. Erich Neumann, among the world's leading Jungian analysts.

My meeting with Professor Gershom Scholem was both productive and strange. If I obtained the position at the Jerusalem University Hillel, he agreed to take me on as his doctoral student for two years at the Hebrew University. I was already planning to gain my doctorate in Jewish studies, and in this way I would be able to complete the coursework for it.

During my personal conversation with Scholem, I asked him, "Who is currently writing about spiritual direction and Jewish mysticism? A lot of people can perform nice homiletic spins on the scriptures, but who's really sharp in spiritual direction?" Scholem told me about Rabbi Ahrele Roth. I'd never heard of this Hasidic master by his last name. When I asked Scholem if I could meet Rabbi Roth, Scholem smiled and replied that I was too late by a couple of years. Then I asked Professor Scholem, "How will I find their places?" He jokingly answered, "Go to Meah Sh'arim, and where they shout prayers the loudest, that's where it is!"

Later on, I did go there, and I met with the son of Reb Ahrele, who was very friendly to me despite the fact that I was wearing short pants like any ordinary tourist. I also went to the synagogue of the son-in-law. When I entered it, I heard an amazing sound resembling howling dervishes—the *davenen* (praying) was so loud, so strong, and everybody was making vigorous body movements, *shukkling* very hard.

I *davened* there that *shabbos* morning, and when I took a particular place, somebody gently insisted, "Would you please move." Why? Because this was the *Makom Kavu'a* of that particular person—everyone had his particular power spot—so I stepped to another place in the *shul*, and there I continued my *davening*. It was wonderful.

Among the most interesting experiences of my first visit to Israel was meeting Dr. Erich Neumann in Tel Aviv. Internationally acclaimed as a leading Jungian scholar, he was the prolific author of major works on consciousness, depth psychology, and such profound archetypes as the Great Mother. In graduate school at Boston University, I had avidly read Neumann's intriguing writings and been especially inspired by his first magnum opus, *The Origins and History of Consciousness*. Initially drawn to psychoanalysis, Neumann had completed medical studies at Friedrich Wilhelm University in Berlin, but when the Nazis came to power in 1933, he was barred as a Jew from obtaining an internship. After briefly studying with Carl Jung in Zurich, Neumann and his Zionist wife, Julia, emigrated to the Holy Land in 1934. There, in Tel Aviv, he began his lifelong practice as a Jungian analyst and later became president of the Israel Association of Analytic Psychologists.

During the World War II years, when international communications were disrupted, Neumann had suffered severely from his lack of contact with European colleagues. But I knew that for the past decade, he had been an active lecturer in Europe, notably at conferences of the Eranos Society in Asconsa, Switzerland. Besides his strong interest in women's personality development from a Jungian perspective, he had written about the nature of the human shadow and evil—he was perhaps the first post-Holocaust psychological thinker to do so—in his 1949 book *Depth Psychology and the New Ethic*. Generating controversy among Jung's cohorts in Zurich, he declared in this work, "It is only when man learns to experience himself as the creature of a Creator who made light and darkness, good and evil, that he becomes aware of his own Self as a paradoxical totality in which opposites are linked together. . . . Only then will the unity of creation and of human existence escape destruction."

After meeting Professor Gershom Scholem, I went to visit Dr. Neumann to ask him whether he would take me on for a didactic analysis. We had a therapeutic session that day, during which he made me venture deep inside, and it was wonderful what I discovered.

We also had a conversation that led up to the issue of lunar spirituality. The moon doesn't generate any light of its own, and I quoted from Talmudic literature to that effect. Dr. Neumann retorted that this is not true: it may not produce blazing light like the sun, but it emits dark light. That gave me a lot to think about. He offered to take me on for $10 per session; I would come from Jerusalem to Tel Aviv weekly and have one session in the evening and one the next morning. He said, "I'm ready to take you on, but I never take anyone on without my wife's reading his palm first." To my surprise, I later learned that his wife, who was also a Jungian analyst, was one of Israel's most famous palm readers.

I also went to see Shmuel Yosef Agnon, and that was not such a nice meeting. I went to Talpiot, the bustling section of Jerusalem where he lived, and asked him a variety of questions about his difficult stories—especially the one story that I later used for my doctorate. But Agnon, who would be awarded the Nobel Prize for Literature in 1966, was not friendly at all. He wasn't interested in telling me anything. Upon leaving his home, I asked for his autograph. Agnon gave it to me reluctantly, then sarcastically commented, "Why do you want my signature and ignore my books?"

I also met Moshe Shamir, a well-known Israeli novelist who had written a marvelous short story, which I had translated into English. Called "Astride His Horse on the shabbos," it describes Rabbi Meir and his past teacher, now a heretic.

When our group first arrived in Israel, it was the twelfth day of Tammuz. So instead of going with the rest of the Hillel campus directors straight to Jerusalem, I took a taxi instead to Kfar Chabad, the Israeli settlement of the Lubavitchers, about a thirty-minute drive from the airport. They were celebrating the liberation of the late Sixth Lubavitcher Rebbe, Rabbi Yosef Yitzchak Schneersohn, from Soviet prison in 1927, and it was also his birthday. He had been my Rebbe, of course, until his death in 1950. At Kfar Chabad, I met Shlomo Rosenfeld, who had been one of my friends from the diamond-cutting group in Antwerp during World War II. I felt joyful to connect with him after all those years. Then, in the morning, I took the train for my first visit to Jerusalem.

On board, I noticed several young Hasidim. I said to them, "I see by your outfits that you are Vizhnitzers, so what are you doing on the way to Jerusalem?" They smiled and replied, "We've been asked to go and spend the shabbos with the Vizhnitzer's son-in-law." This son-in-law would later become the Belzer Rebbe, and they had all been invited so that he would have some good guests at the tish. One thing they had to do—each one— was look into a holy book in order to propose something that they had read, and the Vizhnitzer's son-in-law would weave all the verses together spontaneously into an erudite, seamless Hasidic sermon. This feat seemed to me very much like that of the famous story by the eighteenth-century German philosopher Salomon Maimon, in which he describes how the Baal Shem Tov's chief disciple, the Maggid of Mezerich, demonstrated similar, amazing mastery of the Torah.

The Gerrer Rebbe

Having been to the congregations of various Hasidic rebbes, I was eager to see how the Gerrer Hasidim and their Rebbe, Rabbi Yisrael Alter, conducted themselves. I knew that he had escaped from Poland during the Holocaust and settled in the Holy Land in 1940. When World War II ended, he learned that the Nazi regime had murdered his wife, children, and grandchildren. Following the death of his father, Rabbi Avraham Mordechai Alter, the Third Rebbe of Ger, he had become a forceful leader of his growing movement of followers, as well as highly active politically in the nascent State of Israel. Rabbi Alter had a reputation for quick wit coupled with an unpredictable temperament; his visitors never knew when he might attack them verbally or even physically with a Zen master–like slap on the face.

When I came on *shabbos*, a crowd was waiting for Rabbi Alter to enter the room of the *tish*. He came in wearing a Polish tall *spoddek* (fur hat), a *shtreyml* (a round fur hat) different from those you saw worn by the rest of the Hasidim. As he strode in, it was as though the sea of Hasidim were parting to make room for him. But he did not proceed right away to the table. He walked around and scrutinized some of the Hasidim, and I could see how probing and judging his gaze was. They trembled as he looked intensely at them.

Then Rabbi Alter proceeded to his table, and I tried to secure a place where I could see what was occurring. But a lot of the Hasidim had warned me about that, saying, "The crowd will not be gentle with you."

I thought that I had learned enough at Lubavitch about how to manage being jostled and squeezed at the table of a rebbe. But I was wrong. One Hasid dug his elbow into my side; I yielded to him and went to the back, then climbed up on the bleachers to see what was happening at the Rebbe's table.

After wine was presented and people shouted, "L'chayim," and burst into boisterous song, he started to give his Torah discourse. Suddenly, in the middle of his speech, he exclaimed, "Enough!" He didn't even finish his sentence. In a way, I found this shocking. After *shabbos*, one of my colleagues and I went to see Rabbi Alter privately. He sat there impassively smoking a cigar. I gave him regards from a rabbinic colleague in Winnipeg, a Gerrer Hasid, and then translated from my colleague the question, "Why is it that people need a rebbe as an intermediary between themselves and God?" He gazed at me closely and sarcastically answered, "And you couldn't tell him yourself?" When I mumbled something like, "It's better to hear from you than from me," the Gerrer Rebbe firmly replied, "Every Jew can directly approach God, but some people find it easier with a rebbe as a guide."

Recently, I have been considering the question of whether a Hasid chooses a rebbe because of the ethnic connection or because he is looking for the best rebbe to teach him how to serve God most effectively. Is he really the one who gives you the best advice on how to serve God, or is it just because you have an ethnic association? A lot of the followers are particular Hasidim because they come ancestrally from that geographic neighborhood, whether it be in Poland, Hungary, or Russia.

One complaint I have is that these Hasidic groups imported the exilic modes to the State of Israel. They do not look to the spiritual forms that are there. For example, the Belzer *shul* in Jerusalem was trying to rebuild something that had existed in the Jewish Diaspora. The Lubavitchers built a life-size replica of their urban Brooklyn headquarters at rural Kfar Chabad in Lod.

Toward the end of my Israel trip, Professor Bergmann invited me to speak about Hasidic meditation to an intellectual salon he called *Amanah* (loyalty/faith). I started to speak in English because I didn't possess the Hebrew vocabulary to express myself with subtlety. To my frustration, they commented, "We can't understand your English. Could you please speak in Yiddish?" So I gave my presentation in Yiddish, which was later transcribed and published in the *Amanah* journal.

At the time, I was unhappy about my presentation because speaking Yiddish pulled me into how I would have spoken during my Lubavitch yeshiva years, as a young man; it did not express my current psycho-spiritual understanding. Subsequently, I therefore composed a statement in English, which the *Amanah* association dutifully translated and published. Joseph Manella, who was one of their members, translated my booklet *The First Step* into Hebrew, and the association published that, too, in the *Amanah* publications.

Upon my return from Israel, the University of Manitoba raised me from the rank of assistant to associate professor, then when I earned my doctorate, to full professor in 1968. When I returned, I also affixed blue thread *tzitzit* to my *tallit*, because that was something that the nineteenth-century Hasidic rebbe known as the Radziner, who came from the town of Izhbitz in Poland, had done.

On one of my last days during that trip, I passed by a little Yemenite silversmith shop in Jerusalem. I entered and noticed that the owner was selling little signet rings. I asked him if he would engrave one of them for me and inscribe the Hebrew message "Gam Zeh Ya'avor" (This too shall pass), and he fashioned the signet ring exactly as I had envisioned it.

A few months after I returned to Winnipeg, a stranger came to one of the *shuls* where I assisted as rabbi and told me about his family problems and how stressed he felt: everything was seemingly falling apart for him. So I said to this man, "Look, I obtained this special ring in Israel. I'll lend it to you for a while to help you keep in mind that 'this too shall pass.'"

Several weeks later, he phoned me and said, "Can I come and see you again?" I said, "Sure," and he came and gave me two dozen of the rings! He had gotten my ring duplicated because, he said, "I want to keep the ring; it helped me so much." Later on, I ordered those rings from some place in Jerusalem.

When I returned to Israel a few years later, I went to King George Street in Jerusalem where that silversmith shop was located. I said to the owner, "I understand you have these rings for sale." He said to me, "Yes, I do, and do you know what? There's a rabbi in Canada who is also a psychologist, and I'd really like to meet him and shake his hand, because this signet ring inscription is such a wonderful idea. Do you know him?"

I heartily gave him my hand, and since that time, I've put out lots and lots of those rings. Nowadays, I have it in terms of those little rubber bracelets, and they say the same thing.

~

CHAPTER EIGHTEEN

Qumran, USA: Jewish Community

Whereas the leaders of Jewish public worship were mainly interested in the verbal and musical parts of the liturgy, monastic groups sought a more introspective way of serving God. Upon reading the *Manual of Discipline* of the Dead Sea Scrolls, I was impressed that a Jewish monastic group existed before the destruction of the Second Temple; indeed, it became the model for the monasticism of the Christian Church and of various Sufi communities. In seeing that the monastic spiritual group in the center of the larger community was the spring from which all inspiration for faith and observance drew, I felt that if we could establish a contemporary form of Jewish monasticism, it would serve to invigorate the rest of the Jewish religious community. Also, those who served as religious functionaries in the typical North American congregation needed role models, for much of the initial fervor and intentionality had evaporated in such congregations. I felt that if we could make our living by serving those congregations, we could serve as role models for the other persons who worked there.

In 1961, I was able to integrate my various readings about the Dead Sea Scrolls and my exposure in Winnipeg to Catholic monasticism to produce one of my most important writings during what I call my focus on "Jewish restoration" after the Holocaust. Published in *Jewish Tradition* in 1964, it expressed my long-range vision for creating a new template for vibrant Jewish life in the mid-twentieth-century United States—and drew substantially on Judaic historical forms for insight. Though my vision of an urban monastic Jewish community has yet to be realized, some of the ideas in this article became seeds for Jewish Renewal and sprouted with the emergence of America's counterculture in the late 1960s and 1970s.

Toward an Order of *B'nai Or*:
A Program for a Jewish Liturgical Brotherhood

There are ample precedents in Jewish history for liturgical brotherhoods, or *havurot*. Josephus and Philo have apprised us of the work and lives of the Essenes, and the Dead Sea Scrolls, of course, have yielded a *Manual of Discipline*, increasing our knowledge of the constitutional and functional aspects of liturgical group life. Even within normative Judaism, there are many examples of such societies. The following pages are the result of the discussions of concerned individuals who see it as their vocation to establish such a community—an Order of *B'nai Or* (Sons of Light)—and to live its life in our own time.

We take it for granted that the present "business-as-usual" status quo does not express the highest and most desirable dimension of Judaism and that this condition does not necessarily meet with divine approbation. On the contrary, it must act as a stimulus challenging us to overcome it. To be motivated by a wish to "save Judaism," "to make for a more meaningful Jewish survival"—or whatever the current formulation of the *shelo lishma* is—may have salutary effects, but we want it clearly understood that we are interested in *shlemut ha'avoda*, the perfection of the service to God, so that He, be He blessed, may derive *nahat* (pleasure) from us. Or, to put it differently, we are concerned about realizing God in this lifetime, achieving a higher level of spiritual consciousness, liberating such hidden forces within us would energize us to achieve our highest humanity within Judaism. Regardless of the particular formulation of the meaning of *shlemut ha'avoda*, not only do we regard ourselves as working out our own concern, but in our concern we also see God's blessed providence in action, calling us to the life of the *hevrah*, as well as His abiding involvement in it. Responding, we see ourselves as yea-saying partners with Him.

The most serious reason urging against the establishment of such a brotherhood is that this constitutes a forsaking of the larger community. But this is not our intent. In a later section, describing community services, we will deal with this in detail. For the moment, suffice it to say that the means of earning a livelihood for the total community and its individual members would be found largely in serving urban Jewish *zorkey zibbur*, or community needs.

Groups like ours are usually bound by the three vows of poverty, chastity, and obedience. To us, poverty means no private individual ownership of resources. These will be pooled in a common treasury (and their return shall be guaranteed on the event of a member's leaving). That which is owned by the group is considered *hekdesh*, or dedicated to God. A waste of these resources amounts to desecration.

Chastity, to us, means no mitigation of the full implication of this word. The eyes, the mind, language, and the senses have to be guarded, so that they remain in the condition of chastity. Such sexual activity to which the Torah obligates us must be engaged in with chastity. Thus we interpret chastity not to mean total sexual abstinence but that the fulfillment of such *mitzvot* as are tied to sex is engaged in a manner befitting God's continual, ever more intense Presence, as it obtains between husband and wife in the joyous fulfillment of *mitzvah*.

Obedience, to us, takes on a *halachic* character. Any Jewish society receives sanction for its *takanot*, constitution, and statutes by virtue of the principle *al nafshey hatikha d'issura* in that whatever the statutes forbid takes on the forbidden aspect of *t'refah*. Positive levels of obedience take on the character of positive commands. As God's delegate—more *rabbakh k'more shamayim*—the ultimate arbiter of the *takanot* will be the overseer chosen by secret ballot by full members of the community. Any immediate superior delegated by him will also be accorded the same obedience. The overseer's rule will, God helping, not be a capricious use of power. In this sense the overseer is accountable to God and the community.

As various income functions become more clearly defined and take on dynamics of their own, it may very well be that other *B'nai Or* groups will have to split off from the original group. As it is, we have quite a bit of work to do, which may turn out to be more than we can handle. We expect that functions will be split off according to the planning of the group and the promptings that come through the individual member's heart and from Him who ultimately is the holder of our destinies.

Time and time again we must consciously and deliberately center down to our main calling, which is the service of God in prayer. There are *Torah Kolelim* who organically represent the head—the "apostolic" shock troops, representing the mouth and language—but we must be the heart. It is for this reason that our excursions into such means will be closest to our central vocation, but the contemplative aim must remain central and be pursued in sober seriousness.

We are basically dissatisfied with "the world." Our dissatisfaction stems mainly from the fact that as well-adjusted members of it, we would have to live as ardent consumers of goods that we do not really need and that in fact inhibit our best possible functioning in terms of *shlemut ha'avoda*. We have to isolate ourselves from a contaminated environment. Only then can we make sure that the laboratory conditions will be met that will permit us to proceed in our chosen direction.

We believe that the experience of the cosmic and the divine is potentially given to all men (and women) and that depending on one's style of life, one can become a receptacle for the grace of God.

We believe that there is enough psychic and pneumatic know-how available to us within the Jewish framework. To serve God better, we will not even hesitate to borrow extensively from the know-how of others. We feel that the seriousness of the vocation to serve God has largely become lost in the exoteric assertion of the reception of the unique gift of grace, which is the revelation possessed by a group. To put it differently, if I am sure that I possess the clear statement of what God demands of men, this possession ought only to humble me and challenge me to fulfill the demands of that revelation. Yet some "guardians of the revelation" see themselves as exempt from the humbling challenge to live up to it, as if their chosen-ness implied that they need not struggle with their own recalcitrant wills, slothful habits, and so forth. For us, the need to establish a liturgical community actually means that we have become aware of what William Law calls "the serious call to a holy and devout life," issuing daily in the *bat kol* from Sinai.

We are dissatisfied not only with the secular world but with the "religious" world at large. That world lives under the same consumer compulsion as the secular world. Under this consumer compulsion land kosher goods, and their producers are as relentless in driving us to consume them as are others: one is far too busy to obtain the means for consuming and then far too busy to consume all the means. One consumes without having any time left for *Avodath Hashem*. One may become a kosher sensate reprobate. Economically, four hours of work per day, five days per week, yield enough of the necessities of life for people whose only "Joneses" are those who live as frugally as they. With twenty hours of work per week, one should have enough for one's self and one's family to receive all such necessities as will prompt one to be in the best shape for *Avodath Hashem*. We will work forty hours. It is our hope that in the absence of all sumptuousness, there will be no need for ascetic self-denial in the vulgar sense.

We are also dissatisfied with the religious world because it lives the religious life of hardly more than verbal assertion, at best a feeble vote for the good, for God and against sin. We are not interested in formulating a new religion; we seek to live the esoteric implications that inhere in our religion as it is. The esoteric side of any religion tells not only about the core experiences behind the exoteric facade but also how one is to achieve such experience. It may not be "democratic" to hold that the esoteric experience is not given to the masses, but masses are not given to the highest functional striving in the religion to which they give assent. Their assent is static. The static view does not recognize that as a person progresses and grows, new emphases are necessary. Mass people are frightened by the seeming inconsistency in balancing emphases that strike them as contradictions. No static philosophy can express all the levels of the dynamic range of the process of inner growth. This is another reason why we cannot anchor ourselves in any specific philosophy and why our psychological ceiling must remain open.

The exoterically minded will accuse us of antinomianism. We are as antinomian as Yom Kippur and Pesach. If they were to fall on one and the same day, it would be quite impossible to fast and eat *matzot* at the same time. But there is half a year in between.

To gauge the level of the postulant will be the responsibility of his spiritual director, who will give him a temporary theological conceptual framework. Some souls may ultimately not fit the contemplative life but will nevertheless need to be set into growth by being associated with us for some time. We pledge ourselves not to be possessive about them but to allow them free egress whenever they feel that the time has come. Thus, besides being theologically and psychologically open, we must be socially open. It is also conceivable that non-Jews will wish to spend some time with us. They may run into some functional difficulty on their own part, but we have no intention to demand from them that they give up their current faith (or lack of faith) before they join us.

We are not pledged to any particular philosophy. However, in order to communicate with one another and with the Jewish past, we need a comprehensive, subtle, and precise language. We are aware that the terminology will be important to those who join us. We hope that a postulant will outlive a dozen philosophies in his progress from level to level.

All this may give the impression that only persons of high IQ are suitable for the work of the *hevrah*. This is not so. Spiritual generosity is a far greater prerequisite for the communal contemplative life. Simpler souls often have as God's gift to them a better intuitive grasp of unseen realities than intellectually complex ones.

If our community were to be "busy" and wanted to heal all the ills of the world, it would not have time for the very time-consuming exercises with which our purpose burdens us. We must not be busy. We hope to divide our day into eight hours for livelihood work (which we will describe later), eight hours for bodily needs, sleep, and food, and eight hours for intensive and serious spiritual work. We are not worried about recreation in the vulgar sense.

We feel that living the cycle of the liturgy, we will experience joys such as are not given to the pleasure chaser, and the shabbos and holy days will suffice to recreate us in a far more natural and soul-satisfying way.

We are sure that no one will survive for long in the community if not engaged in a noticeable process of sober growth. There must be no emergencies occasioned by the other day segments (except, of course, when a problem of actual preservation arises) that would cut into the eight hours of *Avodath Hashem*. This is the sole purpose of our community, and nothing must interfere with it. This aim, then, would be pursued as relentlessly as we have been pursued by the "Hound of Heaven." There has been far too much romanticism in religion in connection with spiritual advancement. We intend to proceed with this work to achieve a level of craftsmanship that will equal other precise professional skills. Yet we are aware that, despite their apparent vagueness, such inner promptings that are authentically experienced by certain souls are often far more valuable than any book of knowledge. These promptings will have to be clarified by spiritual direction, but the work proceeding from these promptings will have to be pursued soberly and consistently.

We are also convinced that life makes for adaptability and the readiness of organisms to accept education. To have been given the privilege of the use of the bodily senses means to us that these too must be educated to enhance the spiritual life. We will, with God's help, want to find the sensory triggers capable of opening us to a wider consciousness. We hope with His blessed help to learn in the spiritual laboratory what physiological fulcra will be of help in our work. Any kosher means that our community decides are proper and helpful we will want to study in their application and usefulness and learn to control. Depth psychology has given us many insights and placed good tools at our disposal, and we hope to use them.

We dare not give Him worse service than that which is expected on other levels of life and vocation. We hope to winnow from our own Jewish and general religious literature such *eitzot* (counsels, hints, bits of empirical advice) as are to be found in them, to classify them, and to apply them where conditions indicate their use. We hope, God willing, to use every phase of life for the bettering of our service to Him: eating, sexual activity and rest, breathing and body posture, dance and song, sight-light and dark-color schemes, olfactory stimuli, and so forth.

As a result of spiritual direction, we hope to start our own mind-body-spirit phases and to apply such positive or negative feedback as seems needed. We hope in this manner to be able to rediscover some of the pneumatic clues to be found in the observance of *mitzvot ma'asiot*, which transform into *hovoth hal'vavot*, and thus to relearn the art of achieving *Yichud*, the God-one-ing function, which will enable us to be more intensively, more frequently, and over a greater range in *d'vekut*, or absorptive union with our God. All this, then, is based on the assumption that it is still feasible in our day and age to fulfill the commandment of *k'doshim tih'yu* (holy shall you be).

We need to maintain contact with the Jewish world at large and to offer a service that many do not find in their synagogues. Furthermore, a great number of unaffiliated people may be able to overcome their reluctance to seek information and guidance if they were offered such outside the regular synagogue setting. In short, a reading room in a downtown area may supply this need. People are reluctant to sit down in the sanctuary of a synagogue simply to relax for a while, away from their pressing cares and burdens. A chapel in conjunction with a reading room would make this possible for them (and ultimately serve as a model for synagogues). The chapel would also serve as a laboratory for classes to be conducted in the reading room.

An experienced counselor may lend a sympathetic ear to allow a heavy-laden soul to unburden itself. It is conceivable that some psychotherapist will at some juncture wish to refer people with value problems to a counselor affiliated with the reading room. This counselor will, besides possessing clinical training and native ability, need to be an integrated person with a rich inner life. He will be on good terms with people who are situated in the world and will have to avoid being a soul trapper for the *hevrah*. He will, we hope, as a result of his contemplative training, be able to look at his counselee as he stands in God's primeval thought and lead him to realize that potential in himself.

Such souls as will be moved to enter the community will be tested through a probationary period to see if they are motivated by a divine stirring in them or by a need to escape some unwholesome immediacy. In case the two coincide, it would be our principle to have the person first resolve the problems that immediately face him and then enter the community.

For many Jews it is an unknown fact that Jewish answers in depth are available to them. Non-Jewish esoteric and pneumatic societies that promulgate one or two esoteric insights are full of Jews. We acknowledge that we are pained by this, for we think that the majority of Jews who frequent these societies do so not because they are pneumatically fulfilled by them but due to lack of available Jewish facilities. It is hoped that at least some of them will find their way to the reading room and chapel.

We need, too, *atzarot* weekend retreats for our men and women, the object of which would be for these individuals to become reacquainted with their inner selves and with their early struggles to live a God-directed life. Here they could become acquainted with an enlarged repertoire of Jewish experience and striving. Here they could relearn how to *daven* with *kavvannah* and how to learn Torah. Here they could sharpen their spiritual sensitivities. Until such time as we have ample facilities for guests, we may have to conduct our *atzarot* at some kosher hotel during the off-season.

An *atzeret* program might begin with a briefing, a spiritual housecleaning to be followed by an earnest *Minhah*. A half hour of representative study could be followed by a joyous *kabbalat Shabbat*. After *Ma'ariv* all the participants would then gather at a *tish*; with the exception of conversation pertaining to Torah or prayer, silence would be desirable. Now *zemirot* could be introduced. The *tish* would take up the entire evening. Instruction as well as questions and answers could take place right there. After the *bentshen* the group would retire right on the premises. In the morning there would be a *shiur*, a time for meditation before the *davening*; the service would be with the entire group, followed by *Kiddush* and another *tish*. After the second meal, a silent rest period with books would be desirable, followed by another *shiur* and the third meal with *Ma'ariv* and *Havdalah*. A *Melvaveh Malkah* would provide an outlet for discussion and evaluation.

Perhaps the retreat ought to extend through Sunday in order to present an extension into the week of the renewal of the spirit. A group might perhaps wish to experiment with other modes of inner expression, thus bringing to light some of the gems contained in our spiritual storehouse.

Perhaps, and this is not such a remote possibility, we could again infuse the observance of Yom Kippur Katan with contemporary relevance. A Yom Kippur Katan retreat would serve as a periodic stock-taking experience. Most of our self-employed professionals and businessmen can and do, when they so desire, take a day off for whatever purpose they choose. They could convene at the retreat house in the evening, eat in silence, or in fact impose silence for the entire stay, while someone reads to them a passage of, let us say, the *Mesillat Yesharim*. After a period of Torah study, they could, as a *minyan*, and taking their time, retire with *K'riyat Shma Shea Hamittah*, awake at about 5:00 a.m., and perhaps for the first time in their lives, recite the *Tikun Hatzot* (for most of us, the *Tikun Hatzot* has the emotional connotations of a romantic legend). Then, after reciting *t'hillim*, they could study some more, *daven* without hurry, and return to study. They could fast during that day, spend some time on *heshbon hanefesh*, or meditation, then proceed with the Yom Kippur Katan liturgy at *Mincha* time. *Ma'ariv* and supper could be followed by a discussion, after which they should return home.

The idea behind the *atzarot* is not only to give a one-time experience but to demonstrate the practicality of transferring and incorporating into one's own home and synagogue observance some of the dimensions experienced during a retreat.

We are disturbed to note the gradual decline of the comprehensive liturgical repertoire once alive in the synagogue. We feel that we must prevent its complete loss. Who knows whether a generation yet to come will not have to resurrect for use, or at least find roots in, a non-European synagogue tradition? Avraham Tzvi Idelson and others had the holy restlessness that moved them to collect and record for posterity such things as *Die Synagogengesaenge der Orientalischen Juden*. We think it imperative to acquire and perpetuate the skills of praising God in the *nussah* of Italy, Cochin, Baghdad, Yemen, Rhenish Ashkenazim, and so forth.

We are also painfully aware of the lack of *piyyutic* material created in the last 250 years. People engaged in praising God with a vital and joyous desire are always on the lookout for new modes of expressing love and longing. How incongruous is it that in the last thirty years, mostly people living in a secular world have found it necessary to find poetic expression for the spiritual and liturgical feelings that welled up in their hearts. We hope to make these two problems our own.

We think the solution lies in alternating the different *nusha'ot* liturgically, musically, and rhythmically for six out of seven years. The seventh, the Sabbatical year, would be devoted only to a skeletal framework of Talmudic liturgical institutions, which would then be enhanced and clothed with the sinew, flesh, and skin of contemporaneous liturgical expressions from the realms of poetry, prose, music, chanting, and rhythm—on days when instrumental music is *halachically* permissible to the accompaniment of "harp and timbrel," even to the inclusion of such experiments as *musique concrète*. We hope that the people exposed to retreats from time to time will take their impressions with them and bring about the adoption of such liturgical modes to fill the contemporaneous needs of Jewry at large.

Currently the ideal artist is the one who expresses himself. It is quite obvious that only the individuated person has a unique self to express. For us, an individuated self that is not also sanctified has no warrant to clamor for expression. Besides the contribution that sanctified art can make to religious art in general and to Jewish religious art in particular in stimulating other art aspects, particular liturgical values can be realized through rededicated sacramental artistic expression that springs from real spiritual sophistication. Hasidic masters have already shown the way of what can be done in the field of musical creation. Taking ethnic tunes they found appealing, they transformed them into profound religious paeans of praise. But these creations have largely been of an ecstatic nature. They may not lend themselves to a more "Apollonian" mode of worship. On the other hand, their uncomplicated rhythms are also not quite contemporaneous; even on the ecstatic musical side, the lively syncopation of jazz has for the most part introduced vulgarities to the Jewish scene. The field still awaits its artist. The imagination contains the only barrier to the kind of musical creativity that awaits us as a result of the activity of *B'nai Or*. From a *halachic* point of view, abstract painting is to be favored. After some of our people will have become adepts, we hope that they will see fit to arrest and project that which happens in their interior contemplative eidetic field through their skills in painting. The Zohar and the entire Kabbalah, with their visual (differing from the Talmudic aural) emphasis, offer countless themes for the artist who prefers abstract forms. Nowadays, there are more and more pliable media available than ever before. It will be our task to utilize them. Much philosophy and science has been redeemed and made serviceable to God in our faith. The "muses" are still awaiting redemption. Many synagogue appointments, such as arks, *parokhot*, and Torah *mantelah*, are now mass-produced. Though from time to time Jewish artists are employed to design new patterns for them, these do not always correspond to the spiritual business of the *shul*. To design and produce them is a work of love and ardor that stems from the awareness that these things will be utilized in a palpable way for the greater glory of God. This is motivation enough for some of us to pursue this work as a means of livelihood. It is quite conceivable that one of the people who joins us will be an architect or interior designer, or will have leanings in that direction plus innate talent. He would be sponsored by the community to study this field and pursue it. Perhaps much of the bizarre would be obviated, and objects more simple and spiritual would take their place. It stands to reason that people who work at prayer would be able to distinguish between that which enhances worship and that which distracts the mind. At the same time, a person who is engaged in sinking his roots in the classical experience of the past will be able to make use of such traditional forms as are available in our heritage without necessarily copying them.

For work inside the home, we would design such khaki or denim work clothes as would permit us to attach *tzitzit* to them. For occasions of spiritual work, a *tallit*-like coat will be worn. For studying and spiritual work during weekdays, we want to reintroduce the practice of wearing the *t'fillin* all day. Wherever possible, we would like to fulfill the dictum of our sages: "'This is my God, and I will beautify Him.' Beautify Him? Beautify Him in *mitzvot*!"—a beautiful *tallit* and a well-wrought pair of *t'fillin*, the *tallit* stripes in many colors.

Some people at present involved in the teaching of Hebrew do this for extrinsic reasons. It is as good as any other job and better than some. The hours may be convenient and the surroundings congenial—all in all, it's a good way to get through college or seminary.

Every sermon on education points out that we stand in need of dedicated educators capable of empathizing with their students, transferring to them information and, what is more, the proper attitude to utilize this information. Teaching is a holy act, a *mitzvah* in itself. Members of our community will be particularly well suited for the profession of teaching, if this coincides with their talents and inclinations. Knowing that they are engaged in a *mitzvah*, they will know how to resist the temptation to kill time. And besides making sure that the information transfer involves authentic Judaism (i.e., Torah), the skill drills will be in their direction of *t'fillah be'tzibur* and *limud hatorah*. They will foster the stance of piety of body, mind, and soul.

One or two of us in a Hebrew school or a day school may be capable of involving the entire staff of that institution in a wholesome change. We pray and are hopeful that some day there will also be teaching orders. To us, however, the income derived from teaching will afford an opportunity to engage in a contemplative life, and the contemplative life will influence our teaching.

The masculine liturgy is not designed to raise women to spiritual heights. They are bereft of the sacramentals that men experience in such *mitzvot* as *tallit* and *t'fillin*, and they have, therefore, been liturgically dependent on the men's synagogue.

The solution for the problem of women lies in a full separation of their entire spiritual work from that of men. *Halachically*, our women are largely free to experiment with the liturgy and to fit it to their own physiological curves. Chances are that women with different monthly cycles could not act in concert with a *minyan*. Thus, they will largely have to chart their calendars and do their interior spiritual work according to it. In the absence of masculine sacramentals, they would have to invent for their own *minhag* such sacramentals as would be prompted by the stimulus of tradition and reinforced by their own personal insights, aesthetic feelings, and experiences. (We do not refer to such functions as remain en famille but to those that are performed at public worship. While, in the beginning, women might have to be under the direction of a male spiritual director, it is hoped that very soon spiritual direction by women for women may be achieved. We expect a larger turnover in the women's novitiate for such who, after a period of initiation into the spiritual life, wish to return to the world. Furthermore, we do not expect to accept as permanent members women of marriageable age, and those female adepts who are single would remain postulant novices of a higher degree than recent arrivals until they married and remained in the community, when they would be accepted as permanent members. Chances are that fate and exigencies will demand a special classification of nonparticipant dwellers in the community. Thus, for instance, a member's spouse who happens not to be inclined toward this work will have to be integrated on the sidelines of our community.

What we have presented above is a tentative program for our projected Order of *B'nai Or*. It is not yet a rule of our order. That will have to be fashioned as a result of actual communal living; at present, we have not yet begun as a group in any permanent sense. You who read this are asked to help us by letting us know your reactions. And if you are sympathetic toward our hope but feel yourselves not called to join us, we will request your prayers for our sake and reciprocate with ours for you.

CHAPTER NINETEEN

~

Hasidic Counseling: New Explorations

Since the mid-1950s, when enrolled in pastoral counseling at Boston University, I had been interested in the psychological facets of Hasidism. Back then, I had already received approval to write a doctoral dissertation titled *Personality: A Hasidic Interpretation*. But I left Boston University for the B'nai B'rith Hillel position at Manitoba before embarking on doctoral work, and there my plan ended for several years. At United College—now the University of Winnipeg—I established what is now the Department and Clinic of Pastoral Psychology. When it was time professionally for me to obtain my doctorate, I was still committed to the topic of Hasidic counseling and began to look for a hospitable institution. I knew that long before the emergence of modern psychotherapy pioneered by Sigmund Freud, Carl Jung, and Alfred Adler, Hasidic rebbes had advised individual Jews in ways to help them emotionally. I was also aware that both Freud and Adler came from central European Jewish families whose ancestors may well have been Hasidic. The time seemed right for a scholarly analysis of counseling in the Hasidic tradition.

Of course, this topic held more than mere academic interest for me. Since the age of seventeen, as a Holocaust refugee newly arrived in New York City, I had been close with both the Sixth and Seventh Lubavitcher Rebbes. Rabbi Yosef Yitzchak Schneersohn had been my spiritual guide and had led me to Jewish outreach and congregational work, and his son-in-law, Rabbi Menachem Mendel Schneerson, had inspired me to make Jewish education my life's work.

Professor Jakob J. Petuchowski at the Hebrew Union College (HUC) in Cincinnati, with whom I shared wonderful adventures teaching weekend seminars, kindly encouraged me to enroll in his school's doctor of Hebrew letters program. Although he was a brilliant theologian, I must admit that I found journeying intellectually from Hasidism—which was invariably dismissed as "ultra-Orthodoxy" by mainstream media—to the Reform bastion of HUC quite a stretch. This was especially true because, at the time, I considered myself a loyal Lubavitcher. Indeed, I initially tried to secure an aegis other than HUC for my envisioned study of Hasidic counseling. Yet, oddly enough, academic institutions more to the religious center and right were less hospitable to Jewish mysticism than was HUC.

I was amazed and delighted to be treated warmly and respectfully by its faculty, administration, and library staff. Dr. Robert Katz, a human relations professor who had recently authored *Empathy: Its Nature and Uses*, was an exacting and patient dissertation adviser. He encouraged, criticized, guided, and pruned my work, which I titled *The Yechidut*—now published as *Spiritual Intimacy*—and which focused specifically on the rebbe-Hasid therapeutic encounter. During that intellectual process, I grew considerably emotionally as well, ultimately developing autonomy and outgrowing my dependencies upon the Lubavitcher rebbes for my decision making.

Over the course of four years, I developed a structure for my scholarly research that proved effective. I divided my dissertation into chapters on such particular subjects as the social milieu of early Hasidism, the varieties and types of problems for which ordinary Jews (as well as some non-Jews) sought their rebbe's help, the ways in which Hasidic rebbes viewed their counseling work, the precise nature of the core session known as *Yechidut*, and its subsequent impact upon both Hasid and rebbe.

By the mid-1960s, it was already clear to me that the classical rebbe-Hasid encounter took place in a hierarchical context. I realized that the democratic language with which most psychotherapeutic work takes place does not harmonize easily with the Hasidic model. Yet I felt that both approaches were in need of reexamination, in view of the emerging holistic, organic model that allows for the gradations imposed by the system of hierarchy as well as for the democratic values of the rebbe-Hasid relationship.

In the Hasidic setting, a basic presupposition always existed: the rebbe was a complete *tzaddik*. Even when he stated with humility that he was not so at all, his position was imbued with heavy moral expectations that did not allow for a transfer of his modality to those unable to qualify for the loftier rungs of holiness. Does that mean that in a present-day encounter we cannot make our own any part of the rebbe function that is not part of the Hasidic social setting? Not necessarily, for in our experience, the person who serves as rebbe is not always in the rebbe mode. Just as counseling is an active function, so too is rebbe-ing.

Perhaps this notion applies even to the classical Hasidic setting. I once came to see the Seventh Lubavitcher Rebbe, *shlita*, and was denied admittance to his office. A few days later, when I was admitted to see him, Rabbi Schneerson said to me, "The other day, when you wanted to see me, that one whom you came to see was not here. But today he is."

In the Hasidic worldview, the rebbe was a general oversoul, a *n'shamah k'latit*, and the Hasidim who came to him saw themselves as particular souls clustering about him. Today's charismatic religious leader is no less a general soul, but—and this notion is decisive in our context—one *is* not a rebbe; rather, one *acts* or functions as a rebbe. That is, one is in an interactive, reciprocal process with others, and only for the time that one is rebbe-ing. So in dealing with such a dynamic system and process, it is possible that different persons will at times be rebbe-ing in a *chavurah* or an affinity group. Thus, the ultimate function of the rebbe is one of attunement.

The rebbe is the one who, at a given time, functions as the attuned mouthpiece of the group's God presence. As Rabbi Schneur Zalman in a tour de force in chapter 42 of the *Tanya* states, "Each and every soul from the house of Israel has within her [something] of the category of Moses, our teacher, peace upon him, a rootedness . . . deriving from the root of the soul of Moses."

The one function that we can all learn from a rebbe is that of bestowing blessings. In the Hasidic interpretation of Genesis 12:3, all the children of Abraham are heirs to the divine promise: "I shall bless those whom you will bless." The blessing still flows through those who allow it to flow through them. The practice of praying for the counselee and of blessing her or him is also increasing.

I wrote *Spiritual Intimacy* in the mid-1960s. It was a time when behaviorism and psychoanalysis were battling each other for domination of the field. Humanistic psychology was only a fledgling movement, and transpersonal psychology did not yet exist. Also, few scholarly studies had ever been conducted on Hasidism as a way of life; though Martin Buber was acclaimed as among the world's leading philosophers, his books on Hasidism were highly stylized to support his philosophical views and presented virtually no details about actual Hasidic communities. In truth, I was still rooted mainly in Chabad during that period and had experienced little involving other Hasidic groups. For all these reasons, *Spiritual Intimacy* was a product of its time. Since then, I have found in the general scholarly literature on Hasidism much more that could have been incorporated into that study. I hope that scholars of Hasidism, as well as scholars of the emerging psychologies, will be able to add more details that will be helpful to contemporary counselors.

Although I have much respect for transpersonal psychology, I feel strongly that whenever groups are involved in spiritual activity, such as prayer or meditation, then transpersonal sociology is also needed. Don't be surprised if you have never heard this term, for unfortunately, reflecting the individual-istic biases of American social science, the field essentially has yet to exist. Nevertheless, I have found in my own experience leading retreats and work-shops for over fifty years that when people participate in spiritual activities together, various kinds of phenomena may occur that cannot be understood from merely an intrapsychic perspective. As I have pointed out in many writ-ings over the years, it is no accident that Judaism mandates a *minyan*, a prayer quorum of ten individuals, not one, for different things start to happen when a group reaches a certain size. To really understand Hasidism, one needs to recognize that a group setting exists in which there is a strong sense of *we feeling* and that in the rhythms of religious singing and dancing (traditionally among men), a shared limbic energy manifests and creates possibilities of individual transformation and healing.

My time at HUC in Cincinnati was delightful in many ways. Although I did not have to be there consistently while writing my dissertation and my two master's-level theses, my visits when I came to consult with my advisors allowed me to stay at the dormitory. There was a room in the college build-ing on Clifton Avenue that was known as the "bumming room." I had many wonderful conversations there with students who also asked me to lead ritual labs with them. Many years afterward, I would encounter rabbis with whom I had talked in the bumming room, and we reminisced about those times with pleasure. As for my dissertation, which I completed in 1968, it was first published as a resource for students and others through the Department of Near Eastern and Judaic Studies at the University of Manitoba; later it was also made available at the Department of Religion at Temple University.

Though pleased that my dissertation was praised by rabbinic scholars, I was convinced that it deserved a wider audience—especially among those interested in the spiritual dimensions of counseling and psychotherapy. In many ways, my work was way ahead of its time, as few therapeutic thinkers outside the Jungians and creative humanists like Abraham Maslow and Erich Fromm were seeking insights at all from the world's great religious traditions. I had to wait for the zeitgeist to change—and change it did by the early 1980s.

In 1981 I received the galleys of a very interesting book on the teachings of Kabbalah from the perspective of contemporary humanistic and transpersonal psychology. The author was Edward Hoffman, a recent PhD graduate from the University of Michigan who had relocated to the Miami area. I admired his publisher, Shambhala—then located in Boulder, Colorado, where I now reside—which specialized in thoughtful books about spirituality. Shambhala, whose publishing specialty was Buddhism, had one best seller, *The Tao of Physics* by Fritjof Capra, in its impressive backlist. I found Hoffman's book, *The Way of Splendor*, to be quite a useful contribution to transpersonal psychology and invited him to collaborate with me on a popular version of my doctoral dissertation.

Shambhala's editorial team eagerly gave us a contract for the book, which we titled *Sparks of Light: Counseling in the Hasidic Tradition*. We worked on the book during the winter of 1982, when both of us were living in southern Florida, and finished it at *B'nai Or* in Philadelphia. Published in 1983, it still remains in print almost thirty years later. Among the most important conclusions we presented in our book was the relevance of Hasidism for pastoral counseling and psychotherapy in general. I regarded the traditional rebbe-Hasid relationship as an important paradigm for the therapeutic encounter and yet definitely in need of revision and adaptation to the contemporary world. Certainly, the highly patriarchal structure of early Hasidism would have to give way to an egalitarian mind-set.

Thus, at the end of *Sparks of Light*, we presented a list of seven traits that we deemed essential for training the rebbes of the future. These qualities, which still seem vital to us today, encompass the following:

1. An experience of kinship with other beings on the planet—that is, a sense of compassion transcending the bounds of ego, time, and place
2. An inner "awakening" in which one encounters the realm of the transcendent, however fleeting or incomplete that sacred moment may be
3. A thorough understanding—and working through—of one's own emotional imbalances, resulting in a lesser likelihood that one will project his or her problems onto those seeking advice
4. A firm "grounding" in one's own body awareness so that one is comfortable with—neither anxious nor obsessed about—dealing with the sensual world
5. A comprehensive philosophical-intellectual training, enabling one to grasp a variety of "reality maps" of consciousness, not just the everyday reality of human existence

6. A well-developed sense of intuition so that one knows when to discard rote principles and generalizations and rely instead on personal hunches
7. An active participation in a community or network so that one can engage in honest soul-searching with others as friendly critics and guides

So, looking back over my life, what is my take on rabbinic training? I have had many opportunities to participate in this field, beginning with my own training. I felt very fortunate to have the opportunity to observe and serve *rabbanim* in dealing with *halachic* matters—at times serving as a scribe in the issuing of *gittin* (religious divorces)—and, by contrast, observing how most rabbinic training was basically academic. I hoped for and dreamed of another way to go about it. Yes, at the Lubavitcher yeshiva I was also blessed to receive spiritual direction from my *mashpiyim*, the seasoned Hasidim who could teach me about the inner life. However, I found that other rabbinic seminaries effectively provided information but not much nurturing of the inner life of future rabbis.

A big shortcoming of Chabad's rabbinic training at the time was that for all the *halacha* I learned and was tested on, I was never taught any skills for being a congregational rabbi. What I learned was strictly on the job, and it was sometimes bitter learning. My model had been the Lubavitcher Rebbe, and it was a monarchial model. I had been given no conception of how to work rabinically with a synagogue governing board or with synagogue committees. When it came to conducting services, I soon realized that the way we *davened* in our Lubavitcher yeshiva in Brooklyn was not relevant to my Friday evening family service in New Bedford, Massachusetts.

What do I mean? Simply that no more than 5 percent of my congregation were regular weekday worshipers. Because our Orthodox *shul* was less expensive than the Conservative congregation, these relatively secular Jews joined ours. It wasn't possible to make an all-Hebrew liturgical service meaningful for these congregants. It was there that I learned to work with vernacular translations that did not pretend to be modeled after the Episcopalian Book of Common Prayer with its ornate words like "vouchsafe" and "bestow." The melodies I used had to be simple and easily singable. Thus I began to translate some of the liturgical hymns and poems into singable versions so that the Hebrew and English could be sung simultaneously.

When approached by a young man who had dropped out of a Jewish seminary because it did not touch his heart and engage his spirit, I was pleased to help him prepare for ordination. I knew a lot more about what to put into his rabbinic training. Obviously, it was crucial for rabbinic students to read any text in our sacred literature with understanding and know how to apply it in daily life. However, it was also important to teach them how to handle the liturgy for contemporary Jews in a meaningful way. My candidate was ready to learn not only what to do with other people but also how to become spiritually active and effective in his own life. His prayer life became rich and experiential. He would learn to use introspection to understand himself in relation to the liturgical cycle.

My first ordainee in the late 1970s received what I called a "certificate of collegiality," which was a way to express not a hierarchical bestowal but a recognition of our being colleagues from now on in service of the Jewish people. Thank God, the ground rules of that training have persisted in the Aleph's rabbinic training. Every year when I can be present at the *smicha* ceremony held at the annual meetings of Ohalah, I am happy that I have been able to set the track on which we have now ordained more than one hundred Jewish Renewal rabbis.

CHAPTER TWENTY

~

Psychedelics with Timothy Leary

In the summer of 1962, I took LSD with Timothy Leary. It was among the most mind-changing experiences of my life during that period. At the time, my children were growing, and I needed a summer camp to keep them occupied constructively. So I took a position at Camp Ramah in pastoral Connecticut, and they attended for free while I could also keep an eye on them. My job title was religious environmentalist, and my task as rabbi-educator was to create a spiritual environment there. In keeping with the Catholic-Latin nomenclature I had enjoyed in Manitoba, I jokingly dubbed my activity centers as a "tallissarium" for making *tallitot*, a "scriptorium" where we used index cards to make practice inserts for *mezuzot*, and a "hermitage" where one could be alone for twenty-four hours with a Hebrew prayer book and one's spiritual journal. This was all wonderful stuff for me and the campers I taught.

At the end of the summer, we were given the opportunity to take a trip together. We visited the historic synagogue in Newport, Rhode Island, and then the venerable Seamen's Bethel Church in New Bedford, Massachusetts, where I read them Father Mapple's famous sermon from Herman Melville's epic novel *Moby Dick*. Next, we all went to the ashram in picturesque Cohasset, Massachusetts, on that memorable trip.

While my campers strode the grounds, I met Timothy Leary, who taunted me a bit about my religious identity. "So, you're still into monotheism?" he laughed merrily, then invited me to join him personally for an LSD trip. At the time, he was recognized as a brilliant but maverick psychology professor at Harvard University, seeking to forge a new approach to human consciousness by experimenting with psychedelic drugs. Leary's emergence as a countercultural hero and then a criminal fugitive from the American judicial system still lay several years in the future. The U.S. federal government would not outlaw the sale and purchase of LSD for another six years, in 1968. I was charmed by Leary's Irish wit and intelligence and looked forward to my visit.

Next on that trip, I took the group to Boston University, where my mentor Howard Thurman spoke to us about authentic religious experience. After that, we traveled to Bethlehem, Connecticut, where we inspected a residential program for Benedictine nuns. Finally, we visited the Cloisters in New York City. Camp Ramah's director understood my viewpoint about confluent education and experiential learning. So I encountered no administrative conflicts in taking campers under Conservative Jewish auspices to such diverse religious settings. Sometimes, for instance, I awakened Ramah's campers before dawn to see the sunrise—for only then did the Jewish morning prayer service of *shacharit* truly make sense. A lot of things that were later integral to the popular *Jewish Catalogues* coedited by Michael Strassfeld in the mid-1970s originated in these kinds of activities I was initiating.

Prior to our journey to the various sanctuaries that summer, I visited the Lubavitcher community in Crown Heights for its celebration of the twelfth day of Tammuz, on which Hebrew date in 1927 the previous Rebbe, Rabbi Yosef Yitzchak Schneersohn, was freed from Siberian exile imposed by Russian Communist officials. Between his talks, Rabbi Menachem Mendel Schneerson, his son-in-law and successor, was greeting people who raised their wine cup to him with a hearty "L'chayim!" I needed to talk with a friend of mine and stepped outside the great hall at 770 Eastern Parkway. Suddenly, I heard that the Rebbe was asking for me from his seat.

"Where's Reb Zalman? Maybe he went for a retreat or meditation?" This remark provoked laughter among the Hasidim, as I was well known for conducting religious retreats and teaching mediation.

As soon as I entered, the Rebbe said to me, "Drink! L'chayim! One for the retreat and one for the meditation!" I took a large cup, and people poured vodka into it. Raising the cup, I said, "L'chayim!" but the Rebbe did not respond. I thought he was waiting for me to drink the second cup. After I did so, he looked at me and said, "So, drink!" Then I was handed a straight whiskey, and I said "L'chayim!" again. As my fourth cup was now filled with wine, the Rebbe smiled at me and said, "Have a good retreat! Have a good meditation!" After I drank the fourth cup, he vigorously motioned with his hand for everyone to start singing and dancing to a boisterous melody, and I began to dance in the place where I was standing.

Soon after my LSD experience with Leary in the summer of 1962, I wrote a report about it for some of my colleagues. Since some of them were rabbis, I was able to use much Hebrew and Yiddish. I utilized many biblical and Talmudic allusions (of great significance to me) and five years later produced an edited version for general readers. After nearly forty years, it still retains a personal freshness and a vivid picture of that era:

> I take it you have read the text of the Besht's *aliyat han'shamah*, his conscious ascent to inner heights. I want to compare this to my first experience with LSD.
>
> I must begin with a few preliminary remarks.
>
> I once read a science-fiction story about an American soldier who, in about 1990, was captured by the Chinese; they put him into a "blackout tank." I want to tell you about this blackout tank. There have been quite a number of isolation experiments to separate people from sensory experience. At many universities today, there are isolation chambers. They neutralize sight and sound and other stimuli. One of the research questions is, How long can one stand it?
>
> I had often asked myself, What would there be after death? Being rid of sensorimotor responses is like getting rid of one's body. It's a frightful thing. But now one has the proper situation of being able to evaluate a conscious ascent of the soul, an *aliyat han'shamah*, that doesn't involve muscle energies but happens purely in the mind.
>
> Our mystics reported *aliyat han'shamah*, or conscious ascents of the soul. These reports were accepted at face value. When Paul claimed to have been raised to the Third Heaven, he did not have to apologize to his hearers. They accepted such reports and believed them. The climate was well prepared by the visions of Isaiah, Ezekiel, and Daniel. Many Apocalyptics claimed high visions, and the Quran sectaries sought them. The Book of Revelation is one big trip, and in that climate of gnostic questing, Rabbi Akiba and three companions entered into the Paradise. Akiba had a good trip; he entered in peace and left in peace because he trusted God, himself, and the process. It is like flying in a cockpit through a cloud. You can't see anything in front of you, only the milky white, and you don't know if you are moving or will ever get out of the cloud of unknowing. This is the way in which *Abot dR'Nathan* describes it; Moses entered into the cloud and was sanctified there. Contemporaries of the author of the *Abot dR'Nathan* wrote the Heykhalot books, a kind of heavenly geography.

When I read Huxley's *Doors of Perception*, my interest was sharpened. There was some material written by William James, who inhaled all kinds of fumes. This takes us again back to Greece, where the Pythia sat on a three-legged stool and inhaled fumes. Her oracle is not a bipolar statement but monistic—therefore an ambiguous, holistic kind of statement.

I came to Boston University and found that Dr. Max Rinkel was doing some work with LSD. I went to see him, and I asked him if he would let me have some LSD and perhaps a physician to supervise an experiment I had designed. I wanted to run the experiment in the college chapel.

I wanted to sort the subjects with Rorschach tests beforehand in order to be able to predict whether they would have mystical experiences or not. My hope was that Rinkel would let me elicit from the subjects enough information to classify them. I wanted to ask them whether they had any kind of religious experience in the past. Then I wanted to give some of them a placebo and some LSD, then see if there was a difference. I would use everything else, like incense, music, and so on, and then add the drug. Did they feel this was perhaps only a difference in degree, though not a difference in quality, or was there a qualitative difference between their experiences? The psychiatrist did not want to let me have any of the drug because he said that I did not have the proper experimental design, and that was that.

Later I came to Canada and found out that Drs. Abraham Hoffer and Humphrey Osmond were doing some work with LSD in a public psychiatric hospital. I talked to Hoffer, and he said, "Okay. You come to the hospital. I will be very glad to give it to you there." At this point I hesitated, because my instincts and what I had extrapolated from the situation told me that I did not want to be in a "crazy house" in so highly suggestible a state. Also, frankly, I believe in possession and had no wish to be around a psychic garbage heap. Later on, when I talked to Gerald Heard about this, he said that I was right and that I should not take it in a hospital but in congenial surroundings chosen prior to the experiment.

Now then, this summer, we took a fabulous trip with a group of students to a retreat house on the East Coast. At the retreat house, I met and talked with Leary and asked him whether I could try LSD. I told him all the antecedents and that I was quite happy to take it at the retreat house because I had been there several times before and had had a very comfortable, reassuring feeling that all this was very fine. Would he let me have it? He agreed. I told him I would be back the following week with someone who would drive, because I did not want to have to worry about driving home. I did not know how long the thing would last.

We came to the retreat house. Leary was already waiting.

I took some music along, Mozart and some Hasidic melodies on records. I took along my special shabbos clothes so that I should be in the proper setting, for I had planned my meditation beforehand, though I was too excited later to follow it through because too many things were happening too fast. I wanted to know from Leary what the social contract between us was. "Do I owe you anything for it? The drug costs money; so does your time." For me, it was well worth the experience, and at the same time I wanted to know before rather than having to pay afterward. He said, "No, you don't owe me a thing." So I said, "This brings me to a very logical question, or maybe not so logical a question but a paranoiac question: Why the hell are you doing this?" He said, "Because I want to afford people liberation." He said this so simply and so reassuringly. I said to him, "I understand that you want to come along with me"—in other words, that he would have some LSD too. So he said yes. "Will you want to elicit some information? You are doing research. What should I watch out for and tell you about?" He replied, "You don't have to worry about me. I will just come along with you and be there with you, and I will learn a great deal just coming along, if you will have me."

This was very good and warm.

Now a word about the setting. It is a chapel paneled with wood. It has a very warm ceiling. There is a big illuminated symbol in stained glass on top of the altar. There is a fireplace on the side. There is a rug all over the place. There are not too many chairs so that people can sit on the floor. On one side there is a relief in bronze of some religious personages; on the other side, another figure looks at the other three. The lighting is rather dim but comfortable. The person who runs the retreat house is a very wonderful mother type, and the name they call her means "little mother." I had met her several times before, and I had a real sense of confidence in her full spirituality, which is not fanatical or power hungry but permissive and at the same time well guiding. She wore her robe. Leary wore a blue shirt, and she said that evening that she would come and join us a little bit later. Leary asked her if she would have him prepare some LSD for her. She said she didn't need it.

I said to Leary, "Is there anything special that you would want me to remember?" He said, "Yes, the rules of the road are two: trust your traveling companion; when in doubt, float downstream."

Neither Leary nor Mother speaks Yiddish, and not having someone around who did and being in a non-Jewish place with all the symbols that were there, I was not able to express myself at the gut level. In other words, the experience became far too cerebral because it was necessary to translate. A direct dialogue was not possible. Now, she gave me the holy draught and there was a holy moment in drinking it.

In offering the blessing, I thought of the little tale of the Hasid who brought to his Rebbe, the Kobriner, his tale of woe. The Rebbe was about to eat a belated breakfast and interrupted the Hasid's sad tale with the blessing: "Blessed art Thou . . . for the All was made by His word." When the Hasid continued to relate his troubles, the Kobriner chided him, "What is there to say after 'The All was made by His word'?"

I sat waiting for things to happen. The record player was on, there were cushions and blankets on the rug, and there was a fire in the fireplace. Leary had taken some LSD too, and Mother had joined us for a little while. And here I was looking from the corner of my eye for something to happen.

I tried all my old tricks, and I could see that they were not doing anything special except what the old tricks deliver. Nothing special about LSD. When Leary noticed I was sitting there anxiously, he said to me, "Don't push it. It will happen when it is ready. When it happens, you will know that it is happening." I looked again from the corners of the eye, and it was still the same; nothing special about it. Mother joined us. The record was still playing, and I danced through several sides of the Hasidic records and was not winded a bit. I usually get winded because I am heavy, but I wasn't winded then. I usually dance only with my feet, but then I was dancing with all my bones, even my shoulders. As the drug began to take effect, the image of the Lubavitcher Rebbe and his remark to me, "Have a good retreat! Have a good meditation!" suddenly came into my mind's eye. I remember saying to myself, "This is better than schnapps!"

What was Leary doing all this time? First he watched, and then he listened. Then I saw him curled up like a baby in Mother's arms. I still danced, and the coordination was there. Later on it became difficult, but at that time my coordination was still there.

Eventually, it seemed as if I was falling, falling, falling. I would sometimes stand, sometimes walk around, but all the time I was tumbling and falling. It was almost like the music you get with *The Twilight Zone* and some of the movies of dream falling, and it was an eerie kind of thing. And then making a comeback, while my eyes were closed: I could see eons and eras, and not always was it pleasant. Sometimes there were agonies. It was like waves washing across me, and each wave brought a new lifetime to be lived through. Then I would come out of it for a moment.

At this point came the center experience—I can't even today describe it. It has no mythic tag. All the myths in concert together, each one flowing over into the next, and they are all myself, which turns upon and against itself. The central figure ground switch, the yes and the no. Life and death. All the revelations ever wrapped in One. I know and I know again; I recognize myself in all the masters and martyrs, in all the blasphemers, murderers, and rapists, in all animate and inanimate beings, in my freedom and necessity, in all patterns and forms and in all the changes. I bear all the guilt for being and for making being and pain and pleasure and all the ecstasies of the I WANT, I WANT, I WANT, I have, I am, and all this now. I can't suffer it, I want out, and no! I want to stay with it. No! I want to die. No! I want to live, to continue. Yes! I take upon myself all the consequences and I suffer them all. Later . . . behind the scenes a conference; so who'll play villain and who the hero? The show must go on. Which role do you want? Make up your mind and I want to be me. . . .

I don't know if the Hasidic record was still on, but one thing was absolutely clear to me: none of the people in the Chabad *yeshiva* and none of the other close friends I have were with me through all these tumblings, the *gilgulim*, the reincarnations. Mendel T. was with me. It may well be that Mendel really was another part of me, and none of the others were. People I would expect to find, great friends from my *yeshiva* days to whom I have vowed eternal loyalty, were not there, and Mendel was.

There was one moment when I was in Spain during the Inquisition, and dying took quite a long time. One more little moment, one more little moment, another two seconds, and it will be all over. And then whoosh, another wave came by and a few moments of lucidity (not that the other moments were not lucid), a few moments in which the coordinates of here and now and the place where I was were clearly established.

The business with time is very curious. I kept my eyes open and started looking around, and there were these wavy movements and a great deal of shimmering. Nothing I looked at stood still; everything was possessed with a life of its own. A point I would focus on would suddenly step out of its field and approach and engulf me, then step back, and then another point would come out.

Then on the "inside," I was enveloped in light, in pure light. It was luminous and milky white. I was completely lost and dissolved in it. It's not that I could say that I was in the light, but the light was there, and I was not quite there in it. I just wasn't. And then came the black light. The black light was even a stronger kind of feeling, the absence of feeling. And then I finally came to. I remember standing and thinking that if anyone were to look at me at that moment, he would have positively thought that I was some kind of catatonic. I began to see where they would call this psychotomimetic. And with it came a great deal of compassion for the people who were involved in mental illness—not so much for them as for the problems they must have in communication.

Leary wanted to know when I came out, "Where are you now?" I said to him, "Eons and eons later. It is about 2:30 in the morning." He said, "How come you Jews know so well?" And I turned back to him and said, "Silly, we have shabbos every week." I did not have my watch on at that time; I had put it away. (Among our Hasidim there is a custom. When you come to a *fabrengen*, and you sit down and you are going to spend the night drinking, thinking, talking, and singing, you put away your watch.)

And then we had some more conversation. If I had had a tape recorder then, it would have only recorded some mumbling, and yet I knew precisely what he was saying, and he knew what I was saying because it was at a speed far closer to the speed at which we were both living. Before long, we gave up using words; we were just using gestures and movements and laughing our heads off. One of the conversations was, "Is it only happening in my head or is it really there?" The joke was that the language on the inside and on the outside, with its everyday meaning, was completely senseless. What is animate? what is inanimate? By this time we had walked over to the bronze reliefs where the religious images were. They were not just standing still but were moving out of the bronze as if they were alive.

One of the things that we talked about was time. What is time? Which concepts do we invest in order to keep our concepts located so that we don't lose ourselves? It really is just a game, and that word "game" is very important. Yes, it was very much like Hermann Hesse's novels *The Glass Bead Game* and *The Journey to the East*. As we had a conversation, there was a great, wonderful feeling of laughter; a feeling that this world was really a tremendous joke; of how we take this world so seriously and how we insist on points of view; of how we insist that there are absolutes rather than realizing that they are constantly shifting in the reality that our emphases might have. All the fine distinctions between logic, metaphysics, ethics, and aesthetics seemed to be such nonsense, such thorough and complete nonsense. Why should anyone do anything? Because it is so beautiful to do it that way. And why was anything beautiful? Because it was so right. And why was anything right? Because it made such perfect sense and formed such a great logical sequence, so that metaphysics was proven by aesthetics, and aesthetics was proven by ethics, and ethics was proven by both of them.

We sat down and pondered things, and this was a very lovely moment, when everything was so intensely significant that you don't even want to communicate. You just want to sit down and take it all in. How significant it is. I had warned him before that I was a hugger and a kisser, and he said, "Well, if you feel like it, then just go right ahead." So I hugged and kissed him. By that time, Mother had decided that she would leave her two boys to enjoy their flight of consciousness and would turn in for the night. We both walked behind her, walked her to the door like two children, wishing her, "Sleep well, Mother."

The question that preoccupied me was, What is the purpose of the individual in this whole business of the universe?

So I looked into the fire, and my thoughts began to wander to the subject of hell. First I had said to myself, Will I get hurt? And it was very interesting to see. I would not have gotten up for myself because my fingers so fascinated me at that time, why should I move them? Everything was so right. When Leary shivered, I felt the cold.

I am so glad he came along. I love him so dearly, and if he is shivering, I will go and put on another log as part of the game. I wondered how I managed to coordinate. I put the piece of wood on the fire. When I kept looking into the fire, at how the wood was consumed, my thoughts wandered off to being hurt, hurt being hell, and in hell, oh-oh—over here are a whole bunch of demonic punishers, avenging angels making all sorts of ugly faces and teasing me and trying to get me angry. I am still looking at the fire. They are all there, at the edge of my field of vision. Leary turned around; the noise from the fire now sounded almost as if they were ready to pounce.

What am I going to do? And I close my eyes for a moment: "Oy, Rebbe, what am I going to do?" "What Reb Zussia did." R'Zussia said that when God tells him that he has to go to hell, he will gird his loins and say, "For God's sake," and he will jump into *Gehenna*. There, you can't do any more good deeds, right? But then if God wills that he go to hell, he will go to hell; then he has one more fulfilled command. So he will jump. So I sort of said, "OK . . . come on demons, come and get it!" Suddenly they were still at the edge of my field of vision. They were good white angels. And they were having such a great deal of fun, as if I had sort of found them out, that they were not really demons. There was a great sense of rejoicing.

We go into the kitchen. The table is moving. Nothing stands still. Mumble, mumble, we talk back and forth, and I tell him that Theodore Reik is right where he says something about totem and anti-Semitism, "we" Jews are sheep, and "they" are cats and dogs and lions and all sorts of beasts. It is existentially so, and you cannot talk it away. To be able to say that you are hungry and eat me—that's another part of the game. So he does not have to eat me any more. I was so happy, and I started to dance.

I started to dance with him, and I said, "Oh, this is great! This is great! So inexpensive! How much fasting one would have to do in order to get there! How much sensory deprivation! To be able to get oneself into this realm with a mere sip! How great! How inexpensive! This is great! This is the greatest thing that ever happened!"

Here is a person who is sort of suspect in the eyes of the world as not being a responsible person, member of the community. But he said, "You see what the problem is? How can we use this drug? Can you give it to students? Can you give this to kids? What is going to happen when kids are going to get into a car and they will want to drive, or one says he wants to walk on water?"

So I said, "Who would do such a damn thing? This is beautiful, heaven."

"Well," he said, "This is my worry."

And I said to him, "Tell me, what do you do with a guy who has bad karma? In other words, somebody who has all sorts of hells?"

And he said, "I don't have that kind." There were times when just by the fact that he touched my hand while I was tumbling, he gave me a great deal of reassurance. To be alone could be terrible, and that is perhaps the most danger-ous aspect, inexperienced people taking it alone; you know, it's important to have good people around. Good people never bring out bad karma in others. We went and had a couple cigarettes outside.

We went out into the lit garden. It was still night. It must have been 3:30 or 4:00 a.m. All the trees had faces and low reaching arms, which were very threatening, but if you said, "Nice, nice trees," they became very friendly. I kept on saying, "Such a pity that he has to play the tree game, when I can play the human game." I walked over to the trees, saying, "*Sha, sha* trees. In the next *gilgul* [incarnation] I will be a tree, and you will be a human being."

When it began to dawn, I took the *tallit* (prayer shawl) and said, "Tim, I am going to pray. Let's be together." So I opened up that *tallit* and the *t'fillin* (phylacteries) and took his hand and tied it to my hand and put the headband around him too, and he was under the *tallit*, swaying in rhythm with me.

The only trouble was, I could not *daven* (pray). Every word was a cosmos. I had to skip. The slow prayer seemed to swallow me; I could not move from my word. It kept me locked in its sense. Each stress of difference between polarities—Jew-Gentile, man-woman, day-night—locked me in its cyclic set of necessities. I wanted to escape these polarities and just be in prayer with Tim vis-à-vis God.

We stand around the trees, and they seem to sway and *daven* along with us, and all the while the visual back-and-forth flow is still happening. Sometimes there would be a focus zooming back and forth, like when you try to fall asleep, and you look at the ceiling, and the ceiling moves so far, far away or closes in on you. We came to "Thine, O Lord, is grandeur and might." I just overflowed with tears, and I couldn't go on. "And Thou believest them all!" I was ready to give up and die, so that He could live in me better. Words came out of their wrappers. They said, "Look at me." And I would look at each word, and I would see things in that word that I never saw before.

Leary? He was swaying along with me and reassuring me with a squeeze of his hand. So, finally I finished *Shmoneh Esreh*, the silent prayer, and I knew that I could not go on. So I took off the *tallit* and *t'fillin* carefully. The *t'fillin* were super special, almost as if they had halos. The leather thongs were alive, snaking, hanging down. I put them down carefully and covered them with the *tallit* because I couldn't wrap them up. It was just too much. I sat down again and tried to meditate. Mother had gotten up and started to look around. It was interesting to see her face and that of her assistants. I always see her as an exceptional woman, but then she looked like a *mameniu*, a frail mother. I wanted to pick her up and carry her so that she wouldn't have to walk.

All the people who were at the service . . . I could read them like a book. And I looked at Jerry, who had come along with me, and I had such pity for him because he looked like a prisoner of a desk. I could see him at age forty-five trying to protect himself with all sorts of little defenses and having a job and a desk. And I had snatches of compassion: "Oy, that's all that he is going to be, such a poor game for him this time."

Then there was the service. Every word in the service was so right. You didn't have to say amen all the time; it was so obvious. All the mysteries that otherwise get whispered here were so real and obvious. We started breakfast, and I washed my hands very sacramentally.

By the way, when I put the *t'fillin* away, I kept on saying to myself, "You know, I shouldn't even have put you on. It's shabbos. It's the shabbos." And I kept on feeling as though it were shabbos. I mustn't travel today. I could see the sense of why one mustn't travel on *Shabbatim*; right here it's so good, why go elsewhere? They've got here everything that they need. There was some toast and butter, and they always buy for me Kasanov's kosher rye and some jam. I sat right next to Mother, and Leary sat on the other side, and all the other people were there at the table and Jerry.

Breakfast was over, and there was the arduous task of putting the *t'fillin* together, because on the one hand I knew that the *t'fillin* had to be put together, and on the other hand I couldn't disturb the beautiful snaking of the thongs and the way the light hit it, and why should I even bother with it? I finally put everything together, and we said good-bye and started out, and I strapped myself into the front seat.

Jerry is driving. Jerry had to go to New York, and I was quite willing to go with him now. I wanted to see what the road was going to be like. I gave him directions because my mind was so clear now, but I asked him to ask me all the time, because I might get so lost in just looking.

Nu, we are on the way, and I look at cars, and I could tell you which car had been in an accident before, despite the fact that it had a nice paint job. You could see where a car was sagging. While Jerry was phoning, I had taken out my *Hok L'Yisroel*, and I started to study. In Deuteronomy, Moses describes how he went up in the mountain and what happened, and I read that thing and all the harmonies were there. I kept on saying to myself, "Oy, if only I could study always like this! Who needs commentaries? Rashi has only one harmony and I have a whole orchestra here." And the letters, since they were hand-set letters, now I look at the thing, I couldn't know much of the difference, but there, every little bit of visual distortion with emphasis, and I could see almost the furniture and the quoins exerting pressure on the letters of the print and the chase in which they were locked. How the paper got the imprint of the type.

So we get on the road and, there, now we are on the parkway already. I see willows shaking in the wind, and that is Van Gogh. You know, you remember the way in which the trees were crouching, yeh? Cypresses look as if they are all saying something. And I said to Jerry, "Now I understand the story of Reb Ber, who when he looked at a pot could tell you that this pot was turned on a wheel by a one-eyed potter."

The highway was quiet, even the cop who was standing there taking tolls. I ask Jerry not to stop at the exact-change booths because I want to see the faces of all the people there. I must have smiled, because everyone smiled back so sweetly. "Poor guy, you are standing here a whole day. Cars are coming by and you are just an adjunct to a machine. But you are a human being, and I love you."

Finally we got to Jerry's place and looked around the house a little while, and then it was really getting late. Since I hadn't slept the night through, I was saying the night prayer and already slowly, because by that time already I had more control. Everything was terribly rich but not as painful. The next morning I woke up; I hollered to Jerry, "It's gone, it's gone!" You know, it was completely gone. The same everyday walls.

I had to put the world back for myself. This, too, is a wonderful experience because the world is taken so much for granted, and under LSD it gets all scrambled up and needs to be put back into order. There is much in Hasidism about this. It is called "*Tigun* and *Tohu*"—making order from chaos. Except that here you don't just put back together the dualistic world—no, the world is orderly, and all the monistic insight has to be accommodated. This seems to me the most significant addition LSD makes to the arsenal of psychotherapy.

Now, my immediate reaction was, if you could only give everyone some LSD in the bottle of milk they would get the next morning, all the ills of the world would be solved. If Soviet premier Nikita Khrushchev and President John F. Kennedy could have felt the compassion that I felt, what would there be to worry about? Everything is going to turn out all right. After the summer passed, and I came back to my home, I started to rethink the whole situation again and was very eager to tell everyone about it.

Then, coming back to work, I started having some misgivings. I kept on worrying, first of all, about Leary. I had written a note to Mendel saying, "You know, I had LSD this summer, and you were with me all the time; I sort of feel that I want to share this with you." I got back a note from him saying, "I suppose that you ought to read the article in *Esquire* and in *The Reporter*, and so on." I finally managed to get hold of *The Reporter* and *Esquire*, and I read them. I was angered by their distortions about LSD research.

Then I got the printed material from Leary and Richard Alpert, and I kept reading Abraham Maslow's book on peak experiences, and I wrote to Maslow that what he was writing about in his book sounded suspiciously like LSD. And he replied, no, this was *not* LSD. He had been told that quite a number of times by people, but he didn't think that he wanted to climb Mount Everest by using a cable car. This was his reaction.

So was it a genuine *aliyat han'shamah* (ascent of the soul)? I would have sworn on the trip to New York afterward that it was. Now I couldn't swear to it. I was being swept by the experience. I didn't go anywhere. The sense of going to a destination, raising my questions with a heavenly mentor, and coming back with a specific answer didn't occur. But then I did go to the place where the mentor has to go for his answers—was this not better?

It also wasn't Jewish enough for me. A universe in which everything was happening, regardless of whether it was kosher or not, wasn't Jewish enough. Under LSD, I did not replicate other peak experiences. Later, when the shabbos came, I found some things in a regular shabbos that weren't in LSD, but again, I had no shabbos experience with LSD. Now every shabbos has some echo of the LSD experience.

I started to reread some Hasidic material in order to see whether any parallels with LSD experiences stood out; I found there were many. Things I had read and passed over before now took on a new, psychedelic dimension. I realized that even the Hasidic mystics couldn't always slip in and out of the expanded state of mind at will. It happened. And this isn't satisfactory. The moralizing myth is that the mystic can make it happen. The functional truth is that one is always inactively active and working. Even for them, set and setting were real conditions.

The other item is the question of the morality of the instant and easy attainment that Abraham Maslow raised. To this I want to say—this still is my judgment after misgivings—I don't think that I could retreat from the socioeconomic world in which I have to be active in order to get a certain kind of standard of living and produce the spiritual state I want to produce. So I don't think that I could withdraw into meditation, despite the fact that I might want to go to a hermitage. I can't put in the time to do it in the old-fashioned way, to climb Mount Everest on foot. If we are using a car and vitamins and a whole bunch of other newfangled things, I see no reason why this particular thing is immoral if it can produce what it does. If you have a chance even once a year to remind yourself not to take the social game too seriously, a chance to experience compassion in such a way that you can draw upon the memory, I don't see why this thing is immoral.

All our emphasis in contemporary Judaism is on living the ego and the controlled life, while those who wish to make religiously significant regressions to primary levels of life-death are held to be the modern heretics. Sure enough, Judaism is a delay culture but not one of infinite delay—and after delay, it has to deliver the sanctified regression.

After this first LSD trip, I had several more experiences with hard and soft psychedelics. I had some bad trip experiences and some very ecstatic ones. I hope I have learned from them. Psychedelics certainly had a profound effect on me and in many ways restructured my life. For the better? Who can say? There are times when I am not so sure. Some of the old games I played with an unsophisticated "sincerity" I can no longer play that way. I am not satisfied with my own unconscious deceits. I know myself better, and at times this hurts. I knew more before. I used to think I had more answers. Now I have more questions. I cannot lead others with such great self-assurance as I had. In theology, where before I would spend time arguing for a precise formulation, I now see the other point of view as clearly as my own, and I can no longer invest my views with the same vehement assertiveness. Alan Watts expresses my views on myth and the necessity for a dynamic metatheology far more closely than Maimonides, who is static.

Was it a real *aliyat han'shamah* that night or not? Does LSD turn plain folks into saints? Does a revelation at Mount Sinai turn plain folks into saints? Only forty days after seeing God face to face, the people worshipped a golden calf. So it is clear, is it not, that only moral effort is rewarded by sainthood? But then, what about grace? And if you say grace works by predestination, what about free will? And so it goes . . . ad infinitum.

I am sure that when you have it all figured out, you yourself will provide the next question that starts another round of games. While we exist, what else are we going to do? We exist forever in the now.

CHAPTER TWENTY-ONE

~

My Friend Thomas Merton and the Ecumenical Quest

Among the most remarkable persons I've been blessed to know was Thomas Merton. From the first time we met at the Our Lady of Gethsemani Monastery in Kentucky, until his life was tragically cut short by a freak accident in Thailand six years later, we were staunch colleagues and friends. I continue to be inspired by his hopeful vision of ecumenical harmony and cherishing of humanity's diverse spiritual traditions. In some ways, his outlook is even more important today than when he advanced it during the Cold War and its nuclear tensions.

Merton initiated our friendship in a letter he wrote me in early 1961. It was prompted by his reading of my booklet *The First Step*, which had been given to him by Jerry Steinberg, then a rabbinic student at the Hebrew Union College in Cincinnati. The booklet was aimed at inner growth from a Hasidic perspective. "I especially like the work of Rabbi Nachman and his message of fervor and hope," Merton commented. "In the dark night through which we travel, it is good to hear the voices of those of who have set upon us . . . what is most precious to [God] in His creation."

We immediately began sharing books from our respective faiths: I sent him several works by Martin Buber, and Merton sent me his anthology of the early Catholic mystics titled *The Wisdom of the Desert*, together with a mimeographed article about prayer. From the outset, I was the more active correspondent, a situation about which Merton poetically apologized in December of that year. "You know that whether I write or not, it makes no difference to the profound union between us in the glory of Him in Whose service we are hidden. . . . I wish I knew more about doing *T'shuvah* [penance]. It is the only thing to make much sense in these days."

During the next year, our friendship deepened. Merton very much liked a Jewish mystical novel I sent, *The Last of the Just* by Andre Schwartz-Bart. Tracing the history of Jewish persecution from the Middle Ages through the Holocaust via the lens of the Talmudic legend about the *lamed-vov* (the thirty-six hidden saints who sustain the world), it had been a recent best seller and translated into many languages. "I think it is a really great book," Merton enthusiastically wrote. "It has helped crystallize a whole lot of things I am thinking about. Chief of these is of course no news to anyone: that the Jews have been the great eschatological sign of the twentieth century. Everything comes to depend on people understanding this fact." Among Merton's books that I found most inspiring were his autobiographical *The Seven Storey Mountain, The Sign of Jonas,* and *The New Man.* In early 1962, I had eagerly finalized plans to visit Merton at Gethsemani in the upcoming summer.

I well remember that August day. In Chicago, I boarded a Greyhound bus to Bardstown, Kentucky, and from there took a taxi to Our Lady of Gethsemani Monastery. It was already evening, and the gate was officially closed. Having made reservations to stay at the guesthouse, I arrived with my baggage at the front gate. To my dismay, the entrance bell announcing visitors was attached to a rope with a cross at its end. As a Hasidic rabbi, I really didn't want to grasp the cross, but it was necessary to pull the rope in order to ring the bell. After a moment's thought, I grabbed the rope above the cross and yanked. The bell instantly rang!

Suddenly, a Trappist monk emerged from the shadows, where he had obviously been standing silently all along. Striding over, he opened the gate for me and said, smiling, "An interesting solution to a problem of conscience."

He led me to the guesthouse, and the next morning, after eating breakfast, I was to meet Merton. I had never seen a picture of him, and I had no idea what he looked like. In those days, Pope Pius XII had appeared quite ascetic, and I unthinkingly assumed that Merton, as a fellow clergyman of the Catholic Church, was the same type of person. Suddenly, I felt a tap on my shoulder. I turned around, and there was Thomas Merton—who resembled a football coach! He was husky with broad shoulders and a big grin, and he took me to Shangri-La, his hermitage, which Gethsemani's administrators had given him permission to have. Merton had initially been thinking of joining the Carthusian order of monks, but he had not been born Catholic, and the Carthusians have never accepted converts. Merton wrote about that. However, Merton was permitted to have a cloistered cell, which he had built with the help of other monks.

We were hardly strangers, having written to each other regularly for over a year and a half, so what did we talk about? Everything. The first topic I wanted to discuss concerned the real differences between meditation and contemplation. Nowadays, thanks to the New Age movement of the 1980s, everything involving the mind is simplistically dubbed "meditation" by practitioners of yoga, Buddhism, Kabbalah, and a host of other popularized spiritual paths. But in those days, especially among Catholics, the religious language was precise and clear. Meditation was discursive reflection, and contemplation was something that moved away from words and got to the place where—when grace overcame the individual—he or she would experience infused contemplation, meaning that the *shefa'* descends from the transcendent and fills the mind.

Then we talked about the obstacles to reaching a deep state of consciousness. We gave our views about St. John of the Cross—and why one has to pass through a "dark night of the senses" and a "dark night of the soul." After all, one does not achieve the experience of infused contemplation by opening a box of Cracker Jacks. However, I felt that when I looked at Chabad's spiritual practices like *hitbodedut* (meditative introspection) throughout the week, it very much resembled discursive meditation. One talks to oneself in this way: "There are my beliefs; these are my values." In this light, Abraham Heschel put it wonderfully: "It isn't enough to have conceptual meditation. You have to get into situational thinking." In Chabad, I had been taught about *adata d'nafshey* (soul knowledge): seeing oneself in the picture.

The food at the refectory was vegetarian. It was to be eaten in silence by the monks and the retreatants. However, there was usually a reading of a religious text or the playing of a recorded sermon. That day, the monastery was playing a sermon by Bishop Fulton Sheen, a hugely popular radio and television figure, who was rather conservative in his sociopolitical views. In this particular sermon, Sheen was preaching that God makes a covenant not with individuals but only with corporations such as the church—the *Ecclesia*, or as it is named in the Hebrew Bible, the *Quahal*. Sitting near us was a priest who was also visiting the monastery that day. To me, he had the austere visage of Saint Augustine. Suddenly, he began to roll his eyes in disagreement, and then, after making the sign of the cross, he bolted from the room. As soon as I properly could, I went into the garden to look for him, and this is how I met Father Daniel Berrigan, with whom I had a warm conversation. Later that afternoon, he and his younger brother, Father Philip, joined me and Merton for a lively discussion about how best to integrate both contemplative and meditative practices into our bustling society.

At Gethsemani, there was also a black lay brother who had studied Hebrew to understand the psalms, which he was reciting as part of his monastic vocation. In the chanting in the chapel, his voice was a beautiful *basso pro-fundo*. I had heard that he used to play second trumpet in Louis Armstrong's jazz band before becoming a Trappist monk. Once a year, on the day when the feast of the Annunciation was celebrated, he was given permission to go up on a hill and play his horn. Alas, he did not remain at the monastery. He wanted to be permitted to join as a choir monk-priest, but at that time in the southern state of Kentucky, such a position was barred for African Americans. I stayed in touch with him for a while when he went back to secular life.

Over the next few years, I visited Merton from time to time while working on my doctorate in Hebrew Letters at the Hebrew Union College. It was not very far from Bardstown, Kentucky, where Gethsemani was located. My conversations with Merton were a great delight to me. We both could talk about the inner life without any barriers. Some parts of our correspondence will be in the archives that the University of Colorado is creating for Jewish Renewal.

By February 1964, our relationship had deepened to the point where I could share some of my more intimate concerns—particularly how to find time for spirituality in the midst of my highly active life as a rabbi, professor-scholar, and family man. I wrote him,

> It is so difficult to think about God, always being his errand boy. Then I say to myself, I didn't ask for the errand, it was sent to me. Maybe he wants my errands more than my meditations. I used to make time for intercession while driving to and from campus, which is 13 miles out of town. On my car's wind-shield visor I kept a long list of people's names, and I would glance up at it from time to time. Whenever I had a moment's pause, I would utter that name and offer a few rounds of my favorite psalms, or something else for them, as well as decide to offer charity on their behalf. But I am so time-pressured that I no longer do this.

Later that month, I wrote to Merton something about my inner struggle, as I felt confident about his understanding of mystical experience: the "dark night of the soul."

> Of late, in writing to some of my friends who reacted to Reform Rabbi and [Union of American Hebrew Congregations] President Maurice Eisendrath's statement, in one way or another, I felt that our problem is not so much to come to terms with the Jesus of the Gospels. That is easy. *Midrash* and the early fathers of the Jewish faith parallel the Gospels so closely, that we have no

problem whatsoever in that. At one time, I thought that the Epistles were the farthest away from Judaism. But even this is not quite so. There is enough of the antinomian demand not to seek in the fulfillment of the commandments a defense against the true belonging to God that comes out of a committed faith. This too is not a problem.

And the problem that remains a problem is not something that we can handle conceptually: that is, to come to terms with the Passion, and of this I'm personally convinced, having had some experiences in that direction. If the Passion would merely stand for physical suffering, then it is nothing. Polycarp II and Stephen and countless other martyrs were able to do this being sent on their martyr voyage amidst certitudes and harmonies and glories. . . . It is altogether different. When in taking upon oneself *peccata mundi*, sins of the world, he takes upon himself also the alienation of *peccata mundi*, where there is no support. In fact, there is not even the momentary support that a Kierkegaardian begins with, and in this, you are close to Kierkegaard, but not that close and truly not identical.

In Kierkegaard at least you have the security in committing oneself to leap. And so the initial impetus comes from man's own leaping. What you are describing is the falling in which suddenly the ground from one's feet has been ripped and one falls into a vertigo in which not a single coordinate remains where it is, where every bit of security and suredness is gone and one falls, falls, falls (if only one were sure) into the hands of the living God. At the moment one falls, one is under no assurance that underneath, there are the eternal arms. How gladly one would exchange this for the greatest awe that comes from certitude.

The story is told of how the Hasidic master Reb Zusha loved God and said, "Dear Lord, grant me some of the awe that your angels experience," which God granted him, whereupon Reb Zusha crawled underneath the bed, unable to take any more of this. He implored God, "Please give me back the love that Zusha has for you and take away the angels' awe."

In the late 1960s, Merton became increasingly interested in Eastern philosophy and spirituality. He lectured and wrote prolifically about such topics as Zen Buddhism—thereby provoking increasing criticism from traditional Catholics who felt he was straying dangerously from church dogma. Merton dismissed such criticism as simplistic, but those like me who knew him personally could see that it stung him. Ironically, it was on a religious tour of the Far East—including three meetings with the Dalai Lama—that Merton's life came to an end in December 1968. Although the precise cause of death has always remained a bit of a mystery, it seems that he was electrocuted while taking a shower after participating in an interfaith conference with Catholic and non-Christian monks in Thailand.

Do I think Merton was in danger of losing control of his interest in other religions at the end of his life? My answer is a decisive no. The person who is at the growing edge of something—if he has a direct connection to the trunk of the tree—is safe. The trunk is mostly dead wood, but it gives structure to the tree. The growing edge gives life to the tree, and the two of these must be together. I had the sense that Merton did not want to wreck that balance.

We once had a conversation about Joris-Karl Huysmans (1848–1907)—the French novelist who had written about "the cabbage eaters," those Catholic lay people who came regularly to church—and how crucial it was for them to have the devotional experiences the church used to provide. But now, post–Vatican II (1963), the church in the name of modernism had stripped away the little *sancta* (holy practices) that these ordinary people used to have. Hardly anyone was doing the rosary anymore, there weren't novenas, everything had been turned into the "Big Bertha"—the Mass—and even that had lost its longtime splendor and greatness. Many other items favored in the lives of devout Catholic lay people began to disappear during the 1960s.

Merton and I lamented this trend and asked ourselves, What can be done? He was more hopeful that something would happen, something that later showed itself as contemplative education, led by some other Trappists, such as Thomas Keating and Basil Pennington at St. Joseph's Abbey in Spencer, Massachusetts, but it was only slowly beginning at that time. A kind of prayer of the heart was slowing beginning to become what is now called centering prayer. Merton believed that such innovations would give the religious situation a lift. My sense was that living the liturgical year was important, and it would be good if the church developed a kind of lay tertiary order that would devise more home rituals, and so forth.

Merton and I were both interested in the *upaya* (Sanskrit, literally meaning "means to an end")—the "skillful means"* that people use for their transformation. Here was an element of what I call generic spirituality. Take a specific ethnicity and polity, whether it's church government or *halachic* government, and ask, What is it that works, when it works, with transformation? What helps us with *tikkun hamidot* (repair of one's attributes) and *conversatio morum*? How do I move from my "is" to my "ought"? Here is where yoga, Zen Buddhism, all of these, have wonderful *eitzahs* (teachings). St. John of the Cross called these the *cultalasas*, the counsels that are there. My feeling was that if both of us are, first of all, unabashedly saying that we love God, and if when you please God, I'm happy, and you're happy when I please God, then

---

*From the Bhagavad Gita, 2:50: "Yoga is skill in actions."

we can become close friends. And another thing: "Then they that feared the LORD spoke often one to another: and the LORD hearkened, and heard it, and a book of remembrance was written before him for them that feared the LORD, and that thought upon his name" (Malachi 3:16). When those who fear God and honor His name talk to one another, those dialogues are so precious to God that God has a special book in which he writes them down. So we enter into religious dialogue not by minimizing our differences, but by maximizing our devotion.

What is my view of Thomas Merton's legacy and how it relates to contemporary challenges in the Catholic or Jewish community? For problems arising from the need to adjust ancient worldviews to our modern scientific understanding of a dynamic (evolving) world, it is necessary to read Teilhard de Chardin. Merton did write about big cosmological or metaphysical issues. But he had something important to say about problems arising from recent shifts in worship and piety.

I say this because the Roman Catholic Church lost a great deal in not paying that much attention to the daily office. When you look at Merton's *The Seven Storey Mountain* and *The Sign of Jonas*, you find that he always began with some of the *piyyutim* (religious poetry) that he found in the liturgy. That's what he paid attention to and expanded on. It was a way of "inflating"—in a good sense, from *afflatus*, blowing into it. If an idea touches your heart and you breathe in, just at the beginning, when there is the slightest bit of affect coming, you welcome it, and the feeling builds up.

Merton was doing this, but today people read his writings without recognizing the underlying liturgy, and that's a real pity. The Breviary is dry compared to what it was in other days. Also, Catholics would read the collateral reading, the *lectio divina*, along with the office, so that would give them access to insights of the fathers.

The iconography that the modernists eliminated was a matter of taste. It was the wrong iconography, but iconography is important. I'm not speaking from a "Jewish" perspective: I have in mind windows, pictures, and images. For example, there is a church in Frankfurt-am-Main, Germany, with a pietà made of brown sandstone. I once stood before it and began to cry. To me, that sense of Rachel's weeping for her children—that's the *Shekhinah* (divine presence) in *galut* (exile). At the same time, I see the mother and earth holding the child that is broken. It's very powerful. It's the same thing: if you *daven* in the *siddur*, and you have studied *kavvannot* (preparatory mental exercises) from various Hasidic masters, and you come across a phrase, it gets enlivened because of the interpretations you have studied. All that is nearly lost now.

Monasticism and Jewish Renewal

Do I still believe that Merton and the Catholic monastic tradition have anything to offer Judaism? Absolutely yes, for among the problems plaguing Jewish Renewal today is that everyone wants to be a rebbe. But they haven't been Hasidim long enough to live under discipline. I am still hoping and dreaming that in my lifetime there will be a residential Jewish religious community that will live a liturgical year fully. They would do everything—the whole works. I am not insisting, of course, that such an endeavor should become a permanent *matbe'a* (religious framework) for its participants, but unless you root yourself in that totality of the liturgical life, you can't really grasp the possibilities for renewal. Why? Because changes will be coming to you only externally—and not internally in a profound way.

The sense of days, time as texture, and the texture of a day when you recite *Tachanun* or *Ya'aleh v'yavoh* (two prayers that are not recited daily), or the anomaly of *Hoshanah Rabba* (at the end of Sukkot) with its own liturgy: something happens in the feel of how you live in time. Abraham Heschel was so keen on this issue—to live Jewishly in time and not in space. I agree with his viewpoint entirely.

In my view, the Jewish calendar keeps us rooted in organic time. Pesach takes place on the full moon of the vernal equinox. Sukkot occurs on the full moon of the autumnal equinox. If we live according to this traditional calendar, then we can keep ourselves free of the trends that what I call "commodity time" imposes on us. Therefore, the act of learning basic spiritual practices, including unwavering obedience, does something important for you. In most monastic communities, a novice would have to perform menial tasks in order to do the kind of ego reduction that's necessary for true personal growth.

Late in Merton's life, it became very clear—to some, anyway—that he was experiencing a real tension in his ability to remain loyally inside the Catholic tradition. The administrators at Gethsemani were feeling that, on the one hand, the income from Merton's books was good, their monastery's reputation due to Merton was good, their vocations were good, and many people from all over the world were coming to retreats there. An authentic vitality was manifesting there, and the administrators wanted to keep that going.

However, they also knew that if they allowed Merton too much freedom or leeway, they would have to allow it to others too. And, after all, Merton had taken the vow of stability, so they felt justified in reining in his free-spirited soul. Those who wanted to protect the status quo at Gethsemani kept anchoring Merton in ways that he didn't want to be anchored. With a little more give from them, he would have remained there, in all likelihood, had God granted him the years. Merton would have found a historically valid way to stay within his fold as a Trappist monk.

In keeping with Teilhard de Chardin's concept of the Noosphere, I believe that we can all get together and recognize that just as the lungs, the brain, or the liver cannot function as the entire human body, and every vital organ is needed, so too is every religion a vital spiritual organ of our planet. Once we understand this notion, we can all work together for the divinization of the planet, converging toward Teilhard's "Omega Point." And the means for that forward movement we can find in Merton's spiritual direction. How so? I am referring to prayer, openness to other religious traditions and to poetry, and letting your own tradition work through you.

My friend Thomas Merton had large concerns. It's sad that he had to leave so early, because he was just getting into a stride where his ecumenicism was so rich and so full.

CHAPTER TWENTY-TWO

~

Walks with Abraham Maslow

My first encounter with Abraham Maslow was pure serendipity. In late October 1962, I was flying back from Brooklyn, where I had celebrated *Simchat Torah* with the Rebbe and the Lubavitcher community. I was therefore wearing my Hasidic garb. Suddenly, I heard on the loudspeaker, "Could Dr. Abraham Maslow please identify himself to the flight attendant?" When the man next to me raised his hand, I was instantly excited. While working on my master's degree in pastoral counseling at Boston University, I had been captivated by Maslow's emphasis on psychological growth as articulated in his landmark book *Motivation and Personality*. Along with Carl Rogers, Maslow by the early 1960s had become a national figure in what was known as humanistic psychology. The two had just helped to launch the *Journal of Humanistic Psychology* as the new "Third Force" alternative to the then dominant movements of Freudianism and behaviorism, and I was reading everything I could about this budding, innovative field.

Quickly introducing myself as a professor at the University of Manitoba, I asked my famous seatmate if we could chat, and he readily agreed. Of course I didn't know it at the time, but Maslow always loved to talk about his research—sometimes to the extent that his students at Brandeis University felt he neglected to teach about anyone else's ideas, even Sigmund Freud's. Maslow told me that he was on his way to Saskatoon to lecture on the creative process for the Canadian Society for Education through Art.

For several hours, Maslow recounted his latest work on self-actualizing men and women, and then the topic veered to peak experiences: moments of great happiness and fulfillment in human life. Maslow was pioneering research of such ecstatic episodes, which he enthusiastically viewed as indications of superior mental health and high creativity. He also regarded such experiences as having striking similarities to the reports of history's great mystics and sages.

Having recently taken LSD with Timothy Leary, I was eager to hear Maslow's view of psychedelics, and to my surprise, he was harshly negative. "You know, I've discussed this with Tim Leary," he related, "and he knows my viewpoint. I don't think you can have a genuine peak experience by such easy, chemical means. Life isn't like that. Real growth is hard work. As I tell my students, to achieve anything worthwhile in life, you have to sweat for it. Taking LSD to have a mystical experience or a peak experience is like taking a cable car to Mont Blanc instead of climbing it. At best, you get the illusion of growth and enlightenment."

Over the next few years, I corresponded occasionally with Maslow, and then in the fall of 1968, I had the wonderful opportunity to become closer with him. The University of Manitoba allowed me a sabbatical for the 1968–1969 academic year, and I chose a postdoctoral fellowship in ancient Semitic languages with renowned Professor Cyrus H. Gordon at Brandeis University. Despite his erudition, he was a rather controversial figure in Jewish studies for arguing in scholarly works that ancient Greek and Hebrew civilizations both came from the same cultural ancestor.

During my months at Brandeis, I not only broadened my knowledge of ancient Near Eastern languages and literature but found myself pioneering a new form of contemporary Jewish life. At the time, my friend Rabbi Arthur Green was living in the Boston/Cambridge area, and together with like-minded colleagues and friends, we formed an egalitarian group for Torah study, meditation, and worship, based in a commune-like house first in Cambridge and later in Sommerville. We called it Havurot Shalom. What I had wanted to build in Manitoba—an urban monastic fellowship—did not seem very likely to me, and in past summers, I had served on the National Ramah Commissions at various camps, especially the one in Connecticut. In those camps I met various people who learned with me about creativity in the Jewish tradition—such as in making our own *tallitot* and other ritual objects. It was a joy for me to participate with Art Green in dreaming of a new type of rabbinic collegiality. We also wanted to create a seminary without walls (the Aleph rabbinic program emerged much later) and examined the curricula that would make sense for the kind of rabbinate that was truly needed. Many of those who participated with us during that period have been demonstrably influential in American Jewish life in the past quarter century—and this continues through a variety of instrumentalities.

As Havurot Shalom became increasingly known around the United States, *havurot* (Jewish fellowship groups) sprang up in many other places. The egalitarian ethos, coupled with a "do-it-yourself" sense, created an environment in which the Havurah Institute was founded. Since then, the Havurah Institute has continued to meet—parallel with the Kallot of the Aleph Alliance for Jewish Renewal.

In many ways, of course, I have been an early responder to innovations in our culture—allying myself with Marilyn Ferguson's *Aquarian Conspiracy*, as she provocatively titled her best-selling book about the upheaval in American social values toward greater self-actualization. In witnessing the enormously successful *Whole Earth* catalogue launched by Stewart Brand—with its emphasis on creative self-reliance—I saw the necessity for producing a Jewish catalogue that would provide the same upbeat, practical guidance for all aspects of contemporary American Jewish life.

When I taught a course at Brandeis University—psychology of religion with labs—some of the people who had been with me at Camp Ramah and other such institutes eagerly enrolled. They included (now Rabbi) Michael Strassfeld and others connected with the first edition of the *Jewish Catalog*. The layout and graphics very much reflected what was happening in the American counterculture of the time. Inevitably, the unique energy that produced three volumes of the *Jewish Catalog* ran its course. I would often refer to these as the "*mishnah* of the American Talmud," though unfortunately, no subsequent volumes appeared. Nevertheless, these had a big impact on a plethora of Jewish publications since that time, and I am delighted that I was able to participate in that process.

A major feature of my time at Brandeis in those days was my personal time with Abe Maslow. I knew that he had suffered a major heart attack several months earlier and had been medically advised to take daily walks to strengthen his ailing heart. Soon after I arrived on campus in September 1968, I stopped by his office and introduced myself. I reminded him of our airplane conversation some six years before and how I had been dressed in Hasidic garb. He instantly remembered and invited me to accompany him on walks around campus.

Mentally as well as physically, during those autumn months, Abe Maslow was not a man at ease. We talked genially about our mutual interest in Martin Buber's writings and the Hasidic concept of the *tzaddik* as one who self-actualizes and leads others in the midst of the world and not apart from it. But Maslow frequently voiced to me his bitterness that the psychology department he had created at Brandeis had turned rigidly experimentalist and had no intellectual room, or even respect, for his humanistic contributions. He was even thinking of quitting altogether in disgust. To Maslow's unexpected delight, however, a private foundation associated with the Saga Food Corporation, based in the San Francisco Bay Area, offered him a generous two- to four-year fellowship. Abe and his wife, Bertha, immediately left Brandeis after the position was finalized.

I never saw him again, for he died of a second heart attack eighteen months later at the age of only sixty-two. In many ways, Maslow's belief in personality growth and transformation became a vital part of my approach to Jewish Renewal over the years.

CHAPTER TWENTY-THREE

~

Abraham Joshua Heschel: Mentor and Friend

One of the most inspiring people in my life was Abraham Joshua Heschel. Celebrated for his evocative writings extolling the Bible's prophetic, visionary tradition—and its contemporary relevance in matters like the American civil rights movement—he achieved renown far beyond the confines of his early Hasidic upbringing in pre–World War I Warsaw. Perhaps even more than Martin Buber, Heschel brought Hasidic concepts into mainstream Judaism and wider religious thought. He was also a wonderful man to know in person.

When I first got to read his book *The Earth Is the Lord's* in the early 1950s, I was greatly moved. His focus was on what he called the "inner world" of East European Jewry before the Holocaust, and he wrote in a fervently beautiful poetic style. I loved his aphoristic statements like "A *niggun* [Hasidic melody] is a tune flowing in search of its own unattainable end" and "A *maasseh* is a story in which the soul surprises the mind." Ever since that time, I had wanted to meet him. Of course, as Heschel's subsequent acclaimed books steadily appeared in print, I read them avidly.

Our first significant face-to-face meeting occurred in Minneapolis–St. Paul during the late 1950s, when Heschel was a scholar in residence for a few days at a synagogue there. I had sent him some of my writings, and he invited me to get together while he was in the Twin Cities. I eagerly flew in from Winnipeg to visit him. Initially, we had met at the Jewish Theological Seminary while I was a pulpit rabbi in New Bedford, but I had not found it very satisfying. This second time we enjoyed a stimulating conversation

169

about Jewish education and Hasidic philosophy. Here, I felt, was a person who came from a similar East European background to mine and had beautifully refined it to inspire the world.

Later, when I visited Heschel at the Jewish Theological Seminary—he served on the faculty at this bastion of Conservative Judaism—he gave me an intriguing Hasidic text that I hadn't known. He enlarged my outlook, which at the time was limited largely to Chabad and Bratzlaver Hasidic tractates. The more I gave myself to understanding Heschel's way of expressing our Hasidic heritage to the world, the more I learned from him. For instance, I wrote a book-length essay titled *Patterns of Good and Evil*, presenting my view of why "bad things happen to good people." Published in 1965, it represented my attempt to emulate Heschel's poetically unique style. I also learned how he expressed himself in a responsible way—always keeping an eye on what was beneficial for his readers' souls.

In the early 1960s, the main Conservative synagogue in Winnipeg invited Heschel for a weekend of lectures on the Jewish shabbos, perhaps his favorite topic of all. These lectures were extraordinary. He also consented to come to our B'nai B'rith Hillel House to meet with my students. Our group prepared for him a beautiful, handmade *tallit* with blue threads. Knowing that Heschel liked to puff away on cigars, I managed to get some Cuban cigars, which were not available in the United States due to political-economic tensions.

Before Heschel joined our group that day, we had earlier held a seminar on his writings. We were struck by his bold statement in *God in Search of Man* that "awareness of the divine begins with wonder. It is the result of what man does with his higher incomprehension. The greatest hindrance to such awareness is our adjustment to conventional notions, to mental clichés. Wonder or radical amazement, the state of maladjustment to words and notions, is therefore a prerequisite for an authentic awareness of that which is." In the same book, he declared, "Wonder or radical amazement is the chief characteristic of the religious person's attitude toward history and nature."

That evening, one student in our group earnestly asked Heschel, "Sir, how does one come to radical amazement?" He gently smiled and then, in a way that I had never witnessed before in my entire life, he took the whole audience into a remarkable experience of radical amazement. I will not even attempt to describe it here—because that would involve only mere words. Suffice it to say that we were really moved into astonishment by his adroit way of bringing us to that type of spiritual consciousness.

When Heschel was a young man living in Warsaw, he wrote a book of poems published in Yiddish in 1933. At the time, he was still a doctoral candidate in philosophy at the University of Berlin. It was the first book he ever published. In the late 1960s, Professor Edward Kaplan of Brandeis University shared copies of pages from that book with me. I immediately fell in love with it. When Heschel became weak and frail after a major heart attack, I sent him my translation of his poetry. He wasn't quite sure whether he wanted to have either his original Yiddish poems or my English translation published, perhaps because the material had been written so many years earlier.

After Heschel's death in late 1972, his widow allowed for the book to be published by Continuum. It presented his poems in both Yiddish and English translation. However, I prefer my own translation much more, because I had a better sense of his particular usage of symbols and alliteration. So I produced a small printing of what I called a *Nachdichtung*, an après that followed the rhythm and nuance of the original Yiddish, rather than a more literal translation. This edition I shared with his daughter, Professor Suzanna Heschel. In my introduction to this work, I wrote,

> To anyone acquainted with the other writings of Heschel, his use of metaphor, the evocation of images, the way in which the world's problems always placed him in the situational mode of thought, his deep wish to relate, to repair, to soothe and heal, to bring light to a suffering world, are all presaged in these poems. We will leave it to those interested in such matters to trace the development of his images through his writings.
>
> I cannot claim to have "translated" his poems. *Après Heschel*, a *Nachdichtung* of his poems is offered here. While still trying to do justice to English in the same way as Heschel does to Yiddish, I could in no way render fully all the rich connotations of the vast ethical and moral literature of Judaism he put into these poems. As Heschel in his *The Earth Is the Lord's* wrote, "Even the landscape became Jewish." *Shrouded clouds* does not quite do justice to *clouds wrapped in "kittels"* or in no way can I render what Heschel refers to as "my songs hang before me like *Shivithis*" (a *prie-dieu* image of God's Name facing the worshipper on the Eastern wall of the synagogue). Because of this I have left the Jewish images "In the Park" in their Yiddish context. The medium-message relationship of any language always suffers in translation. However, I am aware that A. M. Klein, writing his Jewish poems directly in English, has made his poetry and prose sing in Yiddish. That great genius can serve me as an archetypal, not accessible model.
>
> A translator ought not to write a commentary for a poet. Conversely any attempt to make a poet appear as if he utilized left-brained, denotative language is doomed from the start. So also is an attempt to bring all the connotations a poet wishes to evoke in his readers and to make them explicit. Had the poet himself wished to do so, he would have written essays, and in fact perhaps many of Heschel's images used in his later works made explicit what already was implicit in his poems.

It must be understood, of course, that these poems were written before the Holocaust. "July Sunday in Berlin" could not have been written after the Holocaust. The Heschel who asked the question "What is Man?" who writes about Israel, who frames the loss of Eastern Europe for us in *The Earth Is the Lord's* was an older, wiser, more experienced, more mature Heschel. Nevertheless, the identity of that young poet with that man who was seen as one of the great teachers for all those who live in the Diaspora, and we might add Israel, is clearly evident. That young poet who is in love with love, with life, feeling in all the chastity of his Hasidic upbringing and ideals the pain of the betrayed sister of the street, who asks G-d to let him help was also a key figure in the "clergy concerned over Vietnam," a brother to the martyred, Dr. Martin Luther King, and (be they kept for us for a long life) the Berrigan brothers.

Heschel became a master of the English language, as much or even more than he was a master of German, Yiddish, and Hebrew. It is interesting that his own work on Kotzk, which he wrote in Yiddish, he did not yet offer an English translation (but wrote in English de novo in his *Passion for Truth*); nor has his monumental work on *Torah as Revelation*, written in Hebrew, been translated by him. If he has not approached the task of rendering his poems into English, how dare this translator attempt the task? I can offer nothing but the apology that upon receiving a photocopy of these poems I was overwhelmed by their poignant voice, form, and content. I knew they must be translated. Even if only a small part of the original content could be rendered in English, it would be worthwhile. I had at that time no intent to do the entire work. I had hoped to share it with other friends so that they too might bring their person and greater skills than mine to the task of translation. Finding, however, occasion after occasion where I wished to share with an audience or group engaged in worship a poem Heschel had written, I was moved to translate it and fell in love with this task. I hope that readers will forgive the, often clumsy, touch of that love.

With trembling joy I placed these poems into the hands of my teacher, master, and guide, as the humble gift of a disciple. When he was recovering from his heart attack I sent every once in a while some of them as I attempted these renderings.

While working on Heschel's poems, I clearly saw that some of the basic metaphors that he famously wrote in his many wonderful later books were already gems in this poetry. Upon hearing the news of his death, I composed this poem to the memory of my friend and mentor:

> *IN MEMORIAM,*
> *RABBI ABRAHAM JOSHUA HESCHEL OBM*
> *So you left us, Teacher, Friend*
> *Finished Kotzk and then abruptly left*

You lived with Jacob-Israel, our sire,
And left with him and left us blessed
With the fruit of heart and mind
With fruit of soul and strength.
You sure did pick a difficult time
In which to bring the WHY of being a Jew to us—
But only you did help
when there were none who could
enunciate the paradox:
"Live—by thy blood," and drenched in it.
No other has so eloquently said
That the ineffable is just that,
And yet the glimpses you did show
Us of the light and time which uttered
By Eternity did shape our destiny
As Jews—though not in Space.
And "Who is Man?" You wrote and spoke
Yet louder than your word your work
For peace and truth and kindness here and now.
You Abraham were a Vietnamese, a Priest
Our man in Rome, Jerusalem, New York
At JTS you were the Mentsch, protecting war objectors.
Your sire was known as Israel's lover
You will not less than he be known
Thus, but perhaps your love for all humankind
Will be with us who see you still
With rage prophetic, urging deeds,
With smile encouraging boding Sabbath's bliss.

When Heschel first wrote his books, people granted him the honor of viewing him as a poet and excusing him for expressing nostalgia for pre-Holocaust Jewish life in Eastern Europe. After his involvement with the Freedom Rides in the dangerous Deep South, everybody was glad to embrace him for his ethical and moral courage. But in his early writings, that courage was already there. Nevertheless, Heschel's theology during his lifetime did not gain enough traction with people who were raised in more cerebral environments. Buber with his I-It and I-Thou concepts had been more widely accepted because of the Christian theologians and the interpersonal psychologists who embraced him. But Heschel, who had the courage to say, "God was in search of Man" (his Yiddish poetry was not yet known in the 1960s), made people anxious.

Once I visited Heschel at the Jewish Theological Seminary, and he quoted to me some beautiful Yiddish proverbs by Reb Ahron of Karlin. Because I was unfamiliar with them, he pulled a book from his bookshelf and gave it to me as a present. Then he gazed at me and asked, "How do you understand my writing?"

I replied, "While Buber has brought us to the I-It and the I-Thou, you, sir, have brought us to the He-me relationship: God being the center and we being the object of God's creative wish."

CHAPTER TWENTY-FOUR

~

Leaving Chabad: The Fallout from My Washington, D.C., Lecture

In the fall of 1968, the rabbi of a large Reform congregation in Washington, D.C., had heard about me as an interesting speaker. He sponsored a Sunday morning lecture forum and invited speakers on contemporary topics. His staff asked me what topics I currently presented on, and I replied, "Moses and McLuhan." At the time people were excited about how the "medium is the message," as the celebrated Canadian media analyst Marshall McLuhan had aptly stated, and I had much to say about the medium of religious observances containing the important message. The second topic I proposed was "The Kabbalah and LSD."

After hearing about both topics, the rabbi asked me to do both. So first I offered the lecture on Moses and McLuhan, and it was announced that two weeks later I would be speaking about the Kabbalah and LSD. By that time, all the hippies had passed the word about this controversial topic, and the Reform synagogue was packed that Sunday morning. Among the people who had come with a group of other young hippies was David Deen. I had to catch a plane right after my lecture, and so David and one of his friends drove me to the Washington, D.C., airport, and we became acquainted. The result was that sometime later David came to Winnipeg both to study with me and to function as my secretary at the Department of Judaic Studies.

Soon after my second lecture, Trudy Weiss-Rosmarin, the editor of the influential *Jewish Spectator*, also spoke there, and having heard about my presentation, she wrote a highly negative editorial in her magazine. Among other things, Weiss-Rosmarin stated that she had asked the staff at Chabad headquarters in Brooklyn if I had taken LSD with the consent of the Lubavitcher Rebbe and that they had commented that I had questionable rabbinic credentials from them. This was only a few months after they had published an article of mine in the Chabad family journal and indicated my proper title: *Ha Rav Hatamim*, graduate rabbi of the Chabad yeshiva.

At precisely that time, I was due to have my oral examination at the Hebrew Union College for my doctorate. The president of Hebrew Union College, Dr. Nelson Gluck, initiated an inquiry to determine if I was still a legitimate candidate for the doctorate if my credentials from the Lubavitcher yeshiva were now questionable. To his credit, Professor Jacob Petuchowski vouched absolutely for my rabbinic ordination as well as my master's degree in pastoral psychology from Boston University. Nevertheless, seeking to make sure that Hebrew Union College's reputation would not be sullied by someone who might not deserve a doctoral degree, my examiners were instructed to make certain that I had full mastery of the material in which I was to be examined.

Thank God I was able to do well. My major dissertation, *The Yechidut: Counseling and the Hasidic Tradition*, was first published as a resource for students and others through the Department of Near Eastern and Judaic Studies at the University of Manitoba, then later through the Department of Religion at Temple University. In 1983, it was published in popular format by Shambhala as *Sparks of Light: Counseling in the Hasidic Tradition*, with psychologist Edward Hoffman as coauthor. Still later, a more academic edition was later published by Jason Aronson as *Spiritual Intimacy*.

In retrospect, I would not have blamed the Chabad people for trying to remove themselves from the taint of my LSD experience if they had called me to say that, in their view, I had deeply embarrassed them, and they now had to engage in "damage control" at my expense. But because I felt hurt that all the work I had been doing in affiliation with Chabad for over twenty years had now been discounted without their contacting me first, their action caused a deep rift between us.

~

CHAPTER TWENTY-FIVE

The San Francisco Counterculture and Neo-Hasidism

During the heyday of the San Francisco counterculture, I often came down from Manitoba to participate in events organized by the freewheeling Jewish community based in Berkeley. The people at the Aquarian Minyan were my hosts; sometimes we would meet in living rooms, and at other times we would rent a place. My old friend Rabbi Shlomo Carlebach directed his remarkable House of Love and Prayer, which attracted disaffected young Jews. Many of them were hippies at the time—"holy beggars" in Reb Shlomo's poetic parlance—and became drawn to Judaism in what I came to call "neo-Hasidism." Shlomo was not always there, as he often traveled and sang elsewhere, so other people took over the House of Love and Prayer's daily management. It was a liberating, crazy time, and most Orthodox Jews, including the Lubavitchers, could not quite accept how free we were in relating to other Jews and to non-Jews as well.

Throughout my life, I have been blessed to have friends with whom I could share aspects of my inner life. This was especially true during those tumultuous years, as I was close with the Sufi leaders Pir Vilayat Khan and Pir Moineddin Jablonski and, through the Sufis, with both Joe Miller and Dr. Claudio Naranjo. Joe was quite a character: he was an irreverent man with a reverend's license to perform weddings and would take people on long walks. These were famous around town. If you wanted to have a scintillating conversation about life and spirituality, you would take a long walk with Joe. Imagine Golden Gate Park in the 1970s as academia, with Socrates strolling with his disciples. That was Joe. He was a wonderful man. He was loved, grew old, died, and was fondly remembered for his way of declaiming, "You get more stinking from thinking than from drinking, but to feel is for real!"

Dr. Naranjo, a polymath, had studied with Oscar Ichazo. He was trained in psychoanalysis and gestalt therapy and was a pioneer in transpersonal psychology. In Berkeley, he founded a group named SAT, an abbreviation for Seekers after Truth (incorporating and updating much of the Gurdjieff work) and perhaps also referring to the Sanskrit word *Sat* (consciousness). He invited me to share my work on Kabbalah and Hasidism with his people. Claudio had also worked with Bob Hoffman and his famous Fisher-Hoffman process. Later I took that process, now called the Quadrinity Process. It is a profound method by which, in order to feel one's family of origin, one has to "kill" one's parents and also "defend them." In Claudio's view, it was also important to subject one's religious origins to the same process. This meant that one had to scrape off the superstitions that had attached themselves to that religious system, then recommit oneself to that which one found worthwhile within it. He invited me to do the Quadrinity work with people's religion of origin. In the process of working with Claudio's people, I got to know him even better and had many other occasions to work in tandem with him.

One day in 1975, Pir Vilayat Khan invited me to participate in a guru panel that was held at the grand Masonic Temple in San Francisco. What an amazing collection of human beings and great teachers were in attendance! Lamas, swamis, gurus, Hindus, Buddhists, Christians, Sufis—and I sat on the dais with them. Members of the audience asked all kinds of questions of the panel, and its participants responded. After a while in which the questions focused on what happens to men's precious *kundalini* when they ejaculate, and the various participants responded with quotes from Sanskrit sources, I told Pir Vilayat Khan, who was the presiding panelist, that I wanted to respond. I asked the audience if they had ever heard of the Jewish philosopher Martin Buber. If so, were they not aware of his conception of the sacredness of the I-Thou relationship? Why were they so concerned about their own spirituality and not the sexual experience of their partner? There was large applause then, mostly coming from the women.

The next day many of the panelists met with me at the Pauley Ballroom of the University of California, Berkeley. I had announced that this meeting would be called "Torah and Dharma." In response, we even had a zealot picket us with a sign that said, "Torah versus Dharma." There were eleven people on the panel, and ten of them—a variety of Sikhs, Buddhists, Christian sectarians, Hindus, and Sufis—had been born Jewish. The only exception was the chair of the panel: Pir Moineddin Jablonski.

In planning for this meeting, I had eagerly invited Reb Shlomo to participate with us. Unfortunately, his time was committed elsewhere, so I asked him to record for me on a cassette what he would like to share with everyone there. As best as I now can recall, here is what Reb Shlomo said:

> The Izhbitzer [a Hasidic master of the nineteenth century] offers a holy teaching: It is written that a *kohen*, a priest, is not permitted to defile himself, to become impure by touching a dead body. Why is that? Because the Bible says, "The lips of the *kohen* are to guard the teachings of the Torah that we are to seek from him." And the Izhbitzer explains that the reason why the *kohen* must not defile himself to the dead is because it is impossible to come in contact with a corpse without being angry at God for having made it so that everyone must die. Angry people are not good teachers to teach people about God. Because of the Holocaust we, all our Jewish teachers, have become afflicted with the taint of death, so our young people have not been able to hear the loving message about God from them. Then God in his great mercy sent us people from the Far East, people who were not contaminated by the Holocaust, to teach us about God in the way that we could let it into our hearts.

Reb Shlomo's statement made a huge impression on the people of the panel, all of whom said, in one way or another, that if they had been able to find the kind of Judaism that we in Jewish Renewal were teaching, they would not have felt the need to seek other religions in which to become expert.

During those same memorable years, Swami Mukhtanada had opened an ashram in Oakland. At the time I was developing neo-Hasidic meditative techniques with people at the Aquarian Minyan in nearby Berkeley. We arranged to go and visit the Swami, and we brought along the proper gifts of flowers, a challah, and a book on Hasidism in English translation. Before we were to meet him in a private audience, someone from his entourage was sent to warm us up. At one point, he bluntly asserted, "We Hindus are very universalistic, whereas you Jews are particularistic." That remark did not sit so well with me. I asked him to translate a few words for me from the Sanskrit, *karma* and *dharma*, which he translated quite easily into "the laws of cause and effect in the way of righteousness." Then I asked him to translate the word *m'lechcha*, at which moment he began to sputter and said, "This word refers to non-Bharatic people." In other words, that is how one says *goy* to describe people who are non-Hindus. (The literal translation is "eaters of excrement.") We therefore saw that their vaunted universalism had its boundaries too.

Later that day, when we met Swami Mukhtanada, I observed how one young man came to accept him as his spiritual master by handing over his purse as a sign of submission. The Swami opened it, looked inside, and saw that it contained a wallet and a set of keys. He looked at the young man seriously and said, "Good, now keep it for me." I was so impressed by how the Swami managed to honor the submission, yet immediately returned to that young man responsibility for and authority over his own life.

CHAPTER TWENTY-SIX

~

Relocating to Philadelphia

By the time 1975 came around, I had been wishing for quite a while to be able to move to a city where my work of Jewish Renewal—B'nai or P'nai Or—would be able to grow. Winnipeg, with its rather conservative Jewish population of twenty thousand and its cultural lag behind the United States, seemed to me a place where I would not be able to grow my work further. While in Winnipeg in the early to mid-1970s, I increasingly thought about traveling actively to other places to conduct workshops and weekend retreats involving people who were ready to grow with me in new Jewish directions. Many of the places I visited and worked were on each of the two U.S. coasts.

From time to time, I visited Boston and Cambridge, where my friends from the Sommerville chavurah—especially Rabbi Arthur Green, who was its founder, and the people whom I had taught during my sabbatical at Brandeis—were located. However, when Arthur Green went to teach Judaic studies at the University of Pennsylvania in Philadelphia, I was attracted to move there too.

In May 1975, I was invited by Dr. Arthur Waskow—who was then affiliated with a Washington think tank—to come and celebrate with others the tenth anniversary of the passing of Martin Buber. We were all invited to give papers. I decided not to make a formal academic presentation but, instead, an experiential one. Martin Buber, of course, was famous for his concept of the I-Thou relationship. I therefore felt it was important for participants to experience the difference between the relationship of I-It and I-Thou. So I offered to conduct a series of labs that would lead us to experience that exalted mode

181

of being. My plan was to use several of the methods I had developed, which I would later call "socialized meditation."

The Department of Religious Studies at Temple University was seeking to hire a professor in Judaic studies. I applied and was accepted. The department head was professor Paul Van Buren, with whom I had very good relations. So when the school year at the University of Manitoba ended in May, I made arrangements to move to Pennsylvania. However, between May and September, there were three whole months, and I sought to find ways to teach during that time.

I received an invitation from the University of California, Santa Cruz, and there I taught courses in Kabbalistic reality maps and Hasidic tales. I had a wonderful time teaching there. The atmosphere in Santa Cruz in 1975 was free and exciting, and the campus, situated right on the sparkling Pacific Ocean, was beautiful. It was about two hours south of San Francisco by car. I taught my course with experiential labs. I also had time to travel up to Berkeley to be with the people of the Aquarian Minyan.

Earlier I had made strong connections with the Sufis, first at the Lama Foundation, then later in Berkeley, especially with the people who followed "Sufi Sam" (Samuel Lewis, a teacher appointed by Hazrat Inayat Khan, who brought Sufism to the United States). I no longer met "Sufi Sam" in this life, but his successor, Pir Moineddin Jablonski, had become a dear friend of mine. I sought to be initiated into Sufism. Having also worked with Pir Vilayat Khan, I was initiated by him and given the honorary title of sheikh.

He was the one who urged me to make a name change, for at that time, I was a vegetarian. My last name, Schachter, referred to a person who is engaged in the kosher slaughter of animals. So I decided to add the name Shalomi because my father's name was Shlomo. My Hebrew names, Meshullam Zalman, are also derived from a word for peace, and my son's name, Sholem DovBer, and my daughter's name, Shalvi, all point to the issue of peace. I decided to hyphenate my name as Schachter-Shalomi with the intent that when peace would finally be established between Israel and Palestine, I would officially and legally change my name from Schachter to Shalomi. Alas, to this day I have remained yoked to both names.

I also was invited to give a course at the Graduate Theological Union nestled in Berkeley's scenic hills. I got a great deal of pleasure sharing ideas with some of the professors on the faculty. My future colleague at Temple University, Ismail al Faruqi, also taught at that time at the Graduate Theological Union. Having been freed from the restraints of conservative Winnipeg and enjoying the company of West Coast people, I had many wonderful personal experiences that readied me for my move to Philadelphia.

Much of what I wanted to do for what became Jewish Renewal began with my move to Philadelphia. However, the seeds of what grew in Philadelphia were planted during my time in Winnipeg. Since that time, my work has also led me to deal with the issue of aging with awareness—one result of which was my book with Ronald Miller, *From Age-ing to Sage-ing*. In the realm of Jewish Renewal, my home in Philadelphia became an exciting place that served to train rabbis and other leaders who would bring Jewish Renewal into the world. We began biannual meetings—the *Kallah*—involving men and women who had become interested in what we were doing, and when they returned to their local communities, they initiated "living room congregations" too. My students and I continue to serve these communities. In 1997, I turned leadership of Jewish Renewal over to my students. They subsequently founded a rabbinic organization, Ohalah, which now conducts the training of rabbis, rabbinic pastors, cantors, and spiritual directors.

~

CHAPTER TWENTY-SEVEN

Epilogue:
Whither Jewish Renewal?

People have often asked me about succession. I am now in my December years, and there will soon be a time when I will not be around here anymore. Many are wondering what will happen to Jewish Renewal at that point and whether I have made any particular arrangements as to who should next lead. I want to say clearly, no, it's not up to me to decide. Whenever someone asks me today, "How would you define Jewish Renewal?" I answer, "We won't know until 150 years from now, because it is very much a work in progress." The one thing I do know is that Jewish Renewal—to use a contemporary metaphor—must be downward compatible.

That is to say, although we are not driving by looking in the rearview mirror, we must nevertheless always check it. This is like saying that we must remain actively in touch with tradition. If we cannot do that, then what will develop will not be Jewish; it will not be Judaism. However, if we do only that, it will not be Judaism of this time—of this age.

I really don't know precisely which way Jewish Renewal is going to advance. But neither I am worried about this matter, because I view myself as an instrument—what I should do in my remaining time here is more in God's hands than a matter of my own planning. This issue does not have much to do with what I, as a particular individual, want to see happen, but I know that my lifetime has been used to help make a change.

I also know that this situation will occur with other people in a similar way—and that Divine Providence, our Mother the *Shechinah*, our Mother the Earth, the entire divine process, will continue. Concerning that sacred domain, I have trust and faith that this will truly be so.

I do not have any statements to make other than, Don't forget where you came from and pay attention to the future that pulls you. As theotropic beings, we are all being pulled by God to get closer to the intent for which the whole universe was created. The future is drawing us. There is a divine entelechy, a conscious, a teleological life force. And that is why I keep saying, "Don't ask so much the question *Madu'a*—Why are we doing this? What's the past? Rather, ask the question *Lamah*—To what end?"

Amen.

APPENDIXES

~

BRIEF REMINISCENCES

~

Gerald Heard, My Irish Rebbe

I was introduced to Gerald Heard sometime in the early 1960s by a young man named Charles Vernoff, then a student at the University of Chicago and now a professor. I was very pleased because that meeting led to many wonderful things in my life.

When I first met Gerald, I was so surprised to meet someone who was a savant, because I had read about savants. Yet there was such a beautiful humility about him. Here I was, a young rabbi coming to see him, and he was willing to hear in a very open way about the Kabbalah and Jewish spirituality. Later on, I sent him a spiritual poem that I had written, and he would read it from time to time as part of his prayers. He considered himself a tertiary—that is, a lay religious person living in the world. Yet, he was a monk of all kinds of systems. His main religion was Vedanta, but he also included anything else that would draw him closer to God.

When Gerald told me about his book *The Gospel According to Gamaliel*, I couldn't believe how its author had such a remarkably wide view of the Jewish-Christian situation. He understood Jesus as depicted in the New Testament as seen through Jewish eyes. I have since written a foreword to a new edition of this work. *Gabriel and the Creatures* was also wonderful. And *Training for the Life of the Spirit* was an important book for me.

When Gerald wrote *The Five Ages of Man*, it became for me the great inspiration for work that I later undertook under the name of *Spiritual Eldering*. My central notion was that we have role models for every phase of life during youth and middle age, but we have none for what I call the "harvest years."

In our society, once one is no longer economically "productive," then there aren't any roles to perform except killing time. I later saw how it was vital to harness the power that an extended lifespan gives to people if they seek expanded awareness instead of engaging in mindless activities like shuffleboard and golf. When Heard wrote in *The Five Ages of Man* about all the ordeals that people must undergo in order to reach their next phase, that was very important to me. It helped galvanize me to cowrite a book called *From Ageing to Sage-ing: A Profound New Vision of Growing Older*. So these were some of the things that he inspired in me.

But that isn't quite the whole story. As Gerald grew older, we would speak from time to time on the phone. We agreed that when the time came for him to die, he would let me know so that I could be at his side. That intimacy was a remarkable thing between us. However, Gerald suffered a series of strokes and was in a coma for quite a long time, and then he expired. So the circumstances of his dying never happened according to our plan. But the planning itself was very much the kind of heart connection that we shared.

Gerald was the type of person in whom all the great figures of the Axial Age were alive. So if one needed Confucius, he was there. If one needed Lao Tzu, he was there. If one needed Aristotle, he was there. If one needed Jeremiah and Isaiah, they were there. That was the amazing thing, the breadth of his awareness; he was able to channel the authentic, pure mystical teachings of the ages. At the same time, he knew a great deal about physiology and neurology, as well as the spirit. In his books, Gerald would talk about the chemistry of noradrenalin and matters like that. That's why I felt he was a savant; there wasn't an area in philosophy and science about which he didn't have some specific and detailed awareness.

In addition, when people come out of any strong religious commitment, they often verbalize a certain amount of triumphalism: every religion has something like this sensibility, such as the Jewish belief that "nobody else does it as well with God as we Jews!" Therefore, to meet someone like Gerald, who radiated a great sense of universality and ecumenicism, was very rare.

And the other thing that was important was that we could talk about psychedelics. Since the early 1950s, Heard had experimented occasionally with psychedelics under clinical conditions often supervised by Dr. Sidney Cohen—then with the Veterans Hospital in West Los Angeles. Heard never advocated the recreational use of psychedelics; he viewed them only in the context of fostering spiritual evolution and promoting social sanity. When I mentioned to him that I had wanted to experience psychedelics ever since reading Aldous Huxley's *The Doors of Perception*, he was eager to help me.

I considered Gerald not just a peer and associate but also a mentor. I would refer to him as "my *goyshe* rebbe"—my Gentile spiritual teacher, for a rebbe is like a Hasidic master. Gerald was somebody who really had a sense of what's going on inside us. Some people are really natural spiritual geniuses, but they don't have enough introspection to make it work so they can lead other people there. Gerald had the introspection, and he also had the scope. You know if there was any kind of *upaya* (spiritual practice) around, he had tried it out and knew how to use it correctly. He also knew the context from which it came, and he had a cosmology to fit the whole thing together.

I loved his Irish face; it was very beautiful face to me. I used to have his picture up to remind me that one can grow old in this way. I really loved that man! You see, for all the *jnani* (analytical approach to God) stuffed in him, he was really a *bhakti* (devotional approach to God) at heart. And whenever he had any *bhakti* connections, then he would overflow with that joy.

Gerald made two major lasting impressions on me. The first was that my horizon expanded. It was amazing to be in his presence because he had a vast perspective that took in so much and managed to keep it organically connected. The second—and this seems funny now to say—was that in the late 1950s and early 1960s, I often wondered, Am I fooling myself when I'm doing the pious stuff? I might say to myself disparagingly, Look who claims to have just had this epiphany, this theophany! A little later I might even think to myself, Maybe I'm just jazzing myself into believing about transcendence.

But when I met someone like Gerald, I had the sense that it must be true! He was my litmus test for the veracity of higher reality.

APPENDIX B

~

Rabbi Hershel Matt

I used to come to New York City from time to time. Rabbi Hershel Matt was one of the people who belonged to the group that met in Oconomowoc, Wisconsin, at the Union Institute. There we could share with each other the thoughts that we could not share even with our colleagues and our rabbinic organizations. There were Conservative rabbis, Reform rabbis, Reconstructionist rabbis, and myself. We kept it under the radar so that we would not be criticized by more dogmatic people in our respective denominational organizations.

Rabbi Arnie Wolf organized some of the essays that we presented to one other, and some of them were published in a volume titled *Rediscovering Judaism*. My essay was titled "Patterns of Good and Evil." It is part of that book, and we shared these wonderful ideas with each other because the Reform rabbis who wanted to say that they really believed in the living God could say that freely. In those days, the best that you could get from liberal theologians was that they believed in the "fatherhood of God" and the "brotherhood of man." Also in the air during the early to mid-1960s were ideas like Dr. Norman Vincent Peale's "power of positive thinking" and psychoanalysis.

I came to know these colleagues on a deep level. Among the outstanding people in that group was Rabbi Hershel Matt. I would think of him as one of the *lamed-vov*—the thirty-six hidden saints who, according to Talmudic and later Hasidic lore, sustain in every generation the entire world. He led a synagogue in Metuchen, New Jersey. The town was situated just on the other side of the Hudson River, so I would awaken sometimes at 5 a.m. to take a subway to the Port Authority Terminal in midtown Manhattan and then board a bus to Metuchen to attend Heschel Matt's *minyan*.

They used the old Silverman Conservative Jewish prayer book for *shabbos* and Jewish holidays, and they also used a blue-covered weekday *siddur*. Rabbi Hershel Matt—of course, this was way before desktop computers were invented—used a Rolodex with sets of differently colored cards for the various parts of the weekday morning service. One color set was for the morning blessings, another was for the psalms of praise, and a third was for the recitation of *K'riyat Shma* and the *Amidah*. Anyone who led the *davenen* could take the card set for each section and conduct the entire service. I was so impressed by this invention because, in this way, Rabbi Matt had made sure that there would be a whole prayer quorum.

The better I came to know him, the more I felt that here was a person who really lived in the presence of the living God. I truly saw in him the best model of an American Jewish pastor.

~

Breakthroughs in Milwaukee

During the late 1960s, I would often travel from Manitoba to Milwaukee to lead weekend retreats with members of a Reform Jewish congregation. One time they were holding their retreat in a place called the Cenacle Center, which was run by a group of Bavarian sisters/nuns. "Cenacle" means the upper room and refers in Catholic tradition to the place where Jesus is said to have shared the last Passover meal with his disciples. That center served people of various faiths and backgrounds who wanted to come for a religious retreat or seminar. The Bavarians were quite hospitable and would serve refreshments and provide a comfortable setting. What we did during that particular retreat was so unconventional compared to how religious retreats back then were typically presented.

On Friday night, I talked to the congregants about sensory awareness: the kind of experiential activity that Charlotte Selver was innovatively teaching at the famous Esalen Institute in Big Sur, California. Then, after everyone had washed their hands, I asked them to eat *everything*—with the sole exception of the soup—with their hands, touching everything with their fingers as mindfully as possible. That night, we conducted the *shabbos* service with a recorded liturgy; I encouraged them to dance through it, and I used a strobe light to spur an altered state of consciousness. The following morning at breakfast, I asked each person to feed someone else—and not put any food into his or her own mouth—just like in that beautiful parable about the nature of heaven and hell.

The Bavarian sisters, who wanted to make sure that everything was meticulously served, were more than a little embarrassed by what they had already seen. It was definitely not what they expected to happen in their sedate retreat house. By Sunday morning, I could see that my retreat had provoked consternation among them, so I asked their superior if I could speak with them after their morning Mass, and she kindly agreed.

I thereupon explained why I had utilized sensory awareness and dancing during the Friday night service, as well as the "interpersonal feeding" activity. After my explanation, they seemed more relaxed but advised me to venture that afternoon to the Church of the Sacred Heart to see how Father Ed celebrated the Mass with his people.

I immediately postponed my flight back to Manitoba because the sisters/nuns insisted, "If you want to get a seat at the Mass, which begins at five o'clock, then you'd better be there by 4:30 p.m., because you won't have a place if you don't come early enough." I arrived there at 4:15 p.m. and saw how the church was filling up; quite soon, there was no room in the pews. People were dressed in all kinds of hippy outfits. Children settled themselves around the altar space, and toddlers gleefully crawled around the altar.

As the musicians tuned their various instruments, suddenly there appeared Father Ed. As liturgical garb, he wore a vestment made of blue denim with a round peace sign stitched on his surplice. He also wore Birkenstock sandals. Standing at the pulpit and gazing into the audience, he began to recount that he had watched a football game the other day, and one player had kicked a field goal. Father Ed related that a fan nearby started criticizing it mercilessly. "So I asked myself," he said "What is wrong with us? Why do we look at these things in such a negative way? Why can't we see other people in a good way? What is it that makes us so ungenerous with one another?"

After this heartfelt remark, he led the congregation into the general confession, which serves as the beginning of the Mass. And there was such a natural and easy movement that one hardly had the feeling that this was liturgy. He went straight to the heart of the people there. The music was wonderful. They sang among the hallelujahs the song of the "Lord of the dance" and other current songs that seemed to fit the liturgy. When it came to the "kiss of peace," there was such a hubbub that it took ten minutes for everybody to hug one another in the church—and then someone pushed me over to Father Ed.

He and I stayed in touch for a while until he was laicized because he couldn't stand the church politics anymore. It is a pity that clergy like Father Ed and Father Matthew Fox, who was expelled for teaching "Creation Spirituality" and is now an Episcopal clergy, could not be accommodated by the church. They all brought great energy and commitment to the people who worshipped with them.

APPENDIX D

～

The Dalai Lama

His Holiness the Fourteenth Dalai Lama, Tenzin Gyatso, and I have been friends for more than twenty years. As chronicled artfully by Rodger Kamenetz in his book *The Jew in the Lotus*, I was one of eight rabbis in 1990 who traveled to Dharamsala, India, to meet with the Dalai Lama. We enjoyed especially stimulating conversations on topics relating to the Kabbalah, including the existence of angels and reincarnation, for both subjects, of course, have long been part of Jewish mysticism and its flowering in Hasidism. He was enthralled by the seeming similarities between our two grand spiritual traditions, and I composed a special prayer in his honor. Perhaps the most famous exchange reported about our first meeting was his Holiness's poignant question about the secret of Jewish survival in exile through the ages.

Since that exciting encounter, the Dalai Lama and I have met in person several times—sometimes in Denver, close to where I live, and often as invited speakers at various international conferences on global issues. Undoubtedly, the most significant conference—including both him and Archbishop Desmond Tutu—took place in Vancouver, British Columbia, several years ago in 2004. There, at a lively roundtable conversation with them, I presented my paper on the need for a contemporary cosmology based on how the Earth wants to be healed. I raised the issue of what is the human ethic to be derived from that crucial perspective and what are the spiritual methods to live that ethic on a daily basis. "More and more have deep-thinking ecotheologians come to the conclusion that each religion is like a vital organ of the planet," I commented, "and that we, for the planet's sake, need—each

one of us—to stay alive and devout in the most healthy way we can manage."
In that light, I called for fresh ways of thinking and urged, "Creativity does
not reside in the way we are imprisoned to repeat precedent. It is in daring—
to be outrageous, to play with the least probable possibilities, the ones more
weird and spiritual, where we may find answers." It was clear that the Dalai
Lama strongly concurred with my viewpoint.

Long before we actually met face to face in Dharamsala, however, a connection existed between us. In March 1959, Chairman Mao's government
brutally crushed the Tibetan people's uprising against the Chinese Communists' invasion and political takeover of their country. His Holiness, all of
twenty-three years old, was forced to flee for his life in a harrowing fifteen-
day trek on foot through the Himalayas and into northern India. It was not
clear whether India's prime minister Jawaharial Nehru would be willing to
offer asylum to the Dalai Lama, and so I immediately fired off a telegram to
Israeli prime minister David Ben-Gurion to do so. At the time, I was a young
professor in Winnipeg, and nothing came of my suggestion.

Four years later, in 1963, a friend of mine took me along to visit the Buddhist monastery in Washington, New Jersey. Known as Labsum Shedrub,
it was run by Ngawang "Geshe" Wangyal, a Buddhist priest and scholar of
Mongolian origin. He was close with the Dalai Lama and at the time teaching at Columbia University. I enjoyed meeting Wangyal and some of his
younger monks at the Buddhist monastery and suggested that because a new
diaspora was forming for the Tibetans, it would be useful for them to learn
from us Jews how to survive in exile. He listened to my viewpoint thought-
fully.

Once, a few years ago, the Dalai Lama came to lecture at Boulder, Colorado, where I live. When he saw me, he excitedly exclaimed, "The Jewish!"
Then he pulled my beard in a friendly way.

APPENDIX E

~

My Unfulfilled Projects

Though I have been able to achieve many of my goals related to Jewish Renewal, some of my hopes and plans never reached fruition. In this chapter, I would like to describe what some of these have been.

First, early in my career as a Lubavitch-ordained rabbi, I wanted to open a storefront in New York City's financial district. Similar in style to the abundant Christian Science reading rooms, it would focus on Jewish outreach. I originated this idea back in the 1950s when there were no Chabad centers anywhere, and I suggested to the Lubavitcher Rebbe that I would be grateful for financial support in order to create such a center. In my view, 770 Eastern Parkway was not always in pristine condition, and its quiet Brooklyn neighborhood was a world away from the bustle and dynamism of Wall Street. Also, the type of Chabad center I envisioned would provide a way for Jews to come and follow through on the Rebbe's advice for them.

I wanted to utilize what I had learned both in pastoral counseling at Boston University and from *Chasidus*: to be able to help these individuals on their life's journey. In addition, I sought to have a place where Jews could drop in to *daven* the afternoon and evening prayers and say *kaddish*. More specifically, I wanted to have an urn for hot water and coffee for drop-in visitors, as well as a mini bookstore to sell Hasidic books and pamphlets and to give away publications. Unfortunately, when I presented my plan in the form of a "brief" to the Lubavitcher Rebbe, his response was not particularly encouraging, and eventually I abandoned it. Nevertheless, today I notice how much the later distribution of Chabad centers around the globe has been predicated on the brief that I originally submitted for the Rebbe's approval.

Another of my major unfulfilled projects was to obtain a position at the Bani Israel synagogue in Bombay (now called Mumbai), India. The congregation had been founded many centuries earlier, and its members did not have a rabbi at that time. The position was advertised in the newsletter of the Orthodox rabbinic association of which I was then an active member. My plan was to take a professional-quality tape recorder and camera with me and to record the stories and liturgical melodies of the synagogue elders. I anticipated hearing intriguing tales and songs dating back to the ancient era of King Solomon. I also planned to meet some Hindu gurus while I was involved with anthropological and rabbinic work. But, unfortunately, I was not offered the position, and my interesting dream never materialized.

Yet another goal I had was to create a Judaic Institute in Israel for the men and women who had just completed their tour of duty in the army reserves. My idea was to provide a healing social setting for the returning soldiers before they entered busy civilian life. Why? Because Israeli army life was necessarily often harsh, and people needed to be able to relax and become "civilized" civilians again. My aim was to enable these recent army reserve soldiers to lower their vibration level from the one in which they sometimes uttered commands in barking style. I remember noticing that the typical mode of discourse among strangers in Israel—and frequently even among acquaintances—had become much less gentle and much more angry and harsh. But, unfortunately, that plan too never reached fruition.

Another worthy project I wanted to initiate in Israel would have involved outreach work for the Ministry of Religion. My idea originated when I once visited the motor vehicles bureau and observed with dismay how a Moslem cleric was treated rather disrespectfully. Not long after, I had a remarkable meeting in Jerusalem on my way to the Kotel (the Western Wall), which solidified my desire to engage in such work.

It was shortly before the shabbos, and I was ambling through the narrow streets that run from the Jaffa Gate to the approach to the Kotel. I suddenly saw an Armenian priest coming up the street, and the brilliant late afternoon Jerusalem sunlight beautifully illumined his hair and beard. I was wearing my Hasidic garb. As he came along, I wanted to meet him. "Excuse me, sir," I asked, "Do you speak English?" He immediately replied, "Yes." I then asked, "May I have your blessing?"

He quickly, almost furtively, looked up and down the narrow street to see if anyone was watching us. Since there was no one else on the road at that moment, I bowed my head for him, and he gave me a traditional blessing. Then the Armenian priest turned to me and said, "Would you give me a blessing too?" Of course, I eagerly did so, and then we warmly went our respective ways.

This brief incident inspired me to imagine how wonderful it would be for Israel's Ministry of Religion to have an outreach worker to serve as a liaison among the various religious heads in Jerusalem. My notion was that I would get the calendar of all the religious associations there, and depending on their particular holy days, I would visit the heads of those religious groups with a basket of gifts fitting for that holiday. I had the sense that if they saw themselves respected and their various requests delivered personally to the Ministry of Religion, a great deal of needless friction could be avoided. Equally important, goodwill would be created for the Israeli government by the heads of the various religions. Alas, that project likewise never materialized.

I also once explored the possibility of becoming a faculty member of the Jewish Theological Seminary in New York City. During the early 1960s, I became friendly with Rabbi Stephen Schwartzschild, who lived in Fargo, North Dakota. He had a European background like mine, and though our temperaments were rather different, we shared quite a bit in common intellectually and spiritually. We both belonged to the group of rabbis who met informally at the Union Institute at Oconomowoc, Wisconsin, for deep and open conversation.

After I shared with Oconomowoc colleagues my little booklet *The First Step*—in which I presented a simple way to enter meditative work based on Chabad and other traditional Hasidic teachings—Schwartzschild showed my booklet to Dr. Louis Finkelstein of blessed memory. At the time chancellor of the Jewish Theological Seminary, he was impressed by its content. As a result, I was invited to spend the weekend at the seminary, with the possibility of being appointed to the faculty there.

I arranged to offer a workshop for Thursday evening on how to construct a theology you can commit yourself to. (I later learned that one of the professors there threatened to ex-communicate any of his rabbinic students if they attended my seminar.) It went wonderfully. Then, on Friday afternoon, I presented a workshop on how to recite the biblical *Song of Songs* to God as a lover to one's beloved. Next, on *shabbos* morning, I dressed in my Hasidic garb—*caftan* and *shtreyml*—wanting to see how much leeway they would give me. I was intrigued to see that my Hasidic garb did not faze them, and I presented a Hasidic discourse at the *Kiddush* in the presence of professors Abraham Heschel and Saul Lieberman.

That afternoon, I led the *Mincha* prayer, and several faculty members were in attendance. All was going well until, in the middle of the Hebrew service,

I switched to English and chanted it with the same fervent melody as traditionally done in Hebrew. Instantly, I felt psychic darts aimed at me. The next morning, both Louis Finkelstein and Saul Lieberman chastised me for using the vernacular in a prayer service. I respectfully responded that I had done so because the rabbinic students who would be graduating from the Jewish Theological Seminary would surely have to lead at least part of the services in English at their future synagogues. Lieberman caustically retorted, "This is only a palliative." I didn't get the faculty position at the Jewish Theological Seminary because I had used English in a prayer service.

Another academic position that I was interested in, and applied for, led to an interview at Stern College with the dean, and then later on with the president of Yeshiva University. Stern College, of course, has been its undergraduate division for Orthodox women only, and I intended to initiate a set of courses based on traditional Jewish liturgy combined with spiritual direction. At my series of interviews, I was asked to outline for them how I would accomplish this goal. I replied that first I would cancel the daily weekday visits of the ten lads from Yeshiva College to make a *minyan*, so that the liturgy would be conducted by the young women of Stern College. This suggestion elicited some raised eyebrows.

I also explained that I wanted to teach their female students how to put on *t'fillin*. When asked why, I replied that Jewish women needed to know this religious ritual because sometimes their husbands would be leaving home early for work, and in this way, they could effectively show their sons how to put on *t'fillin*. This time, there were nods of agreement among my interviewers. I still chuckle at the way I had artfully phrased my answer.

Finally, I was asked what I would do if a Stern College student came to me for counseling—would I check for guidance with the Lubavitch headquarters? I earnestly replied that if a troubled student came to me for counseling, I would conduct my work according to my own view of what was necessary, and I would not consult with the senior Chabad rabbis. But I could immediately see that my interviewers at Stern College were skeptical. Despite the fact that I had recounted for them that I had worked for both Conservative and Reform Jewish institutions, they were suspicious that I might act as a secret agent for the Lubavitcher movement.

A final unfulfilled project that I would like to relate concerned a man in Israel, when I was living there in 1984, who had great plans about solar energy. He had started a high-tech company with an allied business that dealt with arts and aesthetics, and it was named Lunar. I had heard that he was interested in hiring someone who would be an "industrial Kabbalist," and I was very much interested in that position. I believed that I could bring

Kabbalistic resources and approaches to bear on the entire organization by mapping it against the ten *sefirot* of the Tree of Life.

At that time, I was working on something that I called the "Ten Planner." It was an envisioned computer program for problem solving or long-range planning, using the ten *sefirot* of the Kabbalah as a methodology. The program would systematically divide a problem into various activities using the *sefirot* as a guide. It would allocate time intervals of differing duration for each activity, and it would accomplish this task by asking the user a series of questions.

First, it would ask *Keter* questions. These help us to structure the time allocation for the subsequent phases so users can define how they want to spend their time. *Keter* creates a balanced Tree of Life.

Chokhmah would ask, "What do you want?" The user would reply, "I want *x*."

Binah would say, "Let's figure out what *x* is. What are all its dimensions? What are its inputs? Its outputs? What kind of planning goes into it? What sort of budget is needed?" And *Binah*'s answers would lead to computations and allocations.

Da'at would sneak in as quality control: "How will we know we've achieved what we set out to achieve? I, *Da'at*, am the feedback loop. When our perception doesn't hit these indicators, I'll tell you you've missed the mark."

Chesed: "What are my resources? What's available for spending in terms of time, space, energy, money, and so forth?"

Gevurah: "What limits must I consider for time, space, energy, money, and so forth?"

Tiferet, which encompasses the social dimension: "Who's going to participate?"

Netzach: "What kind of technology do I need to make it happen? Whom do I need with what expertise?" There is also a discussion between *Netzach* and *Gevurah*. *Gevurah* says, "Don't forget your budget," while *Netzach* wants to spend profligately, so everything will be terrific and inclusive. However, *Gevurah* sends down a budget message, saying, "We can't afford everything you want, *Netzach*."

Hod: "How am I going to get this idea to find space in peoples' hearts? How shall I market it? How shall I package it?"

Yesod: "How can I produce it so that today and tomorrow it can keep going and be nurtured in a sustainable way?"

Malkhut: "Release the plan. It has to function by itself, without being connected to the system that produced it."

The above scenario illustrates one way that we might be able to apply the functions of the ten *sefirot* in our world of *Assiyah*.

I was already deeply involved with transpersonal psychology, and I felt that applying it to a corporate entity and its employees and function by utilizing the Kabbalah would be an exciting prospect. Alas, I only had one interview with the principal. Nothing came of my interest at that time, but I know that today the solar part of his company has been built in California.

~

Glossary

Adata d'nafshey: Literally (Aramaic): With one's own soul in mind.

Al nafshey hatikha d'issura: Literally (Aramaic): It is as if a forbidden piece of meat for him. Something that is basically permitted but has become forbidden by a person's decision.

Aliyat han'shamah: Literally (Hebrew): A mystical ascent of the soul.

Amidah: Literally (Hebrew): Standing; the prayer of the eighteen blessings said during the week and the seven blessings on the shabbos and holy days connecting to the world of *azilut*, or divine emanation.

Après: Literally (French): After; often referring to a painting or a problem emulating the original.

Assiyah: Literally: The doing; the world of action and sensation; in prayer, representing the blessings connected with the body.

Atzarot: Literally (Hebrew): Contained days; applied to retreats.

Avodath Hashem: Literally (Hebrew): Service of the Name or service of God.

B'nai Or: Literally: Children of Light; the designation of the Qumran community in opposition to the Children of Darkness.

Basso profundo: Literally (Italian): The lowest bass voice.

Bat kol: Literally (Hebrew): Daughter of the voice; echo, heavenly pronouncement.

Beit Din: Literally: House of judgment; generally, rabbinic court.

Beit Midrash: Literally: House of study.

Bentshen: Literally: Blessing, thanksgiving after the meal; derived from the Latin for benediction.

Beyt Hamidrash: Literally: House of study.

Binah: Literally: Understanding; the third of the ten *sefirot*. Often described in maternal terms, *Binah* is the womb out of which the seven lower manifestations are born or the fountain out of which they flow. *Binah* is also the object of *teshuvah*, the source to which all life returns.

Bracha, brachas: Literally (Hebrew): Blessing(s).

Caftan: The long, black, often silken coat worn by Hasidic men.

Chabad: Acronym of *Chokhmah*, *Binah*, and *Da'at*; a designation of the intellectual Hasidism taught by the Lubavitcher masters.

Chasidus: The teachings of Hasidism.

Chavurah: Fellowship; an intimate community of Jews who share in study, prayer, and an understanding of the religious life.

Chavurot: Plural of *chavurah*.

Chesed: Literally: Grace, kindness; refers to the fourth *sefirah*.

Chokhmah: Literally: Wisdom; representing the right hemisphere of the brain and the first of the *sefirot*.

D'vekut: Literally (Hebrew): Cleaving, deep devotion to God.

Da'at: Literally: Knowledge. Often better translated as "awareness," *Da'at* in some Kabbalistic systems serves as the synthesis of *Chokhmah* and *Binah*, completing the highest or intellectual triad of *sefirot*.

Daven: To pray, especially to chant liturgical prayers in the style of traditionally pious Jews. This Yiddish word is derived from the Latin *divinum*, doing the divine thing.

Davenen: The act of praying, especially chanting liturgical prayers in the style of traditionally pious Jews.

De novo: Literally (Latin): As new.

Die Synagogengesaenge der Orientalischen Juden: Title of a book of the music of the synagogue modes of Oriental Jews.

Ein Sof: Literally (Hebrew): No end, designation for the infinite Godhead.

Eitzahs: Literally: Offers of advice (informal).

Eitzot: Literally: Offers of advice.

Fabrengen: Literally: Spending time together; when the Hasidim gather for celebration, sometimes with the master or at other times among themselves, offering drinks, stories, teachings, and songs.

Gaia; gaian: Earth in Greek as a noun; gaian is its adjective; used in an ecological sense.

Galut: Literally: Exile/alienation.

Gam Zeh Ya'avor: Literally (Hebrew): This too shall pass.

Gan Eden: Literally (Hebrew): Garden of Eden; in broader Jewish terms, refers to Paradise.

Gehenna: Literally (Hebrew): The Valley of Hinnom, purgatory.

Gematria: The mystical study of numerical values for letters of the Hebrew alphabet.

Gevurah: Literally: Heroic strength; refers to the fifth *sefirah* representing divine strictness and rigor.

Gilgul: Literally: The turning of the wheel, representing reincarnation.

Gilgulim: The plural of *gilgul*.

Gittin: Literally (rabbinic Hebrew): Documents; especially refers to documents of divorce.

Goy: Literally: Nation; more broadly, a non-Jew.

Goyeshe: Literally: Like a non-Jew.

Ha Rav Hatamim: Literally: The rabbi who studied at Lubavitcher yeshiva.

Haftorah: Literally (Hebrew): Completion; the prophetic portion appended to the weekly Torah reading.

Halachic: Literally (Hebrew): Pertaining to *halacha*, the process of rabbinic law.

Hamantashen: Confection baked for the holiday of Purim.

Hashomer Hatzair: Literally (Hebrew): The young guardian; a Zionist-Socialist organization.

Hatavat Halom: Literally (Hebrew): The amelioration of a dream.

Havdalah: Literally (Hebrew): Separation; the prayer recited when the shabbos or the holy days are completed, separating the sacred from the secular.

Havurah: See *chavurah*.

Hekdesh: Literally (Hebrew): Something made holy; specifically refers to a hospice for the homeless.

Hevra Kadisha: Literally (Hebrew): The sacred *chavurah* dedicated to serve as a burial society.

Hevrah: See *havurah*.

Heykhalot: Literally: The books of the (heavenly) mansions; early midrashic texts leading to the Kabbalah.

Hitbodedut: Literally: Solitude; in the vernacular, heart-full prayer in solitude taught by the Bratzlav Hasidim.

Hitbon'nut: Literally (Hebrew): Contemplation, general term for Chabad meditation.

Hod: Literally: Glory, elegance; refers to the eighth *sefirah*; also means echo feedback.

Hok L'Yisroel: Literally: Specific measure for Israel; a compendium of sacred texts containing biblical, Talmudic, *halachic*, mystical, and moral sections assigned to each day of the week.

Horra: Balkan dance form adopted by the early kibbutz Zionists.

Hoshanah Rabba: Literally: The great "please save us," referring to the sixth day of Sukkot.

Hovoth hal'vavot: Literally (Hebrew): Duties of the heart; the title of a treatise on spirituality.

K'riyat Shma: Literally: The reading of the *Shma;* declaration of the Jewish faith, "Hear O Israel YHVH is our God, YHVH is one."

K'riyat Shma She'al Hamittah: The *K'riyat Shma* recited before going to sleep.

Kabbalah: From the Hebrew root word "to receive." Often used as a generic term for Jewish mysticism per se, it more precisely refers to its esoteric thought from the late twelfth century onward.

Kaddish: Literally (Aramaic): Sanctification, often in relation to the prayer recited for the deceased by the mourner.

Kallah: Literally: Gathering of all scholars in ancient Babylon. The modern use is the biennial gathering of Jewish Renewalists.

Kashrut: Kosherness.

Kavvannah: Literally: Intention, focus, and fervor in prayer.

Kavvannot: Plural of *kavvannah.*

Keter: Literally: Crown; the *sefirah* presiding over the Tree of Life in the Kabbalah, corresponding to the crown chakra.

Kever: Literally (Hebrew): Grave.

Kiddush: Literally: Sanctification; the prayer recited over wine on the shabbos and holy days.

Kittels: Literally: White shrouds; worn on special occasions and during the High Holy Days and the Passover *seders.*

Klippot: Literally (Hebrew): Shells; energy systems of evil in the Kabbalah.

Kohen: Literally: priest; descendants of Ahron, the high priest and brother of Moses. Kohens have specific religious privileges and obligations.

Kol Nidre: Literally (Hebrew): All vows; the introductory prayer and declaration of Yom Kippur.

Kotel: Literally: Wall; refers to the Western Wall, at times called the Wailing Wall, the last remains of the Jerusalem Temple.

L'chayim: Literally (Hebrew): To life; used as a toast involving a beverage.

Lamah: Literally: Why?; meaning "to what end?"

Landsman: Literally (Yiddish/German): Fellow countryman.

Latke: Pancake.

Lecha Dodi: Literally (Hebrew): Go, my friend; refrain of a popular shabbos hymn.

Limud hatorah: Literally (Hebrew): The study of the Torah.

Ma'amar: Literally (Hebrew): An essay verbally transmitted by a rebbe.

Ma'ariv: The evening prayer.

Maasseh: Literally: In action, as story. Abraham Heschel defined it as a story in which the soul surprises the mind.

Machshavos zoros: Literally (Hebrew): Evil thoughts that divert a person from attention to prayer.

Madu'a: Literally: Why?; meaning "what is the cause?"

Maftir: Literally (Hebrew): The one who completes; the last reading of the Torah on shabbos and holy days.

Malkhut: Literally: Majesty, referring to the last *sefirah* of the Tree of Life.

Mameniu: Literally (Yiddish): Little mother.

Mantelah: Literally (Yiddish): Little coat; the garment in which one dresses the Torah.

Mashgiach: Literally (Hebrew): Supervisor in charge of observance of Kosher laws and/or monitor at a yeshiva.

Mashpia: Literally (Hebrew): Influencer; the one who teaches *Hasidic* texts and serves as prayer coach.

Mashpiyim: Plural of *mashpia*.

Matbe'a: Literally: coin.

Matzos: Unleavened bread.

Melvaveh Malkah: Literally (Hebrew): Accompanying the queen; the celebration at a meal of the departing shabbos.

Meshuggeneh: Literally (Hebrew/Yiddish): A mentally disturbed person.

Mezuzah: Literally (Hebrew): Doorpost; the capsule holding the scripture dealing with God's remembrance, affixed to the right doorpost of an entrance.

Mezuzot: Plural of *mezuzah*.

Mikveh: Literally (Hebrew): Gathering; immersion pool for ritual purification.

Mincha: Literally: Gift; originally a sacrifice, currently meaning the afternoon prayer.

Minyan: Literally: A quorum; traditionally a prayer group of at least ten males, thirteen years or more.

Mishnah: Literally (Hebrew): What is repeated; the earliest postbiblical text of Jewish law and belief. It is believed to have been completed in the early third century CE.

Mitzvot hal'vabot: Literally (Hebrew): The *mitzvot* of the heart.

Mitzvah: Literally (Hebrew): Commandment.

Mitzvot: Plural of *mitzvah*.

Mitzvot ma'asiot: The *mitzvot* observed in action.

Moreh rabbakh k'more shamayim: Literally (Hebrew): Respect for your teacher equals respect for heaven.

Nachdichtung: Literally (German): A poem composed in emulation of an original.

Narishkeit: Literally (Yiddish): Foolishness.

Netzach: Literally: Victory/eternity; representing the seventh *sefirah* of the Tree of Life; also meaning effectiveness.

Niggun: Literally: A sung melody. Abraham Heschel defined it as "a tune flowing in search of its own unattainable end."

Niggunim: Plural of *niggun*.

Nistallek gevoren: Literally (Yiddish): He ascended; phrase applied to the passing of a rebbe.

Nusha'ot: Plural of *nussah*.

Nussah: Literally (Hebrew): The form; applied to the rite of prayer.

Ohel: Literally (Hebrew): Tent; graveside covered by a roof.

P'nai Or: Literally: Faces of light. When we changed the name of our organization from *B'nai Or*, we were respecting feminist sensitivities.

P'shettl: Literally (Yiddish): Diminutive of *pshat*; simple meaning of a text, here applied to a clever *halachic* discourse.

Parokhot: Literally (Hebrew): Cover; curtain over the holy ark.

Pirkey Avot: Literally (Hebrew): Chapters of the fathers. The most popular tractate of the *mishnah*, it is a collection of aphorisms, governing ethics and conduct, attributable to Jewish sages who lived before the end of the second century CE.

Piyyut: Literally (Hebrew): Liturgical poem.

Piyyutic: Poetic.

Piyyutim: Plural of *piyyut*.

Prie-dieu: Literally (French): To pray God; a kneeling stool.

Quahal: Literally (Hebrew): A gathering, a congregation.

Rabbanim: Plural of rabbi.

Rambam: Acronym of Rabbi Moshe ben Maimon (Maimonides), the renowned philosopher-physician, AD 1138–1204.

Rebbe: From the Hebrew for "rabbi"; designation of the head of the Hasidic community, a master teacher.

Ribbono Shel Olam: Literally (Hebrew): Master of the universe.

Ruach Hakodesh: Literally (Hebrew): Holy spirit.

Schmoozing: (Yiddish): Now part of American vocabulary, this refers to having a comfortable conversation.

Seder: Literally (Hebrew): Order; applied to the Passover dinner ritual.

Sefer Torah: Literally (Hebrew): Torah book; applied to the scroll.

Sefirah: Literally: The counting. This word designates a specific divine attribute on the Tree of Life.

Sefirot: The plural of *sefirah*. The ten energy essences are said to be in constant interplay and underlie all the universe. The *sefirot* have historically been depicted in various arrangements, the most significant being the Tree of Life.

Shabbos: Sabbath.

Shacharit: Morning prayer.

Shammas: Sexton.

Shechinah or **Shekhinah:** Literally: She who dwells within; this is another name for *Malkhut*, the divine feminine presence that permeates all existence.

Shefa': Literally: The flow; representing the descent of divine grace.

Shelo lishma: Literally (Hebrew): Not for her name's sake; extrinsic motivation.

Shema: Literally (Hebrew): See *K'riyat Shma*.

Shema Yisrael: Literally (Hebrew): See *K'riyat Shma*.

Shiur: Literally (Hebrew): Measure; applied to a Torah lecture.

Shivithis: Literally (Hebrew): The plural of "I have presented myself before God."

Shlemut ha'avoda: Literally (Hebrew): Perfection of the service.

Shlichim: Literally (Hebrew): Emissaries; also *shluchim*.

Shmoneh Esreh: Eighteen blessings; see *Amidah*.

Shochet: Ritual slaughterer.

Shtibel: Literally (Yiddish): Little room; applied to a space where Hasidism get together.

Shtreyml: The fur hat worn by Hasidic men on special occasions.

Shul: (Yiddish) Synagogue.

Siddur: Prayer book.

Siddurim: Plural of *siddur*.

Simchat Torah: Literally (Hebrew): The joy of Torah; the closing holiday of the autumn season, when we complete the reading of the Five Books of Moses and begin it again from the start.

Smicha: Literally (Hebrew): Laying on of hands; rabbinic ordination.

Sukkot: Literally (Hebrew): The Festival of Booths.

T'fillah be'tzibur: Literally (Hebrew): Prayer with a quorum; public worship.

T'fillin: Literally: Phylacteries, the container of the scriptures celebrating "Let them be a sign on your arm and a diadem above your eyes."

T'hillim: Psalms.

T'refah: Generic Yiddish word used for what is not kosher.

T'shuvah: Penitence.

Tachanun: Literally (Hebrew): Prayers of penitential pleas.

Takanot: Literally (Hebrew): Articles of improved behavior.

Tallit: The prayer shawl.

Tallitot: Plural of tallit.

Talmud: The original corpus of the oral Torah, compiled in writings by sages in the Land of Israel and Babylonia and completed about 500 CE.

Tanya: Literally: It has been taught; the title of the major theoretical work by Rabbi Schneur Zalman of Liady. Its first section was published in 1796 and it comprises the central opus of Chabad Hasidism.

Tiferet: Literally: Splendor; the fifth *sefirah*, representing compassion, balancing between *Chesed* and *Gevurah*.

Tikun Hatzot: Midnight lament.

Tish: Literally (Yiddish): Table; the place of Hasidic celebration presided over by the Rebbe.

Torah Kolelim: Places of Torah study supported by stipends.

Tree of Life: In Kabbalah, the central symbol for the universe and every aspect of it. It comprises ten *sefirot* or divine energy essences.

Tu B'Shevat: The fifteenth day of *Shevat*; New Year of the Trees.

Tzaddik: Literally (Hebrew): Righteous one, often in reference to a rebbe.

Ya'aleh y'vayoh: Literally (Hebrew): May it arise and arrive; an insert into the *Amidah* for specific celebrative days.

Yechidut: Literally (Hebrew): Meeting, one on one, of rebbe and Hasid.

Yenne Velt: Literally (Yiddish): That other world; the afterlife.

Yesod: Literally: foundation; the ninth *sefirah* representing the means of procreation and communication.

Yichud: Literally (Hebrew): Unification; a centralizing *kavvannah*.

Yiddishkeit: Colloquial for living in a Jewish culture; observance of *halacha*.

~

Related Books by the Authors

Zalman M. Schachter-Shalomi

Rivlin, Eyal, with Netanel Miles-Yepez, eds. *At the Rebbe's Table: Rabbi Zalman Schachter-Shalomi's Legacy of Songs and Melodies: Volume II.* Boulder, CO: The Reb Zalman Legacy Project, 2007.

Rivlin, Eyal, with Netanel Miles-Yepez, eds. *Into My Garden: Rabbi Zalman Schachter-Shalomi's Legacy of Songs and Melodies: Volume I.* Boulder, CO: The Reb Zalman Legacy Project, 2007.

Schachter, Zalman. *Gate to the Heart.* Philadelphia: Aleph, Alliance for Jewish Renewal, 1993.

Schachter, Zalman. *Paradigm Shift.* Northvale, NJ: Jason Aronson, 1993.

Schachter, Zalman. *Spiritual Intimacy: A Study of Counseling in Hasidism.* Northvale, NJ: Jason Aronson, 1991.

Schachter, Zalman, with Donald Gropman. *The First Step.* New York: Bantam Books, 1983. (This book was issued in a new edition by Jewish Lights in 2003. That version is called *First Steps to a New Jewish Spirit.*)

Schachter, Zalman, S., and Edward Hoffman. *Sparks of Light: Counseling in the Hasidic Tradition.* Boulder, CO: Shambhala, 1983.

Schachter, Zalman, with Phillip Mandelkorn. *Fragments of a Future Scroll.* Philadelphia: Leaves of Grass Publications, 1975 (rev. 2nd ed., Toronto: B'nai Or Press, 1983).

Schachter, Zalman, and Netanel M. Miles-Yepez, eds. *Wrapped in a Holy Flame: Teachings and Tales of the Hasidic Masters.* San Francisco: Jossey-Bass, 2003.

Schachter, Zalman, with Ronald Miller. *From Age-ing to Sage-ing.* New York: Warner Books, 1995.

Schachter, Zalman, with Howard Schwartz. *The Dream Assembly*. Amity House, 1986 (reissued by Nevada City, CA: Gateways/IDHHB Inc., 1989).

Schachter-Shalomi, Meshullam Zalman Hiyya HaCohen ben Haya Gittel. *The Tree of Life of Sacred Time, or the Ten S'firot in Sacred Time*, edited by Daniel Siegel. Philadelphia: Aleph, Alliance for Jewish Renewal, 1999.

Schachter-Shalomi, Zalman. *A Guide for Starting Your New Incarnation: Teachings on the Modern Meaning of T'shuvah*, edited by Daniel Siegel. Philadelphia: Aleph, Alliance for Jewish Renewal, 2001.

Schachter-Shalomi, Zalman. *Sh'ma: A Concise Weekday Siddur for Praying in English*. Seattle: CreateSpace, 2010.

Schachter-Shalomi, Zalman. *Spiritual Economics: You Can Get Anything You Want in Ad-on-I's Restaurant*, edited by Daniel Siegel. Philadelphia: Aleph, Alliance for Jewish Renewal, 2002.

Schachter-Shalomi, Zalman. *Yom Kippur Kattan and the Cycles of T'shuvah*, edited by Daniel Siegel. Philadelphia: Aleph, Alliance for Jewish Renewal, 1999.

Schachter-Shalomi, Zalman, with Cindy Gabriel. *Experiential Flashes on the Sephirot*. Philadelphia: P'nai Or Religious Fellowship, 1993.

Schachter-Shalomi, Zalman, and Yair Hillel Goelman. *Ahron's Heart: The Prayers, Teachings and Letters of Ahrele Roth, a Hasidic Reformer*. Teaneck, NJ: Ben Yehuda Press, 2009.

Schachter-Shalomi, Zalman, and Michael K. Kagan, ed. *All Breathing Life*. Santa Fe, NM: Gaon Books, 2011.

Schachter-Shalomi, Zalman, with Michael Kosacoff. *The Gates of Prayer: Twelve Talks on Davvenology*. Seattle: CreateSpace, 2010.

Schachter-Shalomi, Zalman, and Netanel Miles-Yepez. *A Heart Afire: Stories and Teachings of the Early Hasidic Masters*. Philadelphia: Jewish Publication Society, 2009.

Schachter-Shalomi, Zalman, and Netanel Miles-Yepez. *A Merciful God: Stories and Teachings of the Holy Rebbe, Levi Yitzhak of Berditchev*. Seattle: CreateSpace, 2010.

Schachter-Shalomi, Zalman, Netanel Miles-Yepez, and Susannah Heschel. *A Hidden Light: Stories and Teachings of Early HaBaD and Bratzlav Hasidism*. Santa Fe, NM: Gaon Books, 2011.

Schachter-Shalomi, Zalman, with Joel Segel. *Jewish with Feeling: A Guide to Meaningful Jewish Practice*. New York: Riverhead Books, 2005.

Schachter-Shalomi, Zalman, with Daniel Siegel. *Credo of a Modern Kabbalist*. Victoria, Canada: Trafford Publishing, 2005.

Wiener, Rabbi Shohama, ed. *The Fifty-eighth Century: A Jewish Renewal Sourcebook*. Northvale, NJ: Jason Aronson, 1996 (a second collection of articles and essays in my honor by my colleagues and students).

Wiener, Shohama, and Jonathan Omer-Man, ed. *Worlds of Jewish Prayer: A Festschrift in Honor of Rabbi Zalman M. Schachter-Shalomi*. Northvale, NJ: Jason Aronson, 1993.

Edward Hoffman

Hoffman, Edward. *Despite All Odds: The Story of Lubavitch.* New York: Simon & Schuster, 1991.

Hoffman, Edward, ed. *Future Visions: The Unpublished Papers of Abraham Maslow.* Thousand Oaks, CA: Sage, 1996.

Hoffman, Edward. *The Heavenly Ladder: A Jewish Guide to Inner Growth.* San Francisco: Harper & Row, 1985.

Hoffman, Edward. *The Hebrew Alphabet: A Mystical Journey.* San Francisco: Chronicle Books, 1998.

Hoffman, Edward. *The Kabbalah Reader: A Sourcebook of Visionary Judaism.* Boston: Shambhala/Trumpeter, 2011.

Hoffman, Edward, ed. *Opening the Inner Gates: New Paths in Kabbalah and Psychology.* Boston: Shambhala, 1995.

Hoffman, Edward. *The Right to Be Human: A Biography of Abraham Maslow,* 2nd ed. New York: McGraw-Hill, 1999.

Hoffman, Edward. *The Way of Splendor: Jewish Mysticism and Modern Psychology,* 25th Anniversary Edition. Lanham, MD: Rowman & Littlefield, 2006.

Hoffman, Edward. *The Wisdom of Maimonides: The Life and Writings of the Jewish Sage.* Boston: Shambhala/Trumpeter, 2009.

Schachter, Zalman M., and Hoffman, Edward. *Sparks of Light: Counseling in the Hasidic Tradition.* Boston: Shambhala, 1983.

Index

Abbey of Our Lady of the Prairies, 109
adata d'nafshey (soul knowledge), 157, 205
Adler, Alfred, 8, 133
Age-ing to Sage-ing: A Profound New Vision of Growing Older (Miller, R.; Schachter-Shalomi), 183
Agnon, Shmuel Yosef, 117
Agudat Yisroel, 13
Ahron of Karlin, 174, 208
Aleph Alliance for Jewish Renewal, 167
Aleph rabbinic training, 139, 166
aliyat han'shamah (mystical ascent of soul), 143, 152, 154, 205
al nafshey hatikha d'issura (as forbidden), 123, 205
Alpert, Richard, 152
Alter, Avraham Mordechai, 118–19
Alter, Yisrael, 118
Amanah (loyalty/faith), 119
Amidah (prayer), 194, 205, 212
Anschluss, in Austria, 19
Antigonos, 30
anti-Semitism, 7–8, 19

appell (roll call), 36
Après Heschel (Schachter-Shalomi), 171, 205
Aquarian Conspiracy (Ferguson), 167
Aquarian Minyan, 177, 179, 182
Aronson, Jason, 176
"The Art of the Fugue" (Bach, J.), 99
Assiyah (world of action and sensation), 111, 203, 205
"Astride His Horse on the Sabbath" (Shamir), 117
atzarot (contained days), 127–29, 136, 142, 195, 205
Auschwitz, 23, 31
Austria, 19–20
Avodath Hashem (service of God), 124, 126, 205
awareness: aging with, 183; of body, 99, 137; creativity for, 198; of divine, 130, 170; expansion of, 190; Hasidic methods for, 98; as sensory, 195–96; shifts in, xiii
Ayn Sof (divine infinity extending infinitely), 111
azihut. See emanation, divine

217

About the Authors

Rabbi Zalman Schachter-Shalomi, better known as "Reb Zalman," was born in Zholkiew, Poland, in 1924. Raised largely in Vienna, his family was forced to flee the Nazi oppression in 1938. After almost three years without roots, they finally landed in New York City in 1941, settling in Brooklyn, where young Zalman enrolled in the yeshiva of the Lubavitcher Hasidim. He was ordained by Lubavitch in 1947. He later received his Master of Arts degree in the psychology of religion in 1956 from Boston University and a Doctor of Hebrew Letters degree from Hebrew Union College in 1968. He taught at the University of Manitoba, Canada, from 1956 to 1975 and was professor of Jewish mysticism and psychology of religion at Temple University until his early retirement in 1987, when he was named professor emeritus. In 1995, he accepted the World Wisdom Chair at Naropa University in Boulder, Colorado, officially retiring from that post in 2004.

Throughout his long career, Reb Zalman has been an unending resource for the world religious community. He is the father of the Jewish Renewal and Spiritual Eldering movements, an active teacher of Hasidism and Jewish Mysticism, and a participant in ecumenical dialogues throughout the world, including the widely influential dialogue with the Dalai Lama, documented in the book, *The Jew in the Lotus.* One of the world's foremost authorities on Hasidism, he is the author of the new book, *A Heart Afire: Stories and Teachings of the Early Hasidic Masters* (co-authored by Netanel Miles-Yepez), and on Jewish law, he has written, *Integral Halachah: Transcending and Including* (with Daniel Siegel). Reb Zalman currently lives in Boulder, Colorado, and continues to be active in mentoring his many students the world over.

Edward Hoffman was born and raised in New York City. Attending Hebrew day school as a child, he was influenced in Judaism by his grandfather Louis Lipitz, a renowned cantor and liturgical composer. Receiving degrees in psychology from Cornell University and the University of Michigan-Ann Arbor, Dr. Hoffman has been a licensed New York State psychologist in private practice since 1984. An adjunct associate psychology professor at Yeshiva University, he has authored/edited more than twenty books in psychology, Jewish studies, and related fields. These include award-winning biographies of Alfred Adler and Abraham Maslow, literary anthologies on family themes such as fatherhood, and several books on Kabbalah and its relevance for contemporary psychology. In 2009, Dr. Hoffman was a visiting scholar at the University of Tokyo in the Department of Religious Studies. His books have been translated into many languages, including Chinese, French, German, Japanese, Portuguese, Russian, and Spanish. He also serves as a senior editor of the *Journal of Humanistic Psychology*. Dr. Hoffman lives in New York City with his wife and their two children. He enjoys playing the flute, swimming, and travel as leisure activities.